THE BEDFORD SERIES IN HISTORY AND CULTURE

D0445908

Pearl Harbor and the Coming of the Pacific War

A Brief History with Documents and Essays

Akira Iriye

Harvard University

BEDFORD/ST. MARTIN'S   Boston ≋ New York

For Bedford/St. Martin's
History Editor: Katherine E. Kurzman
Developmental Editor: Charisse Kiino
Editorial Assistant: Molly Kalkstein
Production Supervisor: William Kirrane
Marketing Manager: Charles Cavaliere
Project Management: Books By Design, Inc.
Text Design: Claire Seng-Niemoeller
Indexer: Books By Design, Inc.
Cover Design: Richard Emery Design, Inc.
Cover Photo: Burning Ships at Pearl Harbor. The National Archives/Corbis.
Composition: G & S Typesetters, Inc.
Printing and Binding: Haddon Craftsman, an R. R. Donnelley & Sons Company

President: Charles H. Christensen
Editorial Director: Joan E. Feinberg
Director of Editing, Design, and Production: Marcia Cohen
Manager, Publishing Services: Emily Berleth

Library of Congress Catalog Card Number: 98-87529

For information, write: Bedford/St. Martin's, 75 Arlington Street, Boston, MA 02116
(617–426–7440)

ISBN: 0–312–14788–0 (paperback)
ISBN: 0–312–21818–4 (hardcover)

Acknowledgments

Map, p. xii, Thomas G. Paterson, *American Foreign Policy: A History.* Copyright © 1977 by D. C. Heath and Company. Used by permission of Houghton Mifflin Company.

Map, p. xiii, from *The Twentieth Century World: An International History,* 3rd ed. by William R. Keylor. Copyright © 1996 by William R. Keylor. Used by permission of Oxford University Press.

Martin Bernd. "German Aggression in Russia and Japan's Final Move South." Excerpt taken from *Japan and Germany in the Modern World* by Martin Bernd, 1995, pp. 249–59, 262–64. Reprinted with permission of Berghahn Books, Inc.

Foreword

The Bedford Series in History and Culture is designed so that readers can study the past as historians do.

The historian's first task is finding the evidence. Documents, letters, memoirs, interviews, pictures, movies, novels, or poems can provide facts and clues. Then the historian questions and compares the sources. There is more to do than in a courtroom, for hearsay evidence is welcome, and the historian is usually looking for answers beyond act and motive. Different views of an event may be as important as a single verdict. How a story is told may yield as much information as what it says.

Along the way the historian seeks help from other historians and perhaps from specialists in other disciplines. Finally, it is time to write, to decide on an interpretation and how to arrange the evidence for readers.

Each book in this series contains an important historical document or group of documents, each document a witness from the past and open to interpretation in different ways. The documents are combined with some element of historical narrative—an introduction or a biographical essay, for example—that provides students with an analysis of the primary source material and important background information about the world in which it was produced.

Each book in the series focuses on a specific topic within a specific historical period. Each provides a basis for lively thought and discussion about several aspects of the topic and the historian's role. Each is short enough (and inexpensive enough) to be a reasonable one-week assignment in a college course. Whether as classroom or personal reading, each book in the series provides firsthand experience of the challenge—and fun—of discovering, recreating, and interpreting the past.

Natalie Zemon Davis
Ernest R. May

Preface

Japan's attack on Pearl Harbor on December 7, 1941, was one of the most momentous events in the history of the twentieth century. It not only led to war between Japan and the United States, but it also served to merge the conflict in Asia, where Japan and China had been fighting for more than ten years, with the war in Europe, which had begun in 1939. The United States, hitherto an ostensibly neutral country in the two separate wars, became a major participant in both, to emerge ultimately as the greatest military power in the world. "Remember Pearl Harbor" became not simply a wartime slogan in the United States to avenge Japan's surprise attack, but also provided a point of departure for postwar defense doctrine and military preparedness for the cold war. Japan, for its part, was punished for its offense: Japan was destroyed by U.S. military power, including two atomic bombs, and after its defeat became a nation distrustful of military power and committed to the pursuit of economic objectives.

Because of its drama, its lasting impact, and its controversial nature, Pearl Harbor provides an excellent starting point to introduce students to the study of contemporary history. There is ample data enabling students to examine such issues as how decisions were made by governments, what information they had at their disposal, how closely civilian and military officials cooperated, what ideas and assumptions guided them, and, most important, how miscalculations and missed opportunities changed the course of history. At the same time, because the Pearl Harbor attack has given rise to so much controversy, the episode compels students to sift through conflicting interpretations and arrive at their own conclusions.

There are many ways of studying the Pearl Harbor story. In this book, two approaches were adopted. Part One seeks to help students understand the immediate background of the Pearl Harbor attack through an examination of the negotiations between the United States and Japan in November 1941. Because Japan's decision to attack U.S. territory was in response to a perceived deadlock in these negotiations, they provide crucial raw material for comprehending what was on the minds of Japanese and U.S. leaders in those hectic days. Part Two, in contrast, offers a broader international context for the U.S.-Japanese crisis — a crisis that involved many countries besides the two main players. It is important for students to keep in mind the international context in which the United States, Japan, China, Britain, the Soviet Union, Germany, and many other countries were trying to safeguard their interests. It is my hope that these two approaches in combination will give students a deeper and more nuanced understanding of what the world was like in the late fall of 1941 and what forces produced the Pearl Harbor tragedy.

The legacy of Pearl Harbor is still alive today. Governments and armed forces continue to plan for the possibility of a surprise attack, quite possibly a surprise nuclear attack. Because the ancient doctrine, "If you want peace, prepare for war," seemed to have been vindicated by Pearl Harbor, nations persist in arming themselves. At the same time, not just military but political, economic, and other attempts have been made to prevent another Pearl Harbor, as well as another world war. Believing that Pearl Harbor was not just an isolated event manufactured by a handful of irrational men, but instead was a product of an age in which international order disappeared and anarchy seemed to rule, nations and governments since the end of the Second World War have tried to reestablish some semblance of order in the world. To the extent that such order exists today, its origins, too, can be traced back to those gloomy days of 1941. It is my hope that this book will be read not simply to establish the basic facts about this important historical event, but also to comprehend the global forces that contributed to the Pearl Harbor story — and have reshaped the world since the end of the war.

ACKNOWLEDGMENTS

I am grateful to Ernest R. May, who first suggested that I do a volume on Pearl Harbor for the Bedford Series. At Bedford/St. Martin's, I have been the beneficiary of the professionalism and commitment of the entire staff, especially Chuck Christensen, Joan Feinberg, Katherine Kurzman, Molly Kalkstein, Emily Berleth, Nancy Benjamin, and above all Charisse Kiino whose cheerful, unfailing, and efficient help made the final product as much her work as mine. Before I even began thinking about the book's contents and organization, and again after I completed the first draft, I consulted many professional colleagues, all of whom gave me their most generous and insightful assistance. I am particularly indebted to Sumio Hatano, Tsukaba University; Waldo Heinrichs, San Diego State University (Emeritus); Frank Ninkovich, St. John's, New York; Michael Barnhart, State University of New York, Stony Brook; John Dower, Massachusetts Institute of Technology; Roger Dingman, University of Southern California; and Miles Fletcher, University of North Carolina, Chapel Hill; as well as two anonymous readers of the manuscript, for their valuable suggestions. I have also benefited from my long conversations with Ambassador Takeo Iguchi who, as the son of one of the Japanese embassy officials in Washington who played an important role in the Pearl Harbor story, has generously shared with me his insights as well as the material he has collected. The study of the origins of the Pacific war has become more and more an international scholarly undertaking, as illustrated by the essays included in Part Two, which were written by historians from China, Britain, Germany, and Russia as well as the United States and Japan. I am truly grateful to the international community of scholars for their commitment to seeking the truth and their willingness to share the products of their research with one another. That has perhaps been one of the unforeseen but most gratifying consequences of the Pearl Harbor tragedy. Finally, I would like to record my sincere thanks to the Law School of Waseda University, which provided me with office space and a computer to finalize the manuscript in the summer of 1998.

Akira Iriye

Contents

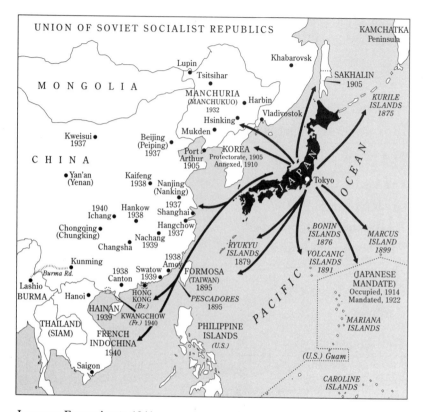

Japanese Expansion to 1941

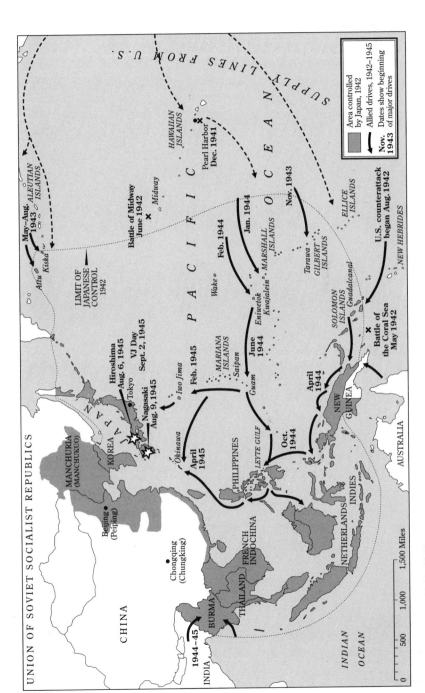

The Pacific War, 1941–1945

PART ONE

Introduction:
"The Day of Infamy"

In the most limited sense, *Pearl Harbor* refers to Japan's attack on the U.S. fleet in Hawaii on the morning of Sunday, December 7, 1941. Japanese fighter planes destroyed or damaged most of the U.S. battleships moored in Pearl Harbor and killed more than two thousand American military and civilian personnel. Simultaneously, Japanese forces began an offensive in other parts of the Pacific and Asia: the islands of Wake and Guam, the Philippines, Hong Kong, Singapore, and the Malay peninsula. Several hours *after* these assaults, the Japanese government declared war on the United States (as well as on Great Britain). The American people, who had hitherto not been united over the question of war or peace in the Pacific and in the Atlantic, were outraged by the "sneak attack" and overwhelmingly supported President Franklin D. Roosevelt's decision to retaliate. On December 7, the United States declared war on Japan. It was a day, Roosevelt declared, that would "live in infamy."

This book contains a number of primary sources, from both Japan and the United States, that focus on the immediate antecedents to Pearl Harbor, followed by ten secondary works that explain the positions of various countries that played significant roles in the unfolding drama of the Pacific war. Besides the two principal actors, China, Britain, Germany, Indonesia, and the Soviet Union are represented. Pearl Harbor was both a bilateral and an international drama. As you study the event, try to put yourself in the position of a Japanese or an American leader in the fall of 1941. Imagine how that leader may have viewed the world situation and tried to turn it to his or her country's advantage. Both the Japanese and the Americans knew, of course, that at that moment a war was raging in Europe and that China and Japan had been fighting each other intermittently for more than ten years. Few, however, could have foreseen precisely how these two wars might merge into a global conflict — or known how to prevent such a development. To understand the significance of Pearl Harbor, therefore, it is important to look first at the two separate wars and then to examine how those wars eventually became one, the Second World War. Did both the Japanese and the Americans want that particular outcome? If not, what did they do to prevent the two wars from becoming one world conflict? The drama of Pearl Harbor must be understood within such a global framework.

THE WAR IN EUROPE

In September 1939, war came to Europe as Germany invaded Poland and, in retaliation, Britain and France declared war on Germany. One year earlier, Britain and France had tried to "appease" Germany by signing the Munich Agreement, in effect ceding a portion of Czechoslovakia to Germany. By the late summer of 1939, however, both London and Paris had determined that further German expansion must be stopped. The Soviet Union, rather than coming to the rescue of Poland or joining forces with Britain and France, had signed a nonaggression pact with Germany and marched its troops into Poland, thus effectively dividing that hapless nation into two halves, the western part under German control and the eastern part under Soviet control. In the spring of 1940, Germany seized Denmark and Norway, and then it commenced its *blitzkrieg,* or lightning attack, on France and the Low Countries (the Netherlands, Belgium, Luxembourg), conquering them one by one. By June, most of Europe lay prostrate at Adolf Hitler's feet. The major exception was Britain, which resisted German aggression virtually alone, with Prime Minister Winston S. Churchill declaring that the British people would mobilize their "blood, sweat, and tears" until the menace was eradicated. Unable to conquer Britain by bombarding its cities, Germany switched to a naval strategy, preying on British and neutral ships in the Atlantic in the hope of starving the island nation into submission.

The situation changed dramatically on June 22, 1941, when Hitler launched Operation Barbarossa, an armed assault on Soviet territory in violation of the 1939 nonaggression pact. Hitler judged that by conquering the Soviet Union, which he was confident could be accomplished quickly, the combined might of most of Eurasia could then be harnessed to bring Britain, finally, to its knees. Hitler's optimism proved premature. The European war, including both the Atlantic theater and the Eastern front (the Soviet Union), divided German resources, and in neither theater was Germany able to win a decisive victory. As tensions grew between the United States and Japan, one key question was how the European conflict would affect trans-Pacific relations.

Japan was a German ally. In September 1940, these two countries joined Italy in signing a treaty of alliance, the Tripartite (Axis) Pact, that bound them together in case one or more of them went to war with the United States. In other words, should war come between Germany and the United States, Japan would be obligated to come to the assistance of the former, and vice versa. Knowing full well the implications of the Tripartite Pact, U.S. leaders tried to keep Germany and Japan separate for as long as possible. This could be done, of course, if the United States refrained from going to war against either country. By the summer of 1941, however, the U.S. Navy was already involved in the Atlantic theater of the European war. President Roosevelt, determined to prevent Britain's defeat, sent troops to Iceland, drew a line down the middle of the Atlantic Ocean and declared the area west of the line off-limits to German naval vessels, and, starting in September, authorized U.S. warships to shoot on sight any German ship suspected of violating that policy. In the meantime, Washington sent food and weapons to Britain under the Lend-Lease program enacted in March 1941, and U.S. leaders intended to extend the program to the Soviet Union. In other words, the United States was engaged already in an undeclared war against Germany.

Japan, on the other hand, was not involved in the European conflict. In April 1941, it signed a neutrality treaty with the Soviet Union, and Tokyo honored it when Germany attacked the Soviet Union and pleaded with Japan to commence military action in Siberia. From the standpoint of the United States, Japanese neutrality in the European war was welcome. By the fall of 1941, it was becoming clearer that the United States would soon be directly involved in the war. It made sense for the United States, then, to focus on the European conflict for the time being and not become involved in the Asian war, which would inevitably bring both Japan and Germany in a war against the United States.

THE WAR IN ASIA

The war in Asia had begun in September 1931, when the Kwantung Army (the Japanese army stationed in China's northeastern provinces, commonly known as Manchuria) manufactured an incident and attacked

Chinese forces in Mukden, an important city in southern Manchuria. Within a few days, the city fell to Japanese military control, but the incident did not end there. The Kwantung Army, supported by the supreme command in Tokyo, went on to conquer all of Manchuria. The area was detached from China proper and became the nominally independent state of Manchukuo, actually a puppet regime under Emperor P'u-yi, "the last emperor." He had abdicated his throne when the Ch'ing dynasty, which had ruled China since the seventeenth century, was overthrown in 1911.

China, a republic since that time, was now governed by the Nationalists under Chiang Kai-shek. There was serious domestic opposition to his rule from the Chinese Communists, various warlords, and even some Nationalists who had fallen out with Chiang. Determined to unify China proper and implement economic reforms, he preferred not to resist Japanese aggression by force. To do so would be too costly and would drag him away from his center of power. The result was that Manchuria stayed under Japanese control while the Nationalists steadily expanded their rule in the rest of China. This was perhaps an inevitable development since no country, however sympathetic to China, was willing to come to its assistance at the risk of war with Japan. The early 1930s were a period of profound economic crisis all over the world, and potential supporters of China, such as the United States and Britain, had to focus on domestic economic recovery. (The United States did issue the so-called nonrecognition doctrine, declaring that it would not recognize the legitimacy of the consequence of any Japanese action that violated the principle of China's territorial integrity.) The League of Nations censured Japan without imposing any sanction. The Soviet Union, while less affected by the economic crisis, was then carrying out its Five-Year Plan of industrialization and did not want trouble with Japan.

Japan, indeed, had chosen its timing well. By the mid-1930s, it had extended its empire to the Asian continent without fighting China and without incurring any sanction on the part of other powers. There was, however, a domestic price for such expansionism. The army, flush with the success in Manchuria, grew in influence in Japanese politics and demanded more and more of a say in the country's foreign affairs. The political parties, the bureaucrats, and the business community, who before 1931 had been generally oriented toward a more peaceful foreign policy in cooperation with the Western powers, were put on the defensive. Some of them were even assassinated outright by army extremists and their civilian supporters. The emperor, who under the constitution was the sovereign monarch and ratified all decisions by the government as well as the military, was a weak figure who did not resist these trends.

Privately, he sometimes expressed his misgivings, for instance about the way Japan was alienating the United States and Britain by its aggressive action, but he did little to reverse course.

The situation changed drastically after 1937. Not only did China decide to fight Japan, but the powers that had remained largely uninvolved now took sides in the conflict. The Chinese-Japanese crisis soon escalated into an international crisis. The story begins on July 7, 1937, when skirmishes between Chinese and Japanese troops a few miles outside of Peiping (as Beijing was called then) grew into a full-scale conflict — although neither side initially wanted it that way. The Japanese were seriously divided; the army, in particular, considered the Soviet Union its primary target, and many of its officers, even those who had carried out the Manchurian conquest, now insisted on containing the crisis in North China. But others, including the civilian government under Prince Fumimaro Konoe (sometimes spelled Konoye), believed that this was an opportunity to "punish" the Chinese, entrench Japanese power more deeply on the continent, and establish a "new order" in East Asia. The Chinese under Chiang Kai-shek, unlike earlier, were more confident of resisting Japanese power. The Communists and other dissidents were calling for a war of resistance; the Chinese economy had begun to recover from the impact of the world depression and from the loss of Manchuria. Apart from a few politicians who believed a war against Japan would merely strengthen the Communists at home and the Soviet Union abroad, most believed that this time the nation would have the support of other countries.

They were right in this last regard. On the battlefield, Japanese forces captured one city after another, but the United States, Britain, the Soviet Union, and the League of Nations all deplored such aggressive behavior and began to discuss possible sanctions. Although nothing specific emerged at this time, even the condemnation of Japan at the Brussels Conference later in 1937, where these countries met with China to discuss the war, was significant. Japan was losing international sympathy, something that was further confirmed when its army entered the city of Nanjing (Nanking) in December and brutally assaulted its civilian population, killing, according to official Chinese estimates, some three hundred thousand people.

The war, however, dragged on, draining Japan's resources while the Chinese retreated step by step into the vast hinterland to continue their struggle. One year passed, then another, without any visible sign of a decisive victory on the part of Japan. Thus between 1939 and 1941, Japan tried a political solution: to set up a pro-Japanese government in Nanjing — the Nationalist regime had moved its headquarters to Chongqing (spelled Chungking in those days) — and to negotiate an end to the war with the Nationalists. However, the puppet regime in Nanjing was no match for the Nationalists in obtaining the people's loyalty, and besides, its offices were infiltrated by Nationalist and Communist agents. The result was that Japanese forces became bogged down in what came to be called the China quagmire.

Faced with this impasse, the Japanese adopted a new slogan: "the Great East Asian Co-prosperity Sphere." The idea was that a "Great East Asia," comprised of Japan, Manchukuo, China, and (although kept vague at that time) parts of Southeast Asia, would establish a new international order seeking "coprosperity"—Asian countries sharing prosperity and peace, free from Western colonialism and domination. The new slogan was thus meant to appeal to the anti-Western sentiment of the Asians who had experienced European and American colonialism. Japan was hoping to coalesce all Asians in this struggle to rid the region of Western power and influence.

Such a vision was filled with contradictions. To begin with, even as the coprosperity sphere portrayed the image of Western domination of Asia, Japan was trying to establish its own hegemony over China by force. The Chinese would never accept a Japanese-led campaign for Asian liberation unless the Japanese renounced such leadership. Besides, at the very moment that the Japanese leaders were embracing the new slogan, they were entering into a partnership with Germany and Italy through the Axis alliance. Ironically, they were relying on these European nations to help them rid Asia of Western influence.

Undaunted by such contradictions, many people in Japan, including some in the army, were envisioning a grand alliance of Japan, Germany, and the Soviet Union, a worldwide coalition of antidemocratic countries. Such a combination would create a formidable bloc of power, encompassing the Eurasian continent as well as significant portions of the Pacific Ocean. Only the United States and the Western Hemisphere would remain outside the new power configuration, assuming that Britain would fall to Germany sooner or later.

These were the developments that provided the context for U.S. foreign policy, which was ultimately to lead to a confrontation with Japan.

THE AMERICAN DILEMMA

The United States was never "isolationist," if by the term one means being determined to stay out of foreign wars. To be sure, during most of the 1930s the nation was preoccupied with the Great Depression, and President Roosevelt well understood that before the nation became embroiled in international affairs, it first would have to mobilize its people and resources to solve the economic crisis. The various New Deal programs were carried out with little regard for events in Europe or in Asia.

By the late 1930s, however, the Roosevelt administration judged that the country had sufficiently recovered from the worst effects of the Depression and that it was in a better position to respond to developments abroad. To Roosevelt and his advisers, these developments were definitely turning the world into a more dangerous place. Not that Japanese aggression in China or Hitler's dictatorship in Germany alone presented a direct threat to U.S. security, but the American leaders believed that the nation's democracy, which had so far survived the Depression, as well as democratic governments and free people elsewhere would be jeopardized if forces of aggression and totalitarianism were allowed to spread unchecked. As Roosevelt stated as early as October 1937 in his "quarantine speech," unless the peace-loving nations of the world cooperated to "quarantine" aggressors, they would never enjoy their peace and freedom. He repeated these ideas again and again to bring home the message that isolation or neutrality was simply impossible and unrealistic. More and more American people came to agree with him. Although few before 1941 advocated that the nation join the Asian or the European war, their sympathies were overwhelmingly with the victims of aggression. In various public-opinion polls, they endorsed programs to assist China and Britain "by all means short of war."

There was a dilemma, however. The United States was, by 1941, the richest country in the world; it was quickly mobilizing itself by producing tanks, military aircraft, and warships and by adopting a peacetime draft; it was sending millions of dollars of aid to China and to Britain. But military leaders as well as Roosevelt recognized that the nation was not quite ready for war, certainly not ready for a two-front war against Germany and against Japan. They continued to draft war plans, and by the spring of 1941, U.S. strategists were in close touch with their counterparts in Britain. Should entering the war become inevitable, their preference was to concentrate on the European war first. This was because they perceived Germany to be the greater threat. But how could the United States predict how war would come about or ensure that there would be no conflict with Japan while it fought in the Atlantic? Should Washington avoid provoking Japan by discontinuing its assistance to China? Would not such a policy enable Japan to succeed in conquering China, thus becoming an even more formidable foe of the United States?

The German invasion of Soviet territory in June further complicated U.S. strategy. The German-Soviet war dashed whatever hopes the Japanese might have entertained about an antidemocratic coalition. Now the Soviet Union was on Britain's side, and that meant on the side of the United States, which quickly decided to extend its assistance to the Soviet Union under the Lend-Lease program — good news from the British and U.S. points of view. However, the dilemmas concerning a two-front war remained; indeed, if the United States became involved in the German-Soviet war in the eastern front, it would have to contemplate a three-front war.

TOWARD PEARL HARBOR

Japan and the United States responded to the new German-Soviet conflict in ways that brought the two nations a step closer to their own war. Their vision of a Japanese-German-Soviet alliance against the Anglo-American powers shattered, the Japanese had to decide whether to "go north" and attack Siberia in violation of the neutrality treaty they had just signed with the Soviet Union. Such an attack, in combination with the German assault in the west, would place the Soviet Union in an extremely difficult position and might even bring down the Stalinist regime. The Japanese army and some civilian leaders were interested in such a strategy and made plans for "going north" sometime in the fall; the Kwantung Army of Manchuria, the key ingredient in the attack, needed reinforcements and supplies. Mobilization, specifically for a Soviet war, would take time.

At the same time, the Japanese military — especially the navy — and certain civilian leaders judged the timing just right for "going south" — to invade various parts of Southeast Asia that were rich in resources, especially oil, rubber, and tin, all essential ingredients for Japan's industries and growing war machine. Japanese troops had occupied the northern part of the French colony of Indochina (consisting of Vietnam, Laos, and Cambodia today) in July 1940, when France fell to Germany. They had met with little resistance, and now, a year later, Tokyo's supreme command decided to occupy the rest of Indochina, believing that while the world's attention was focused on the German-Soviet war, such action would meet with little international protest or interference. This new move was considered crucial in preparing the nation for further advances in nearby areas such as the Dutch East Indies (Indonesia), Malaya, and Burma, the latter two being British colonies. (Thailand, lying between

Indochina and Malaya, was an independent country, although its foreign policy was coming under Japanese control.) The "southward advance" might or might not be coordinated with the planned "northward advance," but it would clearly serve to complete the establishment of the Great East Asian Co-prosperity Sphere.

The occupation of southern Indochina, however, proved to be a fatal step that ultimately led to the war with the United States. Just as the Japanese coveted the resources of Southeast Asia and were making plans to capture them by force if necessary, the Americans were determined never to allow such bounty to fall into Japanese hands. A successful Japanese conquest of the European colonies in Asia would further harm British prestige, isolate Australia and New Zealand, injure the interests of Europeans in the region, and turn Japan into a much more formidable antagonist. To clearly signal that the United States would not tolerate such a course of events, President Roosevelt froze Japanese assets in the United States, and Britain and the Commonwealth countries followed suit. This meant that Japan's trade with these countries would become extremely difficult; Japanese businessmen would have to seek authorization to release funds to pay for their purchases — a cumbersome process. Because petroleum was the main item Japan was importing from the United States, the freeze in effect brought a virtual halt to oil shipments across the Pacific. This was the so-called de facto embargo of oil.

Why did the United States take such harsh measures if, as noted earlier, it had decided to concentrate on the European theater and did not want to become involved prematurely in a two-ocean war? One reason was, of course, to deny oil for use by the Japanese military as they contemplated a southern advance. Another was Roosevelt's concern with the vicissitudes of the German-Soviet war. He was determined to prevent the collapse of the Soviet Union and kept warning Japan against joining Germany in attacking the Soviet Union. To indicate that this was not empty rhetoric, Washington needed to show some muscle. Hence the freezing of Japanese assets and the de facto oil embargo. Of course, the United States could have conciliated Japan and desisted from retaliating against the Japanese occupation of southern Indochina, keeping Japan preoccupied with Southeast Asia and reluctant to implement its northern strategy. Available evidence suggests, however, that Roosevelt and his aides believed that such a soft approach would only embolden the Japanese in the north as well as in the south.

The picture, then, was becoming clear by early August, when President Roosevelt traveled to Newfoundland to meet Prime Minister Winston S. Churchill to discuss the war. (Such a meeting alone shows that the United States was by then fully, if indirectly, involved in the European war.) The two leaders not only reaffirmed their commitment to the defeat of Germany and the support of the Soviet Union; they also agreed that Japan must be stopped from going further south. How this was to be done, however, was never made clear. For the time being, the United States would keep Japanese assets frozen, refuse to sell oil to Japan, and continue to assist the Nationalists in China in their struggle against Japanese forces.

It was at this time — August 1941 — that the Japanese began complaining of an "ABCD encirclement": their nation being encircled by America, Britain, China, and the Dutch. (In the East Indies, the Dutch followed the U.S. lead in foreign policy even after the fall of their homeland to Germany.) From the Japanese perspective, the United States not only was standing in the way of Japan's war effort in China, but also, in collusion with the British and the Dutch, denying Japan its legitimate interests in Southeast Asia. More and more Japanese leaders, including the emperor, were coming to the conclusion that to break this impasse it was necessary to strike south even at the risk of provoking the British, the Dutch, and the Americans. The Americans were the most formidable potential antagonists, and so, from then on, much Japanese deliberation focused on the question of whether to prepare for war with the United States and, if so, when the nation should strike. (It was always assumed that Japan would start such a war at a time of its own choosing.)

On September 6, Japan's top leaders met in the presence of the emperor (hence the meeting was called an "imperial conference") and decided to prepare the nation for war against the United States by early November. At the same time, however, the emperor, Prime Minister Konoe, and others decided to try last-minute negotiations with the United States. The rationale was rather simple. Because Japan's sense of crisis derived from the perceived "ABCD encirclement," the situation would change if Washington agreed to resume trade with Japan and to desist from further assisting China's war efforts against Japan. However, because the United States was not likely to accept such an agreement without some reciprocal concessions on Japan's part, the latter would consider possible terms it would offer in return — for instance, concerning the possible withdrawal of some Japanese forces out of China. U.S. and Japanese officials had been engaged in intermittent "conversations" over China and the Axis alliance since spring, but they would now be converted into serious diplomatic negotiations to avoid a Pacific war.

On Washington's part, such negotiations were not unwelcome if only to gain time while the nation was getting ready for war. In the early fall of 1941, crisis mounted in the Atlantic, where an "undeclared war" was already being waged against German submarines, as noted earlier. A formal war could come at any moment, and so, it would be prudent to postpone a showdown with Japan for as long as possible. Thus, when Konoe expressed a strong wish to meet with Roosevelt personally in order to break the impasse in U.S.-Japanese relations, the president showed some interest. Secretary of State Cordell Hull, however, opposed such a meeting unless there was prior agreement regarding some of the differences between the United States and Japan, especially on China. When, in mid-October, Konoe was replaced by General Hideki Tōjō as prime minister (and concurrently as war minister), the Americans were not very sanguine that anything good would come of last-minute negotiations. But Tōjō made it clear to the American ambassador in Tokyo, Joseph C. Grew, that the emperor was eager to preserve the peace and that Japan was prepared to undertake negotiations with the United States in earnest.

The stage was thus set for last-minute negotiations in Washington. Would they go anywhere? What issue might be resolved? Through the primary souces in the following pages, you will be able to put yourself in the position of the Japanese and American negotiators and determine whether a settlement of differences could have been negotiated or whether, given the two nations' contradictory positions and interests, all negotiations were doomed to failure.

The Documents

Reproduced in this section are documents focusing on the U.S.-Japanese negotiations in November 1941. Read them as if you were a U.S. or Japanese official. Assume that you are interested in a negotiated settlement of the differences between the two countries. What concessions might you make to avert war? What issues are so critical that you would advocate going to war rather than compromise?

Now assume that you are Japanese. Would you consider the U.S. memorandum (the so-called Hull note) of November 26 an ultimatum and thus decide on war? In that case, would you support a surprise attack on U.S. territory? As an American official, would you agree with the timing and the contents of the Hull memorandum? If you were President Roosevelt and aware of the contents of the final Japanese message on December 7, is there anything you could do to avert the Pearl Harbor tragedy? Keep these questions in mind as you read the following documents.

Apart from the immediate circumstances of Pearl Harbor, what were the broad causes of the Pacific war? Were these causes open to negotiated solutions? Do the documents indicate that there was a fatal lack of communication between Washington and Tokyo? Were the two countries' differences as much historical and cultural as they were geopolitical?

Imperial Conference
November 5, 1941

Japan's negotiating position (Proposals A and B) was formally adopted by the imperial conference of November 5, 1941. The document that follows is a record of the Japanese leaders' deliberations on these proposals. Participating in the conference, besides the emperor, were Japan's top civilian and military leaders: the prime minister, the foreign minister, the finance minister, the president of the Planning Board (an agency for war mobilization), the president of the Privy Council (an organization of senior statesmen whose constitutional function was to advise the government), the war minister, the navy minister, the army chief of staff, and the navy chief of staff.

Because Japanese cabinets changed frequently—Hideki Tōjō was the fourteenth prime minister since 1931—and military appointments usually coincided with the formation of new cabinets, the individual biographies of the men who took part in the meeting are less important than the positions they held. As you will note, they expressed their views more often as spokesmen for the offices they held than as individuals. In this connection, it is important to keep in mind that Tōjō was at that time both prime minister and war minister. He had served as war minister in the cabinet of Prince Fumimaro Konoe (1940–41) and had adamantly refused to agree on concessions to the United States on the issue of Japanese troops in China. When the emperor turned to him to form a new cabinet in mid-October 1941, however, Tōjō considered that his mandate had changed: He was now speaking for the entire government, not just for the army. Even his decision to appoint himself war minister can be understood as a means of controlling the army in the event that the cabinet and the emperor adopted a policy on China that was contrary to the army's past positions.

The extreme difficulties that Tōjō and his colleagues foresaw in arriving at a compromise settlement on China can be gleaned from the minutes of this imperial conference. They indicate that the Japanese leaders persisted in the view that U.S. assistance to China had been the major reason for the prolongation of the war on the continent and that once the United States ceased such assistance, Japan could "settle" the war and withdraw its forces from most areas of China. Such an arrangement would still allow Japan to

Nobutaka Ike, *Japan's Decision for War: Records of the 1941 Policy Conferences* (Stanford, Calif.: Stanford University Press, 1967), 209–20, 222–39.

retain control over the northeast (Manchuria) and other parts of China, so the Japanese must have recognized that there was little chance the United States would agree to the scheme. That is why Japan's leaders were interested in ascertaining whether the United States might agree to a temporary arrangement (modus vivendi) that would shelve the thorny issue of China for the time being and focus on the question of Southeast Asia. In a nutshell, Japan pledges to desist from further "southern advances" and the United States resumes trade with Japan, especially shipments of oil.

The record of the imperial conference indicates the extreme seriousness of the shortage of oil and other resources that Japan faced. If the United States agreed to resume trade with Japan, the situation would obviously be alleviated, and there would be no urgent need to undertake a "southern advance." On the other hand, if the U.S.-Japanese crisis persisted, it would become imperative to obtain those vital resources in Southeast Asia — by use of force if necessary. Such action would almost certainly result in war. This dilemma was evident in the deliberations of the Japanese leaders.

Given their preoccupation with the question of natural resources, were Japan's leaders being realistic in pinning their hopes on a deal with the United States that they believed could avoid war? What important concessions did the Japanese think they were making? Why was China so important to them? What was their view of Germany, their official ally? What seems to be the main reason for Japan's risking war with the United States?

Agenda: "Essentials for Carrying Out the Empire's Policies"

I. Our Empire, in order to resolve the present critical situation, assure its self-preservation and self-defense, and establish a New Order in Greater East Asia, decides on this occasion to go to war against the United States and Great Britain and takes the following measures:
1. The time for resorting to force is set at the beginning of December, and the Army and Navy will complete preparations for operations.
2. Negotiations with the United States will be carried out in accordance with the attached document.
3. Cooperation with Germany and Italy will be strengthened.
4. Close military relations with Thailand will be established just prior to the use of force.
II. If negotiations with the United States are successful by midnight of December 1, the use of force will be suspended.

Summary of Negotiations with the United States of America

We will negotiate with the United States and seek to reach an agreement on the basis of attached Proposal A or attached Proposal B, both of which express, in a more moderate and amended form, important matters that have been pending between the two countries.

PROPOSAL A

We will moderate our position on the most important matters pending in the negotiations between Japan and the United States: (1) stationing and withdrawal of troops in China and French Indochina; (2) nondiscriminatory trade in China; (3) interpretation and execution of the Tripartite Pact; (4) the Four Principles.* This will be done as follows:

1. Stationing and withdrawal of troops in China:

We will moderate our position on this point as follows (in view of the fact that the United States — disregarding for the time being the reason for the stationing of troops — attaches importance to the stationing of troops for an indefinite period, disagrees with the inclusion of this item in the terms for peace, and urges us to make a clearer statement of our intentions regarding withdrawal):

Of the Japanese troops sent to China during the China Incident, those in designated sections of North China and Inner Mongolia, and those on Hainan Island, will remain for a necessary period of time after the establishment of peace between Japan and China. The remainder of the troops will begin withdrawal simultaneously with the establishment of peace in accordance with arrangements to be made between Japan and China, and the withdrawal will be completed within two years.

Note: In case the United States asks what the "necessary period of time" will be, we will respond that we have in mind 25 years.

Stationing and withdrawal of troops in French Indochina:

We will moderate our position on this point as follows, since we recognize that the United States is apprehensive that Japan has territorial ambitions in French Indochina and is building a base for military advance into neighboring territories:

Japan respects the sovereignty of French Indochina over her territory. Japanese troops currently stationed in French Indochina will be immediately withdrawn after the settlement of the China Incident or the establishment of a just peace in the Far East.

---

*The basic policies that Secretary of State always insisted should guide the conduct of nations: respect for the territorial integrity of states, noninterference in their internal affairs, equal commercial opportunity, and the use of peaceful means for changing the status quo.

2. Nondiscriminatory trade in China:

. . . The Japanese Government will recognize the application of the principle of nondiscrimination in the entire Pacific region, including China, if this principle is applied throughout the world.

3. The interpretation and execution of the Tripartite Pact:

On this point we will respond as follows: We do not intend to broaden unreasonably the interpretation of the right of self-defense. Regarding the interpretation and execution of the Tripartite Pact, the Japanese Government, as it has stated on previous occasions, will act independently. Our position will be that we assume that the United States is fully aware of this.

4. Regarding the so-called Four Principles put forward by the United States, we will make every effort to avoid their inclusion in official agreements between Japan and the United States (this includes understandings and other communiqués).

PROPOSAL B

1. Both Japan and the United States will pledge not to make an armed advance into Southeast Asia and the South Pacific area, except French Indochina.

2. The Japanese and American Governments will cooperate with each other so that the procurement of necessary materials from the Netherlands East Indies will be assured.

3. The Japanese and American Governments will restore trade relations to what they were prior to the freezing of assets. The United States will promise to supply Japan with the petroleum Japan needs.

4. The Government of the United States will not take such actions as may hinder efforts for peace by both Japan and China.

Notes

1. As occasion demands, it is permissible to promise that with the conclusion of the present agreement Japanese troops stationed in southern Indochina are prepared to move to northern Indochina with the consent of the French Government; and that the Japanese troops will withdraw from Indochina with the settlement of the China Incident or upon the establishment of a just peace in the Pacific area.

2. As occasion demands, we may make insertions in the provisions on nondiscriminatory trade and on the interpretation and execution of the Tripartite Pact in the above-mentioned proposal (Proposal B).

Statement by Prime Minister Tōjō

The Conference is now opened. With His Majesty's permission I will take charge of the proceedings.

At the Imperial Conference of September 6 "Essentials for Carrying Out the Empire's Policies" was discussed, and the following was decided by His Majesty: our Empire, determined not to avoid war with the United States, Great Britain, and the Netherlands in the course of assuring her self-preservation and self-defense, was to complete preparations for war by late October. At the same time it was decided that we would endeavor to attain our demands by using all possible diplomatic measures vis-à-vis the United States and Great Britain; and that in case there was no prospect of our demands being attained through diplomacy by early October, we would decide immediately on war with the United States, Great Britain, and the Netherlands.

Since then, while maintaining close coordination between political and military considerations, we have made a special effort to achieve success in our diplomatic negotiations with the United States. In this interval we have endured what must be endured in our efforts to reach an agreement, but we have not been able to get the United States to reconsider. During the negotiations, there has been a change in the Cabinet.

The Government and the Army and Navy sections of Imperial Headquarters have held eight Liaison Conferences in order to study matters more extensively and deeply on the basis of the "Essentials for Carrying Out the Empire's Policies" adopted on September 6. As a result of this, we have come to the conclusion that we must now decide to go to war, set the time for military action at the beginning of December, concentrate all of our efforts on completing preparations for war, and at the same time try to break the impasse by means of diplomacy. Accordingly, I ask you to deliberate on the document "Essentials for Carrying Out the Empire's Policies."

There will be statements by participants on matters for which they are responsible.

Statement by Foreign Minister Tōgō

I respectfully submit that the essence of our Empire's foreign policy is to establish a system of international relations based on justice and fairness, and thereby contribute to the maintenance and promotion of world peace.

The successful conclusion of the China Incident and the establishment of the Greater East Asia Co-prosperity Sphere would assure the existence of our Empire and lay the foundations for stability in East Asia. To achieve these objectives, our Empire must be prepared to sweep away any and all obstacles.

With the conclusion of the basic treaty between Japan and China on November 30 of last year, our Empire recognized the Nanking Government, marking a great step in the China Incident. Since then we have cooperated with that government to foster its growth and add to its strength. On the other hand, we have continued to put military pressure on the Chiang Kai-shek regime, in an effort to get it to reconsider. Its continued resistance after four and a half years of our holy war depends a great deal, it is clear, on aid from the United States and Great Britain.

Since the outbreak of the China Incident, both the British and American Governments have obstructed our advance on the continent. On the one hand, they have aided Chiang; on the other hand, they have checked our activities in China or have stepped up their economic measures against us. Needless to say, Great Britain, which has acquired more interests than anyone else in East Asia, took all kinds of measures to obstruct us from the beginning. The United States, cooperating with her, abrogated the Japanese-American Trade Agreement,* limited or banned imports and exports, and took other measures to increase her pressure on Japan. Particularly since our Empire concluded the Tripartite Pact, the United States has taken steps to encircle Japan by persuading Great Britain and the Netherlands to join her and by cooperating with the Chiang regime. Since the start of the German-Soviet war, she has taken unfriendly action against us by supplying oil and other war materials to the Soviet Union through the Far East, despite warnings from our Government. As soon as our Empire sent troops into French Indochina after concluding a treaty on the basis of friendly negotiations with the French Government for the purpose of defending ourselves and bringing the China Incident to a conclusion, America's actions became increasingly undisguised. Not only did she cut off economic relations between Japan and the United States, with Central and South America going along with her, under the guise of freezing our assets; but also, in cooperation with Great Britain, China, and the Netherlands, she threatened the existence of our Empire and tried harder to prevent us from carrying out our national policies. Accordingly, our Empire, which is the stabilizing force in East Asia, was compelled to try to overcome the impasse by showing firmness and determination.

*The agreement was signed in 1911 and provided the legal framework for the bilateral trade. In July 1939 Washington notified Tokyo of its intention to terminate the agreement within six months, and in January 1940 it was abrogated.

President Roosevelt has stressed, as his national policy, the rejection of "Hitlerism"—that is, policies based on force—and he has continued to aid Great Britain, which is almost tantamount to entering the war, by utilizing the economically superior position of the United States. At the same time, as I have stated before, he has adopted a policy of firm pressure on Japan. In the middle of April of this year unofficial talks were begun, seeking a general improvement in relations between Japan and the United States. Our Imperial Government, desirous of promoting stability in East Asia and peace in the world, has since then continued the negotiations with a most sincere and fair approach. For a period of more than six months we have tried to reach an amicable settlement by showing patience and a spirit of compromise. In particular, the previous Cabinet tried hard to break the deadlock by suggesting a conference of the two heads of state, and in this way it displayed its sincerity. Late in September it presented a compromise proposal for the improvement of relations between the two countries. The American Government, however, maintained an extremely firm attitude, stuck to the proposal of June 21, which might be considered its original position, and refused to make any concessions. Recently, in discussions since the formation of the previous Cabinet, there have been some optimistic reports that the United States has shown a willingness to compromise substantially; but in fact, she has not made any concessions. Moreover, she has taken many measures to tighten the encirclement of Japan—strengthening of military facilities in the South; encouragement to Chiang through economic assistance, supplying arms, and sending military missions; meetings with military leaders in Singapore and Manila; and holding frequent military and economic conferences in Batavia, Hong Kong, etc. There has been nothing to demonstrate her sincerity. Hence we cannot help but regretfully conclude that there is no prospect of the negotiations coming to a successful conclusion quickly if things continue as they have in the past.

A close study of the June 21 proposal shows that it contains some points that we could accept. But in general it is a reaffirmation of the Nine-Power Pact;* and it was feared that it might destroy the policy we have pursued at great sacrifice since the Manchurian Incident; this in turn might block the creation of a New Order in East Asia and endanger our position as the leader in that area.

---

*Signed at the Washington Conference of 1921–22. It proclaimed such principles as China's territorial and administrative integrity and the open door (equal commercial opportunity).

... In Europe, although Germany and Italy will be able to achieve their first goal, the conquest of the Continent, we cannot anticipate an overall conclusion soon, and the war there is likely to be prolonged. In reality we could not expect Germany and Italy to give us much cooperation.

As I see it, the situation is becoming more and more critical every day, and negotiations with the United States are very much restricted by the time element; consequently, to our regret, there is little room left for diplomatic maneuvering. Moreover, the conclusion of a Japanese-American understanding would necessitate great speed in negotiations, partly because of the time required for domestic procedures on the American side. For this reason we have been required to carry on negotiations under extremely difficult circumstances. The prospects of achieving an amicable settlement in the negotiations are, to our deepest regret, dim. However, the Imperial Government will endeavor on this occasion to make every effort to arrive at a quick settlement in our negotiations. We would like to negotiate on the basis of the two proposals in the attached document, which assure the honor and self-defense of our Empire. . . .

In case the present negotiations should unfortunately fail to lead to an agreement, we intend to strengthen our cooperative arrangements with German and Italy, and to take a variety of measures so as to be prepared for any situation.

Statement by President of the Planning Board Suzuki

I am going to give a summary of the outlook with regard to our national strength, particularly in vital materials, in case we go to war against Great Britain, the United States, and the Netherlands.

First, if we can constantly maintain a minimum of 3 million tons of shipping for civilian use, it will be possible to secure supplies in the amount called for by the Materials Mobilization Plan for the fiscal year of 1941, except for certain materials. . . .

Second, if the yearly loss in shipping is estimated to be between 800,000 and 1 million tons, the maintenance of the 3 million tons of shipping mentioned above should be possible if we can obtain an average of about 600,000 gross tons of new construction each year. . . . Building the foregoing 600,000 tons of shipping is considered possible if we rationally utilize the present civilian shipbuilding capacity of 700,000 gross tons and the engineering and forging capacity of about 600,000 gross tons and if we take such measures as standardizing and lowering the quality of the ships to be built, giving overall control of shipbuilding operations to the Navy, and securing a labor force, as well as allocating 300,000 tons of steel, copper, and other necessary materials.

Third, in order to build 600,000 gross tons of new ships, more than 300,000 tons of ordinary steel will be needed. This can be secured if steel available for civilian use can be maintained at 2.61 million tons and this is allocated on a priority basis, with the allotment being kept to a minimum. . . .

Fourth, in order to maintain the shipping needed for production, it will be necessary to follow the plan agreed upon between the Army, Navy, and the Planning Board when it comes to determining the amount of shipping and the length of time such shipping will be needed for the Southern Operation. . . .

. . . Since it is estimated that for a certain period of time during the 1942 operation in the South ships for civilian use would be reduced to a minimum of 1.6 million gross tons, and civilian shipping capacity to around 2.6 million tons [for this period], it is expected that steel production during this period would decline to 3.8 million tons in terms of yearly production, and that other important materials would decline by around 15 per cent. . . .

In the second half of 1941, particularly in the fourth quarter, transportation capacity will decline because of operations in the South; so we plan to hold the decrease in production to 150,000 tons by mobilizing sailing ships with auxiliary engines, utilizing iron foundries that can use coal shipped by rail, increasing the use of stored iron ore, collecting more scrap iron, and so on. Thus we estimate that actual production will be about 4.5 million tons, as against the 4.76 million tons called for in the Plan.

Fifth, concerning rice, I think it will be necessary to consider substitute food, such as soybeans, minor cereals, and sweet potatoes, and to exercise some control over food in case the expected imports of rice from Thailand and French Indochina called for in the Food Supply Plan for the 1942 rice year (from October 1941 to September 1942) are reduced owing to operations in the South. That is, if the expected imports from Thailand and Indochina are reduced by 50 per cent, the food supply will be down to 93 per cent of the amount called for in the Plan; and if the imports decrease by 75 per cent, the supply will go down to 91 per cent. However, if imports from Thailand and French Indochina can be increased by using more ships after the completion of the first phase of military operations, it may be possible to prevent the reduction from becoming too large. . . .

Sixth, if we can occupy important points in the Netherlands East Indies in a short period of time, we can expect to obtain the following major items . . . :

Nickel ore
Tin (for anti-friction alloy and gilding)
Bauxite (raw ore for aluminum)
Crude rubber
Cassava root, theriac (for industrial alcohol)
Copra, palm oil (glycerin, substitute machine oil)
Sisal (substitute for Manila hemp)
Corn (animal feed and foodstuff)
Industrial salt
Sugar

Among the above items, crude rubber, tin, and bauxite would most seriously affect the United States if their supply is cut off.

Seventh, the total supply of petroleum, in case of operations in the South, will be 850,000 kiloliters in the first year, 2.6 million kiloliters in the second year, and 5.3 million kiloliters in the third year. If an estimate is made of the future supply and demand of petroleum, including 8.4 million kiloliters in our domestic stockpile, I believe we will just be able to remain self-supporting, with a surplus of 2.55 million kiloliters in the first year, 150,000 kiloliters in the second year, and 700,000 kiloliters in the third year. Concerning aviation fuel: it is expected that, depending on consumption, we might reach a critical stage in the second or third year.

That is, according to a study of the supply and demand of petroleum resulting from the occupation of the Netherlands East Indies, which was made jointly by the Army and the Navy at Liaison Conferences, the quantity expected to be obtained from the Netherlands East Indies is 300,000 kiloliters in the first year, 2 million kiloliters in the second year, and 4.5 million kiloliters in the third year. . . .

The oil surplus or shortage each year:

The surplus or shortage, calculated with a presumed loss of 100,000 kiloliters in the first year, 50,000 kiloliters in the second year, and 20,000 kiloliters in the third year, is given below. Estimate One [assumes a demand of] 800,000 kiloliters in the first year, 750,000 kiloliters in the second year, and 620,000 kiloliters in the third year. . . . If a reserve of 200,000 kiloliters, equivalent to approximately two months' need, is taken into account, the supply-and-demand relationship is as follows: in Estimate

One, 180,000 kiloliters surplus the first year, 440,000 kiloliters shortage the second year, and 28,000 kiloliters shortage the third year. . . .

Overall supply and demand of liquid fuel:

If civilian demand is assumed to be 1.4 million kiloliters each year, and military demand is added to it, the overall demand is 5.2 million kiloliters in the first year, 5 million kiloliters in the second year, and 4.75 million kiloliters in the third year.

On the other hand, the potential supply, including stockpiles, production, and expected procurement from the Netherlands East Indies, less a minimum of 150,000 tons for reserve, is: 7.75 million kiloliters in the first year, with a remainder of 2.55 million kiloliters; 5.15 million kiloliters in the second year, with a remainder of 150,000 kiloliters; and 5.45 million kiloliters in the third year, with a remainder of 700,000 kiloliters. In this estimate, domestic production is calculated at 250,000 kiloliters in the first year, 200,000 kiloliters in the second year, and 300,000 kiloliters in the third year, while synthetic petroleum is estimated at 300,000 kiloliters, 400,000 kiloliters, and 500,000 kiloliters respectively.

In brief, it is by no means an easy task to carry on a war against Great Britain, the United States, and the Netherlands — a war that will be a protracted one — while still fighting in China, and at the same time maintain and augment the national strength needed to prosecute a war over a long period of time. It is apparent that the difficulty would be all the greater if such unexpected happenings as natural disasters should occur. However, since the probability of victory in the initial stages of the war is sufficiently high, I am convinced we should take advantage of this assured victory and turn the heightened morale of the people, who are determined to overcome the national crisis even at the cost of their lives, toward production as well as toward [reduced] consumption and other aspects of national life. In terms of maintaining and augmenting our national strength, this would be better than just sitting tight and waiting for the enemy to put pressure on us. . . .

Statement by Finance Minister Kaya

Although the budget of our country has constantly increased since the beginning of the China Incident and has reached more than ¥7.99 billion in the general account and ¥5.88 billion in extraordinary military expenditures (agreed upon by the 76th Diet Session), or a total of over ¥13.2 billion, we have been able to secure large amounts in taxes and assure large savings, thanks to the efforts of various institutions and of the people. On the whole, we have been able to carry on operations smoothly. However, it is clear that when we begin military operations in the South, additional large expenditures of Government funds will be needed to cover them. Can our national economy bear the burden of such large military expenditures? Especially, are they feasible when the probability is high that the war will be protracted? Will there not be unfavorable effects on finance? Isn't there danger of a vicious inflation as a result of these expenditures? . . .

The . . . absorption of funds by taxation or national savings will be possible if the Government's economic policies are adequate, and if the people are fully aware that the destiny of their country is at stake and are willing to exert every effort and make extreme sacrifices. Moreover, we anticipate that the Government's policies will not be in error because the Government itself will carry them out. We believe the people will make every effort and endure sacrifices because they are the subjects of our Empire. Hence we must judge that it is possible. . . .

The areas in the South that are to become the object of military operations have been importing materials of all kinds in large quantities. If these areas are occupied by our forces, their imports will cease. Accordingly, to make their economies run smoothly, we will have to supply them with materials. However, since our country does not have sufficient surpluses for that purpose, it will not be possible for some time for us to give much consideration to the living conditions of the people in these areas, and for a while we will have to pursue a so-called policy of exploitation. . . . We must adopt a policy of self-sufficiency in the South, keep the shipment of materials from Japan to that area to the minimum amount necessary to maintain order and to utilize labor forces there, ignore for the time being the decline in the value of currency and the economic dislocations that will ensue from this, and in this way push forward. Of course it is to be recognized that the maintenance of the people's livelihood there is easy compared to the same task in China because the culture of the inhabitants is low, and because the area is rich in natural products.

Statement by Navy Chief of Staff Nagano

. . . Hereafter we will go forward steadily with our war preparations, expecting the opening of hostilities in the early part of December. As soon as the time for commencing hostilities is decided, we are prepared for war.

We are planning and getting ready with great care because success or failure in the initial phases of our operations will greatly affect success or failure in the entire war. It is very important that we carry out our initial operations ahead of the enemy and with courageous decisiveness. Consequently, the concealment of our war plans has an important bearing on the outcome of the war; and so, in putting our whole nation on a war footing in the future, we would like to maintain even closer relations with the Government and attain our desired goal.

Statement by Army Chief of Staff Sugiyama

. . . Army strength in the several countries in the South is gradually being increased. Roughly speaking, Malaya has an army of about 60,000 to 70,000 and about 320 airplanes, the Philippines have about 42,000 men and about 170 airplanes, the Netherlands East Indies have about 85,000 men and about 300 airplanes, and Burma has about 35,000 men and about 60 airplanes. Compared to strength before the outbreak of the war in Europe, enemy strength has been increased about eight times in Malaya, four times in the Philippines, two and one-half times in the Netherlands East Indies, and five times in Burma; it totals well over 200,000 in these countries. It is anticipated that the rate of increase will rise as the situation changes.

The ground forces in these regions, although varying from one region to another, are composed for the most part of native soldiers, with a nucleus of about 30 per cent white, "homeland" soldiers. They do not have sufficient education and training, and their fighting ability is generally inferior. It should be remembered, however, that they are thoroughly acclimatized, and used to tropical conditions. As to the fighting ability of the enemy air force, I assume that it cannot be taken lightly when compared to the ground force, since the quality of the aircraft is excellent and their pilots are comparatively skilled . . .

1. On the timing of the commencement of war:
From the standpoint of operations, if the time for commencing war is delayed, the ratio of armament between Japan and the United States will become more and more unfavorable to us as time passes; and particularly, the gap in air armament will enlarge rapidly. Moreover, defensive preparations in the Philippines, and other American war preparations, will make rapid progress. Also, the common defense arrangements between the United States, Great Britain, the Netherlands, and China will become all the more close, and their joint defensive capability will be rapidly increased. Finally, if we delay until after next spring, the weather will permit operational activities in the North, and also there will be a higher probability that our Empire will have to face simultaneous war in the

South and in the North. Thus it would be very disadvantageous for us to delay; and it is to be feared that it might become impossible for us to undertake offensive operations.

In addition, weather conditions in the area where important operations are going to take place are such that no delay is possible. Accordingly, in order to resort to force as soon as preparations for the operations we contemplate are completed, we would like to set the target date in the early part of December.

2. On the prospects of the operations:

Since the principal Army operations in the initial stages in the South will be landing operations against fortified enemy bases, conducted after a long ocean voyage in the intense heat of the sun while repelling attacks from enemy submarines and aircraft, we expect to face considerable difficulties. However, if we take a broad view of the situation, the enemy forces are scattered over a wide area and moreover separated by stretches of water, making coordinated action difficult. We, on the other hand, can concentrate our forces, undertake sudden raids, and destroy the enemy piecemeal. Therefore, we are fully confident of success, given close cooperation between the Army and the Navy. As for operations after we land, we have complete confidence in our victory when we consider the organization, equipment, quality, and strength of the enemy forces.

After the initial stage in our operations has been completed, we will endeavor to shorten greatly the duration of the war, using both political and military strategies, particularly the favorable results from our naval operations. Nevertheless, we must be prepared for the probability that the war will be a protracted one. But since we will seize and hold enemy military and air bases and be able to establish a strategically impregnable position, we think we can frustrate the enemy's plans by one means or another.

We will firmly maintain in general our present posture with respect to defense against the Soviet Union and operations in China while we engage in operations in the South. In this way we will be able to strengthen our invincible position vis-à-vis the North, and there will be no problem in carrying on in China as we have been doing. With regard to China, the favorable results of the operations in the South should particularly contribute to the settlement of the China Incident.

3. On the situation in the North resulting from operations in the South:

The Red Army has suffered massive losses at the hands of the German Army; and there has been a marked decline in the productivity of the Soviet armament industry. In addition, the Red Army in the Far East has sent westward to European Russia forces equal to 13 infantry divisions, about 1,300 tanks, and at least 1,300 airplanes since last spring. Its war potential, both materially and spiritually, is declining. Consequently, the probability of the Soviet Union taking the offensive, so long as the Kwantung Army is firmly entrenched, is very low.

However, it is possible that the United States may put pressure on the Soviet Union to permit America to utilize a part of the Soviet territory in the Far East for air and submarine bases for use in attacking us; and the Soviet Union would not be in a position to reject these American demands. Hence we must anticipate the possibility that we might see some submarines and aircraft in action against us from the North. Consequently, it cannot be assumed that there is no danger of a war breaking out between Japan and the Soviet Union as a result of such causes and changes in the situation. Thus our Empire must conclude its operations in the South as quickly as possible, and be prepared to cope with this situation.

4. On the relationship between operations and diplomacy:

Up to now, in accordance with the decision of the Imperial Conference of September 6, we have limited our preparations for operations so that they would not impede diplomatic negotiations. But from now on, given the decision for war, we will take all possible measures to be ready to use force at the beginning of December. This will have the effect of goading the United States and Great Britain; but we believe that diplomacy, taking advantage of progress in war preparations, should be stepped up. Needless to say, if diplomatic negotiations succeed by midnight of November 30, we will call off the use of force. If they do not succeed by that time, however, we would like to receive the Imperial Assent to start a war in order not to miss our opportunity, and thereby to fully achieve the objectives of our operations.

[A summary of the question-and-answer session between President of the Privy Council Hara and others follows.]

Hara: The topic of today's Imperial Conference is the extension and execution of the decision of the Imperial Conference of September 6. The decision of September 6 was primarily on the development of Japanese-American negotiations; but, to my regret, the negotiations have not led to agreement. . . . I should like to skip over the technical points of diplomacy and ask what is the present status of the negotiations. What are the important points? What has been definitely agreed upon, and what has not?

Tōgō: . . . Concerning attitudes of both countries toward the European war: The two parties have virtually agreed upon the matter of preventing the expansion of the war. On this matter, what the United States wants is to exert military power against Germany as a right of self-defense, while Japan promises not to exert military force in the Pacific region.

Concerning the question of peace between Japan and China: The two parties have not agreed upon the question of stationing and withdrawing troops. Japan shall station troops in necessary places for the necessary period of time, and shall withdraw other troops under certain conditions in a certain period of time. Nevertheless, the United States demands that we proclaim the withdrawal of all troops; but we cannot accept the demand.

Concerning activities of both countries in the Pacific region: The United States demands that there be no discrimination in trade in the entire Pacific region, including China; whereas Japan cannot agree to the demand unconditionally because of the problem of obtaining resources in China, and so on. On the other hand, since the United States contends that this principle [of nondiscriminatory trade] should be maintained throughout the world, we have said in the negotiations that we would agree to their demand if it is possible to maintain the principle throughout the world.

Both parties have agreed not to solve political problems in the Pacific region by military force. Concerning this, the withdrawal of troops from French Indochina is a problem we have not agreed on. . . .

Tōjō: Since the Foreign Minister might be unfamiliar with some matters pertaining to the previous Cabinet, I will make some supplementary remarks.

The American reply received on October 2 does endeavor to force upon Japan the Four Principles: (1) respect of territorial integrity and sovereignty; (2) noninterference in internal affairs; (3) non-discriminatory trade; and (4) disapproval of changing the status quo by force. The Four Principles are a condensation of the Nine-Power Treaty. If we agree to (1), the agreement will involve even Manchukuo, which the Americans have not recognized, to say nothing of the China Incident. If we agree to (2), there is a danger that this might lead to the abolition of agreements with the Nanking regime: i.e., the Japanese-Chinese treaty for trade and communications. Although (3) might be regarded as proper from a common-sense viewpoint, we cannot concede it where it concerns the self-preservation and self-defense of our Empire. This would also be the attitude of the United States and of

Great Britain. Nondiscrimination would also change our rights in nearby areas, which are prescribed by Article 6 of the Japanese-Chinese treaty. Concerning (4), we think that we could probably accept it in the Southwest Pacific, but not in the areas vital to our national defense and vital for procuring resources, such as China. The United States demands that we accept these principles. We cannot do so, because we carried out the Manchurian Incident and the China Incident in order to get rid of the yoke that is based on these principles. The new Foreign Minister and the new Finance Minister say that it is dangerous to agree to these principles. The previous Cabinet conceded what should not have been conceded for the sake of reaching an agreement in the Japanese-American negotiations. Although the American proposal of October 2 uses flowery words, the spirit and attitude expressed in the proposal remain unchanged. The United States has not conceded a single point; it simply makes strong demands on Japan.

The important points are as the Foreign Minister has stated. In concrete terms:

With reference to our attitudes toward the European war, they "appreciate Japan's attitudes" and add, "If Japan would reconsider the matter, it would be most beneficial." That is to say, they are demanding that we clarify our attitude toward the Tripartite Pact. Approval of the Four Principles and their local application are serious questions. More serious is the question of the stationing and withdrawal of troops. What they insist upon is Japan's acceptance of the principle of withdrawal of troops. They urge us to proclaim the withdrawal both at home and abroad, while suggesting that we could probably make some arrangements for stationing troops secretly. As I understand it, withdrawal of our troops is retreat. We sent a large force of one million men [to China], and it has cost us well over 100,000 dead and wounded, [the grief of] their bereaved families, hardship for four years, and a national expenditure of several tens of billions of yen. We must by all means get satisfactory results from this. If we should withdraw troops stationed in China under the Japanese-Chinese treaty, China would become worse than she was before the Incident. She would even attempt to rule Manchuria, Korea, and Formosa. We can expect an expansion of our country only by stationing troops. This the United States does not welcome. However, the stationing of troops that Japan insists upon is not at all unreasonable.

Concerning the Japanese-American conference of heads of state, we do not agree with each other. The United States insists that the meeting be held after the major questions have been agreed upon; whereas Japan proposes to settle the major questions at the talks.

Hara: I have acquired a preliminary understanding of the contents of Proposals A and B as a result of the explanation just given. I shall now ask questions in detail.

Under (1), "Stationing of troops," does "disagrees with the inclusion of this item in the terms for peace" mean that it is not acceptable to include the stationing of troops in the Japanese-Chinese peace treaty?

Tōjō: Yes. That is, the United States makes it a principle that troops must be withdrawn, and objects to including stationing of troops in the terms.

Hara: Do they mean that we should write the withdrawal of troops into the treaty, but still negotiate with China on stationing troops?

Tōjō: The United States seems to be suggesting that we negotiate with China on stationing troops, which she maintains should be dealt with as an unofficial matter. . . .

Hara: Item 3 of Proposal B reads "to restore [trade relations] to what they were prior to the freezing of assets." What about sanctions imposed prior to the freezing of assets?

Tōgō: Our sending of troops into French Indochina directly caused the issuance of the order freezing our assets. The situation should be restored to what it was before the Indochina incident. Japan would prefer that we returned to the state of affairs prior to the abrogation of the trade treaty, but I think it would be better to seek first of all a relaxation of tension. Since the United States will not be completely satisfied because this item is conditional, as stated in Note 1, we think we should first proceed to return to the situation prior to the freezing order, and after this has been achieved carry on negotiations with the United States on various matters. However, in the case of oil, its export was prohibited even before the freezing order; so I would like to make an agreement whereby Japan would be able to buy the amount she needs, and not be limited to the amount prior to the freezing order.

Hara: It was because of the China Incident that the United States put restrictions on trade with us. The freezing order resulted from our advance into French Indochina. Nonetheless, we want to settle the China Incident; therefore, I think we should negotiate and settle all these questions, including the China Incident, with the United States at one and the same time. Aren't our demands in Proposal B too weak? We plan to proceed with negotiations first on the basis of Proposals A and B, and then go on to other questions. How is the United States likely to react to these proposals?

Tōgō: I shall explain what led us to put in Point 3 in Proposal B. Although we desire to return to the situation prior to the abrogation of the trade treaty in one stroke, as you have said, a most serious situation — namely, war — would result if the United States did not agree with us. Therefore, if we offer as many concessions as we can afford, and still the United States does not agree with us, then we will know that she intends to go to war, and at the same time our moral position will be made clear both at home and abroad. Answering your question on the overall situation, we cannot expect to settle matters quickly by means of Proposal A. I am afraid we cannot settle matters even with Proposal B. Take, for example, the withdrawal of troops from French Indochina. The United States, I think, will not agree to the China Question in (4) of Proposal B either, for she has never agreed to it. I suppose it will also be very difficult for her to agree to Item 2 of the Notes, since she has been requiring us to observe it. I, however, do not think that Japan's demands are unreasonable. If the United States wants peace in the Pacific, or if she reflects on the fact that Japan is determined, I think that the United States must give some consideration to our demands. But since this means that Japan will coerce the United States with force [in the background], it is not impossible that she may resist us. Moreover, we have only a short time left. Since we will send instructions to begin negotiations after His Majesty has made the decision, and because we must conclude them by the end of November, we have only two weeks for negotiations. This cannot be helped because of other needs. Consequently, I think the prospect of success in the negotiations is small. As Foreign Minister, I hope to do my best. To my regret, there is little hope for success in the negotiations.

Hara: I should like both the Army and Navy Chiefs of Staff to explain what will happen if the negotiations break down. Please state it in such a way that it can be understood with the use of common sense. Regarding operations in the South, the field of battle in the map we have here covers the entire region. What is the scope of operations, and how successful are our military operations likely to be?

Sugiyama: Targets of this operation are military and air bases in Guam, Hong Kong, British Malaya, Burma, British Borneo, Dutch Borneo, Sumatra, Celebes, the Bismarck Islands, and small islands southwest of the Bismarck Islands. The numerical strength of the enemy in these places is more than 200,000, while the number of enemy aircraft is 800. There are other forces in India, Australia, and New Zealand, which I assume would participate sooner or later. The Army will carry out operations under these conditions in cooperation with the Navy, and its major efforts will be made in the Philippines and Malaya. The operation is planned to start in Malaya and the Philippines simultaneously, and then to move toward the Netherlands East Indies. In this way, it is estimated that it will take 50 days to complete the operation in the Philippines, 100 days in Malaya, and 50 days in the Netherlands East Indies; and that the entire operation will be completed within five months after the opening of the war. However, in case the American fleet comes to attack us, and our Navy goes out to meet it, or in case the United States and the Soviet Union attack us in the North — although the probability of this is low — the periods mentioned above would probably be extended for some time. I believe, however, that we would be able to carry on a protracted war if we could bring under our control such important military bases as Hong Kong, Manila, and Singapore, and important areas in the Netherlands East Indies.

Hara: . . . Although it is said that there is a force of well over 200,000 men and some aircraft in these areas, there are also warships. Can we destroy their fleet in a short period of time?

Nagano: The ratio of our fleet to that of the United States is 7.5 to 10; but 40 per cent of the American fleet is in the Atlantic Ocean, and 60 per cent is in the Pacific. I do not believe that Great Britain will be able to send a large fleet against us; probably her fleet would consist of a battleship, ten or more cruisers, and some aircraft. As to the method of fighting battles, the United States would need considerable time if she should withdraw ships from the Atlantic Ocean and come to attack us. However, a part of their naval force might be able to obstruct our operations in the South, although the strength of that naval force would probably be insufficient to engage in a decisive battle. Consequently, they would have to bring the Atlantic Fleet into the Pacific. Great Britain might send a part of her fleet because she would not want to lose Singapore. In this case it is possible that Great Britain and the United States might combine their fleets. Our Navy has plans for this contingency, although the method of fighting battles would be different from the other case. The combined force of Great Britain and the United States has weak points. We are, therefore, confident of victory. We can destroy their fleet if they want a decisive battle. Even if we destroy it, however, the war will continue long after the Southern Operation.

Hara: Although the Army Chief of Staff has stated that the operation would last 50 to 100 days, I would imagine that landings could not be carried out unless we could deal with the enemy fleets now in the South Pacific. What is your opinion on this?

Nagano: I assume that, among enemy fleets, the surface fleets operating in the vicinity of our fleets would temporarily retreat. We would destroy them if possible; even if we could not, they would not be able to do much. But it is submarines that we would attempt to overwhelm. It would not be difficult to dominate the enemy fleets now in the Pacific Ocean.

Hara: I shall ask about the Soviet Union. While it is stated that our plans are to occupy the greater part of the South Pacific in about 100 days, it is usual for predictions to turn out wrong.... Although I believe that our Supreme Command's plan is most realistic, would you transfer some troops in the South to the North in case the war is prolonged, and the Soviet Union starts a war against us? What would happen in the Chinese theater? I should like to hear your views on this, just to be certain.

Sugiyama: It is difficult for the Soviet Union to conduct a major operation in winter. In light of the present situation, the probability of the Soviet Union entering the war is low. Even if the Soviet Union and the United States should combine forces, they would be unable to carry out a major operation. Even if there were combined operations, they would be only nominal ones for the Soviet Union. We are prepared to deal with their winter operations.

What we are most concerned with is a possible United States–Soviet alliance concurrent with a delay in our plans to occupy Malaya in 100 days and to complete occupation of the Netherlands East Indies in five months. This is dangerous. I think we should be able to meet this situation adequately by using Army corps now in the home islands and forces to be transferred from China.

Hara: I think it is clear that the Soviet Union would not attack us immediately. I also assume that the alliance between the United States and the Soviet Union would be as you have described it. I should like to ask further if we can ignore the possibility that our trade and maritime commerce might be hindered by the activities of the Soviet Navy, and by the enemy fleet stationed in the South Seas. Can we assume that the transportation of materials and other goods would not be affected by interference from the Soviet Union and enemy ships in the South Seas?

Nagano: If the Soviet Union starts a war, and if her submarines become active, we would not be able to send sufficient forces against her, since our Navy would be carrying out operations in the South Seas. We would put up a defense against her activities; and then, as our operations in the South Seas progressed, we would fight actively against them. In the South Seas there are enemy warships, submarines, and aircraft. We are, therefore, prepared to suffer considerable damage once we have begun operations. . . .

Hara: Am I to understand that materials can be secured even if the Soviet fleet and the navies of Great Britain, the United States, and the Netherlands interfere?

Suzuki: The Army and the Navy have already made studies concerning the loss of ships.

Hara: Although (4) under I in "Essentials for Carrying Out the Empire's Policies" discusses relations with Thailand just prior to resorting to arms, it would seem that we will not be able to confer with her if this must be done just before we use force. What do you think about this point? If we allow time for negotiations, Great Britain will learn about them. In that event, the intentions of the Supreme Command will become known to the enemy. What is meant by "just prior"? If you are going to use coercion, it will be coercion, and not negotiation for a close military relationship. This approach would affect our relations with Thailand in the future.

Tōjō: Since diplomatic and military affairs are closely interrelated here, I will answer. With the idea of winning Thailand over to our side we have been working on [Prime Minister] Pibun Songgram to set up close military relations ever since the time of our advance into southern French Indochina. As you have pointed out, there are delicate points. It is necessary from an operational point of view for us to make landings in Thailand. It will not do to let this be known too early. Therefore, we cannot do other than push the matter by force if they do not agree with us at the talks just before we act.

Hara: . . . It would not be desirable to fail to get an agreement on Japanese-American negotiations. We have endured hardships for four years because we are a unified nation under an Imperial family with a history of 2,600 years. It seems that Britain already has war weariness. I wonder about Germany. It also seems that there is an antiwar movement in Italy. I believe that the favorable situation in our country results from our national polity with the Imperial family as its head. Nonetheless, our people want to settle the China Incident quickly.

Statesmen must give serious consideration to the wisdom of waging war against a great power like the United States without the prospect of the China Incident being settled quickly. At the last Imperial Conference it was decided that we would go to war if the negotiations failed to lead to an agreement. According to the briefings given today, the present American attitude is not just the same as the previous one, but is even more unreasonable. Therefore, I regret very much that the negotiations have little prospect of success.

It is impossible, from the standpoint of our domestic political situation and of our self-preservation, to accept all of the American demands. We must hold fast to our position. As I understand it, the Japanese-Chinese problem is the important point in the negotiations, and there is suspicion that the United States is acting as spokesman for the Chungking regime. If Chiang, relying on American power, should negotiate with us, I doubt that the negotiations could be completed in two or three months. It would be nice if he would capitulate in the face of Japan's firm determination; but I think there is absolutely no hope for this.

On the other hand, we cannot let the present situation continue. If we miss the present opportunity to go to war, we will have to submit to American dictation. Therefore, I recognize that it is inevitable that we must decide to start a war against the United States. I will put my trust in what I have been told: namely, that things will go well in the early part of the war; and that although we will experience increasing difficulties as the war progresses, there is some prospect of success.

On this occasion I would like to make one comment to the leaders of the Government. Although the China Incident is one cause for war between Japan and the United States and Great Britain, another is the German-British war. I do not believe that the present situation would have developed out of just the China Incident. We have come to where we are because of the war between Germany and Great Britain. What we should always keep in mind here is what would happen to relations between Germany and Great Britain and Germany and the United States, all of them being countries whose population belongs to the white race, if Japan should enter the war. Hitler has said that the Japanese are a second-class race, and Germany has not declared war against the United States. Japan will take positive action against the United States. In that event, will the American people adopt the same attitude toward us psychologically that they do toward the Germans? Their indignation against the Japanese will be stronger than their hatred of Hitler. The Germans in the United States are considering ways of bringing about peace between the United States and Germany. I fear, therefore, that if Japan begins a war against the United States, Germany and Great Britain and Germany and the United States will come to terms, leaving Japan by herself. That is, we must be prepared for the possibility that hatred of the yellow race might shift the hatred now being directed against Germany to Japan, thus resulting in the German-British war's being turned against Japan.

Negotiations with the United States have failed to lead to an agreement. A war against the United States and Great Britain is inevitable if Japan is to survive. However, we must give serious consideration to race relations, exercise constant care to avoid being surrounded by the entire Aryan race — which would leave Japan isolated — and take steps now to strengthen relations with Germany and Italy. Paper agreements will not do. I would like to call the attention of the officials in the Government to the following point: don't let hatred of Japan become stronger than hatred of Hitler, so that everybody will in name and in fact gang up on Japan. I hope that our officials will deal adequately with international affairs in the future.

Tōjō: The points of the President of the Privy Council are well taken. Ever since the previous Imperial Conference, the Government has not given up its earnest desire to somehow break the impasse in our negotiations with the United States. It is natural for the Supreme Command to devote itself exclusively to military operations, since it sees little hope for the negotiations' success. However, in the hope that there might be some way to break the impasse, the Government sought a settlement, even though it meant some sacrifice of freedom in military operations. That is, we pursued diplomacy and military planning at the same time. There is still some hope for success. The reason the United States agreed to negotiate with us is that they have some weaknesses: (1) they are not prepared for operations in two oceans; (2) they have not completed strengthening their domestic structure; (3) they are short of materials for national defense (they have only enough for one year); and so on.

They will learn how determined Japan is from the deployment of our troops, which we will carry out on the basis of the present proposal. The United States has from the beginning believed that Japan would give up because of economic pressure; but if they recognize that Japan is determined, then that is the time we should resort to diplomatic measures. I believe this is the only way that is left for us. This is the present proposal. This is the last measure we can take that is in line with what President Hara has called "going by diplomacy." I cannot think of any other way in the present situation.

If we enter into a protracted war, there will be difficulties, as mentioned before. The first stage of the war will not be difficult. We have some uneasiness about a protracted war. But how can we let the United States continue to do as she pleases, even though there is some uneasiness? Two years from now we will have no petroleum for military use. Ships will stop moving. When I think about the strengthening of American defenses in the Southwest Pacific, the expansion of the American fleet, the unfinished China Incident, and so on, I see no end to difficulties. We can talk about austerity and suffering, but can our people endure such a life for a long time? The situation is not the same as it was during the Sino-Japanese War [1894–95]. I fear that we would become a third-class nation after two or three years if we just sat tight. We agreed upon the present proposal as a result of a careful study in the light of the possibility just mentioned. The President should share our views on this point.

I intend to take measures to prevent a racial war once war is started. I should like to prevent Germany and Italy from making peace with Great Britain or with the United States by taking advantage of the results of campaigns in the South. I think the sentiments of the American people are as the President of the Privy Council has indicated, and so I intend to take precautions.

As to what our moral basis for going to war should be, there is some merit in making it clear that Great Britain and the United States represent a strong threat to Japan's self-preservation. Also, if we are fair in governing the occupied areas, attitudes toward us would probably relax. America may be enraged for a while, but later she will come to understand [why we did what we did]. In any case I will be careful to avoid the war's becoming a racial war.

Do you have any other comments? If not, I will rule that the proposals have been approved in their original form.

Plan A and Plan B

November 7 and November 20, 1941

The last act of the Pearl Harbor drama began in November 1941, when the Japanese government, in a last-ditch attempt to avoid war with the United States, dispatched a special envoy to Washington. The envoy, Saburō

Kurusu, was a career diplomat, and his superiors in the Foreign Ministry believed that he would be more adept at negotiating with the Americans than Admiral Kichisaburō Nomura, who had been Japan's ambassador in Washington since early 1941. Nomura was not a professional negotiator, his English left much to be desired, and he insisted on talking with the American leaders without an interpreter. Partly as a result of Nomura's inexperience and ineptness, the earlier "Washington conversations" (informal talks with President Franklin D. Roosevelt, Secretary of State Cordell Hull, and others) had gone nowhere, although it would be unfair to blame him for the breakdown in U.S.-Japanese communication, which was fundamentally caused by the two governments' contradictory policies in Asia.

Nomura and Kurusu were empowered to negotiate with the U.S. government for a possible deal. Japan's terms for compromise consisted of two parts, Plan A and Plan B, which had been approved in outline at the Imperial Conference of November 5. As you will see, Plan A focused on China, and Plan B on Southeast Asia. Because conflicting policies in China were the principal cause of the U.S.-Japanese difficulties, it would be difficult to arrive at a mutually acceptable settlement on the issue of China. Therefore, Tokyo judged, it might be more practical to negotiate a deal with Washington on the Southeast Asian question, which had arisen from the Japanese occupation of French Indochina and the subsequent U.S. freezing of Japanese assets. If Plan A was unacceptable to the U.S., Plan B might hold some promise. Do you think either Plan A or Plan B offered a reasonable basis for a negotiated settlement?

Plan A

(A) *Stationing of Japanese forces in China and the withdrawal thereof:*
With regard to the Japanese forces that have been dispatched to China in connection with the China Affair, those forces in specified areas in North China and Mengchiang (Inner Mongolia) as well as in Hainantao (Hainan Island) will remain to be stationed for a certain required duration after the restoration of peaceful relations between Japan and China. All the rest of such forces will commence withdrawal as soon as general peace is restored between Japan and China, and the withdrawal will proceed according to separate arrangements between Japan and China and will be completed within two years with the firm establishment of peace and order.

Peace and War: United States Foreign Policy, 1931–1941 (Washington, D.C.: Government Printing Office, 1943), 776, 801–2.

(B) *Stationing of Japanese forces in French Indo-China and the withdrawal thereof:*

The Japanese Government undertakes to guarantee the territorial sovereignty of French Indo-China. The Japanese forces at present stationed there will be withdrawn as soon as the China Affair is settled or an equitable peace is established in East Asia.

PRINCIPLE OF NON-DISCRIMINATION

The Japanese Government recognizes the principle of non-discrimination in international commercial relations to be applied to all the Pacific areas, inclusive of China, on the understanding that the principle in question is to be applied uniformly to the rest of the entire world as well.

Plan B

1. Both the Governments of Japan and the United States undertake not to make any armed advancement into any of the regions in the South-eastern Asia and the Southern Pacific area excepting the part of French Indo-China where the Japanese troops are stationed at present.

2. The Japanese Government undertakes to withdraw its troops now stationed in French Indo-China upon either the restoration of peace between Japan and China or the establishment of an equitable peace in the Pacific area.

In the meantime the Government of Japan declares that it is prepared to remove its troops now stationed in the southern part of French Indo-China to the northern part of the said territory upon the conclusion of the present arrangement which shall later be embodied in the final agreement.

3. The Governments of Japan and the United States shall cooperate with a view to securing the acquisition of those goods and commodities which the two countries need in Netherlands East Indies.

4. The Governments of Japan and the United States mutually undertake to restore their commercial relations to those prevailing prior to the freezing of the assets.

The Government of the United States shall supply Japan a required quantity of oil.

5. The Government of the United States undertakes to refrain from such measures and actions as will be prejudicial to the endeavors for the restoration of general peace between Japan and China.

WASHINGTON DISCUSSIONS ON CHINA AND THE TRIPARTITE (AXIS) PACT

As soon as Kurusu arrived in Washington, he and Ambassador Nomura paid courtesy calls to the White House and the State Department. On November 17, the Japanese diplomats met with President Roosevelt and Secretary of State Hull; on the following day, they met again with Hull. The records of their conversations are reproduced here.

Even before these meetings took place, the American leaders knew of the contents of Plans A and B, at least in outline, from deciphered Japanese cables. As you will see later in this collection (see page 158), since 1939 the U.S. Army's code breakers had been reading top secret Japanese cable messages. These were encoded in a system called PURPLE, but the Army cryptographers had developed a decoding machine called "Magic" that was capable of deciphering all PURPLE messages. They were then translated into English and made available to top U.S. officials. The translating skills of those involved in the operation were far from perfect, and they often made careless mistakes, but on the whole the decoded and translated documents accurately conveyed the gist of evolving Japanese policies and strategies. By the time Kurusu arrived in Washington, then, Roosevelt, Hull, and a few other leaders were aware of Plans A and B as they had been cabled from the Foreign Ministry in Tokyo to the Japanese embassy in Washington. Moreover, the Americans knew through intercepted messages that the Japanese considered late November to be the point at which negotiation would cease and steps toward war would be taken.

Given such foreknowledge, ask yourself whether Roosevelt, Hull, Nomura, and Kurusu acted with an appropriate sense of urgency in seeking a negotiated settlement, or whether they were wasting precious time by talking in general terms about the state of U.S.-Japanese relations. In this context, why do you think they spent so much time discussing the Tripartite Pact, the Japanese alliance with Germany? What issue was the most important in preventing a settlement: the Tripartite Pact, the status of China, or the fate of Southeast Asia? Do these documents suggest that Secretary Hull was open to, or against, some sort of negotiated settlement with Japan?

CORDELL HULL

Memorandum

November 17, 1941

I accompanied Ambassador Nomura and Ambassador Saburō Kurusu
to the White House in order that the latter might be received by the
President.

Following several minutes of an exchange of courtesies and formali-
ties, the President brought up the more serious side by referring to the
misunderstandings and matters of difference between our countries and
made clear the desire of this country, and he accepted the statement of
the Japanese Ambassador that it was the desire of Japan equally, to avoid
war between our two countries and to bring about a settlement on a fair
and peaceful basis so far as the Pacific area was concerned.

Ambassador Kurusu proceeded with one line of remarks that he kept
up during the conversation and that was that we must find ways to work
out an agreement to avoid trouble between our two countries. He said
that all the way across the Pacific it was like a powder keg, and again he
repeated that some way must be found to adjust the situation.

Ambassador Kurusu made some specious attempt to explain away
the Tripartite Pact. I replied in language similar to that which I used
in discussing this matter with Ambassador Nomura on November fifteenth, which need not be repeated here. I made it clear that any kind
of a peaceful settlement for the Pacific area, with Japan still clinging to
her Tripartite Pact with Germany, would cause the President and myself to be denounced in immeasurable terms and the peace arrangement would not for a moment be taken seriously while all the countries
interested in the Pacific would redouble their efforts to arm against Japanese aggression. I emphasized the point about the Tripartite Pact and
self-defense by saying that when Hitler starts on a march of invasion across the earth with ten million soldiers and thirty thousand airplanes with an official announcement that he is out for unlimited invasion objectives, this country from that time was in danger and that
danger has grown each week until this minute. The result was that this
country with no other motive except self-defense has recognized that

The following selections are from *Peace and War: United States Foreign Policy, 1931–1941*
(Washington, D.C.: Government Printing Office, 1943), 789–99.

danger, and has proceeded thus far to defend itself before it is too late; and that the Government of Japan says that it does not know whether this country is thus acting in self-defense or not. This country feels so profoundly the danger that it has committed itself to ten, twenty-five or fifty billions of dollars in self-defense; but when Japan is asked about whether this is self-defense, she indicates that she has no opinion on the subject — I said that I cannot get this view over to the American people; that they believe Japan must know that we are acting in self-defense and, therefore, they do not understand her present attitude. I said that he was speaking of their political difficulties and that I was thus illustrating some of our difficulties in connection with this country's relations with Japan.

The President remarked that some time ago he proclaimed a zone around this hemisphere, 300 miles out in the sea in some places and 1,100 miles in others. The President added that this was self-defense.

I then said that Ambassador Nomura and I have been proceeding on the view that the people of the United States and Japan alike are a proud and great people and there is no occasion for either to attempt to bluff the other and we would not consider that bluffing enters into our conversations, which are of genuine friendliness.

The President brought out a number of illustrations of our situation and the Japanese situation as it relates to Germany and our self-defense which serve to emphasize our position and to expose the sophistry of the Japanese position.

Ambassador Kurusu said that Germany had not up to this time requested Japan to fight; that she was serving a desirable purpose without doing so, — this must have meant that she was keeping the American and British Navies, aircraft, et cetera, diverted.

The further question of whether the United States is on the defensive in the present Pacific situation came up by some general discussion in reference to that situation by Ambassador Kurusu, and the President and I made it clear that we were not the aggressors in the Pacific but that Japan was the aggressor.

At another point I said that the belief in this country is that the Japanese formula of a new order in greater East Asia is but another name for a program to dominate entirely, politically, economically, socially and otherwise by military force all of the Pacific area; that this would include the high seas, the islands and the continents and would place every other country at the mercy of very arbitrary military rule just as the Hitler program does in Europe and the Japanese in China. The Ambassador made no particular comment.

There was some effort by Ambassador Kurusu to defend their plan of not bringing the troops out of China. Placing the Japanese on the defensive, the President said that the question ought to be worked out in a fair way considering all of the circumstances and relative merits of the matters involved; and that at a suitable stage, while we know that Japan does not wish us to mediate in any way, this Government might, so to speak, introduce Japan and China to each other and tell them to proceed with the remaining or detailed adjustments, the Pacific questions having already been determined.

Ambassador Kurusu strongly stated that it would be most difficult to bring all the troops out of China at once.

Ambassador Kurusu said that we, of course, desired to bring up both sides of matters existing between our two countries and he said that we would recall that when the Japanese went into Shantung during the World War, this Government insisted that she get out. I replied that my own country opposed a policy of this seizure of new territory by any country to the fullest extent of its ability to do so; that it declined to take a dollar of compensation or a foot of territory for itself; that it insisted that the world must turn over a new leaf in this respect or nations would be fighting always for territory and under modern methods of war would soon destroy and utterly impoverish each other; that in any event his country fared well in this respect.

The question of our recent proposal on commercial policy was brought up by us and Ambassador Kurusu said he had not examined it and that he had forgotten much of the technical side of commercial policy since he was in the Foreign Office. The President made very pertinent and timely reference to the destructive nature of armaments and the still more destructive effects of a permanent policy of armaments which always means war, devastation and destruction. He emphasized the point that there is from the long-term point of view no difference of interest between our two countries and no occasion, therefore, for serious differences.

All in all, there was nothing new brought out by the Japanese Ambassador and Ambassador Kurusu. Ambassador Kurusu constantly made the plea that there was no reason why there should be serious differences between the two countries and that ways must be found to solve the present situation. He referred to Prime Minister Tōjō as being very desirous of bringing about a peaceful adjustment notwithstanding he is an Army man. The President expressed his interest and satisfaction to hear this. The President frequently parried the remarks of Ambassador Nomura and also of Ambassador Kurusu, especially in regard to the three main points of difference between our two countries. There was no effort to solve these questions at the conference. The meeting broke up with the understanding that I would meet the Japanese representatives tomorrow morning.

C[ORDELL] H[ULL]

JOSEPH W. BALLANTINE *

Memorandum

November 18, 1941

The Japanese Ambassador and Mr. Kurusu called on the Secretary, by appointment made at their request, at the Department.

After some preliminary remarks the Secretary took up the question of Japan's relations with the Axis. He pointed out that the public would place their own interpretation upon the implications of a situation wherein on the one hand Japan had an agreement with us and on the other was in an alliance with the Axis powers. He said that our people do not trust Hitler and furthermore we feel that it would be inevitable that Hitler would eventually, if he was successful, get around to the Far East and double-cross Japan. The Secretary cited the instance when Germany, after having concluded an anti-Comintern pact** with Japan had surprised Japan later on by entering into a non-aggression pact with Russia and finally went back on the non-aggression pact by attacking Russia. The Secretary said that he presumed Japan did not know in advance what Germany's intentions were any more than we did. The Secretary expressed great doubt that any agreement into which we entered with Japan while Japan at the same time had an alliance with Hitler would carry the confidence of our people and he emphasized that we would have to have a clear-cut agreement making self-evident our peaceful pur-

---

*A foreign service officer specializing in Japanese affairs. He worked in the Far Eastern Division of the State Department and was the principal aide to Secretary of State Hull during the November 1941 negotiations with the Japanese.

**Signed by Germany and Japan in November 1936. Ostensibly an agreement to cooperate in checking activities by the Communist International operating out of Moscow, the pact contained a secret understanding that neither Germany nor Japan would come to the aid of the Soviet Union if the latter should attack one of them.

pose, for otherwise there would be a redoubled effort by all nations to strengthen their armaments. He pointed out that we are coming out of the Philippines in 1946 and that we are now bringing our marines out of China and in this way we are trying to make a contribution to the establishment of a peaceful world based on law and order. He said that this is what we want to work out with Japan; that we had nothing to offer in the way of bargaining except our friendship. Our commercial program was one, he said, calling for a maximum production and distribution of goods. The Secretary pointed out also that we are even now engaged in efforts to induce the British Empire to reduce its Empire preferences. He said that what we desire is to put our people back to work in a way that can never be accomplished through permitting armies to overrun countries. The Secretary observed that many Japanese spokesmen had spoken of Japan's desire to have a controlling influence in Eastern Asia, but the only kind of controlling influence which was worth anything was one that could not be achieved or maintained by the sword. He dwelt briefly upon what we have accomplished in South America through our peaceful policies and through renouncing the employment of gunboats and armed forces. The Secretary made it clear that we recognized that under present emergency conditions we cannot carry out to perfection our commercial policy which must be modified to meet war conditions, but we can at least establish the principles. The Secretary said, going back to the situation with regard to Japan's relations with the Axis, that a difficult situation was created thereby as far as our public was concerned — as, for example, when telegrams of congratulations were sent to Hitler by Japanese leaders when he commits some atrocity.

The Japanese Ambassador observed that the United States and Russia were not pursuing parallel courses and yet we are aligned with Russia at the present time. He also said he appreciated very well the relations we had developed with South America but that, although Japan would like to imitate us, Japan was not in a position to be so magnanimous — as, for example, in the matter of extending substantial lend-lease aid to other countries. . . . The Secretary then added that he frankly did not know whether anything could be done in the matter of reaching a satisfactory agreement with Japan; that we can go so far but rather than go beyond a certain point it would be better for us to stand and take the consequences. The Ambassador then said that Japan is now hard-pressed and that the Secretary was well aware of how desirous Japan was to reach some agreement with the United States.

Mr. Kurusu said that he had served five years as Director of the Commercial Bureau of the Japanese Foreign Office and that he was familiar with the developments in Japan's commercial policy. He said that the situation with respect to the Empire preferences was one of the factors which had influenced Japan to go into the Axis camp. He said that the United States was an economically powerful country and that the United States was, therefore, in a much better position than was Japan to enter into commercial bargaining. Furthermore, Japan was much more dependent than was the United States upon foreign trade. He felt that what the two Governments should now do would be to achieve something to tide over the present abnormal situation. He referred, for example, to the exchange control situation which had been developed in Japanese-occupied China and expressed the view that that situation could not be done away with in a short time. He said that perhaps after the war was over it might be possible to adopt a more liberal policy but that he was unable to promise anything on the part of his Government. The Secretary asked whether Japan could not now agree in principle on commercial policy. Mr. Kurusu made no direct reply but went on to say that in the early years of American intercourse in the Far East our main interest was in commerce and not religious and cultural activities; that we had pursued a course of idealism, but with American occupation of the Philippines the situation changed somewhat and the United States tied itself in with the European concert of nations.

Turning to the question of the Tripartite Pact, Mr. Kurusu said that he could not say that Japan would abrogate the Tripartite Pact but that Japan might do something which would "outshine" the Tripartite Pact.

The Secretary pointed out that unless peacefully minded nations now start their program of reconstruction it will be impossible to get such a program started later on because the selfish elements would get control of the situation and prevent the materialization of a liberal policy. Therefore, he said it was necessary to get the fundamental principles established so that we might begin to enable the peaceful forces, which were now demoralized, to assert a leadership. Unless we pursue such a course, the Secretary noted, we shall not be able to obtain the confidence of peacefully minded people when the time for putting into effect a reconstruction program arrives. Mr. Kurusu asked whether the Secretary had a concrete formula for dealing with Japan's relations with the Axis alliance. The Secretary made it clear that this was a matter for Japan to work out. He said that if we could get a peaceful program firmly established, Hitler ought to be asked not to embarrass us too much. He asked whether Japan could not work it out in some way which would be convincing to the American people. He said that if it goes the wrong way every peaceful nation will redouble its defensive efforts. The Secretary emphasized again that the public would be confused in regard to a survival of a relationship between Japan and the Axis while Japan had an agreement with the United States.

The Ambassador asked whether it was not important now to make some understanding to save the situation. The Secretary said he agreed but that he felt that the Tripartite Pact was inconsistent with the establishment of an understanding.

Mr. Kurusu asked what could the Secretary suggest. The Secretary said that if we mix the Tripartite Pact with an agreement with the United States it will not be possible to get many people to follow us. The Secretary said that the question arises whether Japanese statesmen desire to follow entirely peaceful courses with China or whether they desire to face two ways. The Secretary went on to say that if the Japanese should back away from adopting a clear-cut position with regard to commercial policy, with regard to a course in China consistent with peaceful principles and with regard to Japanese relations to the European war this would leave us in an indefensible position in regard to the proposed agreement. We would have to say that the Japanese Government is unable to get its politicians into line.

The Ambassador repeated that the situation in Japan was very pressing and that it was important to arrest a further deterioration of the relations between the two countries. He suggested that if this situation could now be checked an atmosphere would develop when it would be possible to move in the direction of the courses which this Government advocated. He pointed out that big ships cannot turn around too quickly, that they have to be eased around slowly and gradually.

The Secretary replied that if we should sit down and write an agreement permeated with the doctrine of force it would be found that each country would be entirely distrustful and would be piling up armaments, as countries cannot promote peace so long as they are tied in in any way with Hitler.

Mr. Kurusu pointed out that a comprehensive solution cannot be worked out immediately, that he could make no promises. He said that our freezing regulations had caused impatience in Japan and a feeling that Japan had to fight while it still could. If we could come to some settlement now, he said, it would promote an atmosphere which would be conducive to discussing fundamentals. The Secretary asked if he did not think that something could be worked out on the Tripartite Pact. The Ambassador said that he desired to emphasize that Japan would not be a cat's-paw for Germany, that Japan's purpose in entering into the Tripartite alliance was to use it for Japan's own purposes, that Japan entered the Tripartite Pact because Japan felt isolated. The Secretary observed that it would be difficult to get public opinion in this country to understand the situation as Mr. Kurusu had described it.

He then asked what the Ambassador had in mind in regard to the Chinese situation and whether the Japanese stood for no annexations, no indemnities, respect for China's sovereignty, territorial integrity and the principle of equality. The Ambassador replied in the affirmative.

The Secretary then said that while he had made this point already clear to the Ambassador he wished to make it clear also to Mr. Kurusu, that whereas the Japanese Government desired to consider our talks negotiations rather than exploratory conversations, the Secretary felt that without having first reached a real basis for negotiations, he was not in a position to go to the British or the Chinese or the other governments involved, as these governments had a rightful interest in these problems. Mr. Kurusu tried to get the Secretary to specify in just which problems each of the respective governments were interested but the Secretary said that he had not yet, for manifest reasons, discussed these problems with these other governments and anything that he might say would be just an assumption on his part. Mr. Kurusu then said that under such circumstances United States and Japanese relations would be at the mercy of Great Britain and China. The Secretary replied that he believed and must repeat that we must have something substantial in the way of a basis for an agreement to take to these governments for otherwise there would be no point in talking to them. Mr. Kurusu said that the situation was so pressing that it might get beyond our control. The Secretary agreed that that was true but he pointed out that the fact that Japan's leaders keep announcing programs based upon force adds to our difficulties. He said he would like to leave the Hitler situation to the Japanese Government for consideration.

Turning to the China situation the Secretary asked how many soldiers the Japanese wanted to retain in China. The Ambassador replied that possibly 90 per cent would be withdrawn. The Secretary asked how long the Japanese intended to keep that remaining 10 per cent in China. The Ambassador did not reply directly to this but he invited attention to the fact that under the existing Boxer Protocol Japan was permitted to retain troops in the Peiping and Tientsin area. The Secretary pointed out that the question of the Japanese troops in China was one in which there were many elements of trouble. American interests even had suffered severely from the actions of the Japanese forces and we had a long list of such instances. The Secretary made mention of the great patience this Government had exercised in the presence of this situation. He said the situation was one in which the extremists seemed to be looking for trouble and he said that it was up to the Japanese Government to make an extra effort to take the situation by the collar. He said also that the United States and Japan had trusted each other in the past, that the present situation was one of Japan's own making and it was up to the Japanese Government to find some way of getting itself out of the difficulty in which it had placed itself. The Secretary went on to say that the situation was now exceptionally advantageous for Japan to put her factories to work in producing goods which are needed by peaceful countries if only the Japanese people could get war and invasion out of mind. The Ambassador said that our conversations had been protracted and if the American Government could only give the Japanese some hope with regard to the situation it might be helpful. He added that our country was great and strong. The Secretary replied that our Government has not made any threats and he has exercised his influence throughout to deprecate bellicose utterances in this country. He added that the Japanese armed forces in China do not appear to realize whose territory they are in and that the people in this country say that Hitler proposes to take charge of one-half of the world and Japan proposes to take charge of the other half and if they should succeed what would there be left for the United States? Mr. Kurusu suggested that Japan would have to move gradually in China, that one step might lead to another and that what was important now was to do something to enable Japan to change its course. The Secretary asked what was in Mr. Kurusu's mind. In reply to a suggestion that it was felt in Japanese circles that we have been responsible for delay the Secretary pointed out that we could more rightly accuse the Japanese of delays, that he had met with the Japanese Ambassador promptly every time the latter had asked for a meeting and had discussed matters fully with him. The Secretary added that when Japan's movement into Indochina in July took place this had caused an interruption of our conversations and it was then that the Secretary could no longer defend the continued shipments of petroleum products to Japan, especially as for the past year he had been under severe criticism in this country for not having cut off those shipments. Mr. Kurusu asked whether we wanted the *status quo ante* to be restored or what we expected Japan to do. The Secretary replied that if the Japanese could not do anything now on those three points — getting troops out of China, commercial policy and the Tripartite agreement — he could only leave to

Japan what Japan could do. The Secretary said that it is our desire to see Japan help furnish a world leadership for a peaceful program and that he felt that Japan's long-swing interests were the same as our interests. The Ambassador said that he realized that our Government was suspicious of the Japanese Government but he wished to assure us that Japan wanted to settle the China affair notwithstanding the fact that Japan desired to keep a few troops in China for the time being. The Secretary then asked again what the Japanese had in mind. Mr. Kurusu said that it was Japan's intention to withdraw Japanese troops from French Indochina as soon as a just Pacific settlement should be reached and he pointed out that the Japanese Government took the Burma Road* situation very seriously. The Secretary asked, if there should be a relaxation of freezing, to what extent would that enable Japan to adopt peaceful policies. He explained that what he had in mind was to enable the peaceful leaders in Japan to get control of the situation in Japan and to assert their influence. The Ambassador said that our position was unyielding and that it was Japan's [sic] unyielding attitude toward Chiang Kai-shek which had stiffened Chinese resistance against Japan. He asked whether there was any hope of a solution — some small beginning toward the realization of our high ideals. The Secretary replied that if we do not work out an agreement that the public trusts the arming of nations will go on; that the Japanese Government has a responsibility in the matter as it has created the conditions we are trying to deal with. The Ambassador then suggested the possibility of going back to the status which existed before the date in July when, following the Japanese move into southern French Indochina, our freezing measures were put into effect. The Secretary said that if we should make some modifications in our embargo on the strength of a step by Japan such as the Ambassador had mentioned we do not know whether the troops which have been withdrawn from French Indochina will be diverted to some equally objectionable movement elsewhere. The Ambassador said that what he had in mind was simply some move toward arresting the dangerous trend in our relations. The Secretary said that it would be difficult for him to get this Government to go a long way in removing the embargo unless this Government believed that Japan was definitely started on a peaceful

---

*Built in 1938, connecting, through mostly mountains and jungles, southern China with Burma, a British colony. In July 1940 Japan demanded the closing of the road, which the Japanese viewed as the last remaining channel for bringing supplies from the outside world to the Chongqing regime. Britain acquiesced to the closing for three months, and in October the Burma Road was reopened.

course and had renounced purposes of conquest. The Ambassador said that the Japanese were tired of fighting China and that Japan would go as far as it could along a first step. The Secretary said that he would consult with the British and the Dutch to see what their attitude would be toward the suggestion offered by the Japanese Ambassador. In reply to a question by the Secretary the Ambassador replied that the Japanese Government was still studying the questions of commercial policy involved in our proposal of November 15. He said he assumed that what we had in mind was a program for dealing with the situation after the war. The Secretary replied in the affirmative, so far as the full operation of a sound program is concerned, but added that it should now be agreed upon as to principles.

When asked by the Secretary as to when the Ambassador would like to confer with us again the Ambassador said that he would get in touch with his Government and would communicate to the Secretary through Mr. Ballantine.

DISCUSSING PLAN B

The White House and State Department meetings of November 17 and 18 indicated the hopelessness of arriving at a satisfactory solution to the China problem, and the stage was set for last-minute negotiations on the basis of Plan B. It was presented by the Japanese emissaries to Secretary of State Hull on November 20, and between that day and November 26, the U.S. and Japanese negotiators met on two additional occasions to discuss the plan. In the meantime, there was intensive activity among U.S. officials to counter Japan's Plan B with their own proposals.

Because the future of U.S.-Japanese relations, indeed the fate of the world, hinged on the discussion of Plan B, it is very important to study carefully the record of the conversations as well as the various drafts prepared by U.S. officials. Most U.S. military leaders wanted to delay the coming of a Pacific war in order to focus their efforts on the defense of Britain and the Soviet Union. General George Marshall, chief of the General Staff, hoped that putting more aircraft (B-17s) in the Philippines would make it possible to stop a Japanese southward advance by March 1942. Even if a showdown with Japan over China, Southeast Asia, and the Asian-Pacific region was ultimately inevitable, the situation in Europe might improve by the spring of 1942 and then the United States would be better prepared to fight a two-front war.

Could such a war, then, be postponed through a last-minute deal with Japan? The documents here suggest that many U.S. leaders thought it was worth trying. Plan B proposed, in essence, Japan's pledge not to invade Southeast Asian countries in exchange for a resumption of U.S. oil shipments to Japan. If such a deal could be struck, it would keep Japanese forces out of the British and Dutch colonies in Asia and the Pacific. There were rough estimates in Washington — confirmed after the war in Japanese documents — that without additional supplies of petroleum Japanese naval vessels would not be able to operate beyond two years at most. To resume shipments of oil would obviously change the picture. However, Japanese vulnerability itself would remain, for the United States could always threaten to resume embargoing of petroleum. Therefore, it might make sense for the United States to consider accepting part, if not the entirety, of Plan B as a strictly temporary expedient.

Would you agree with such reasoning? All of these drafts were written for discussion within the U.S. government, and none was actually presented to the Japanese, but if one of the draft proposals had been presented to Japan in response to Plan B, would the Japanese have accepted it? Would war have been avoided? You will note that within just a few days the proposed U.S. response to Japan's Plan B became more and more complex. Does this suggest a mounting sense of urgency to reach an agreement with Japan or rather a growing reluctance to compromise?

JOSEPH W. BALLANTINE

Memorandum

November 20, 1941

The Japanese Ambassador and Mr. Kurusu called at their request at the Department. Mr. Kurusu said that they had referred to their Government the suggestion which the Ambassador had made at a previous

The following selections are from *Peace and War: United States Foreign Policy, 1931–1941* (Washington, D.C.: Government Printing Office, 1943), 799–807; *Papers Relating to the Foreign Relations of the United States, 1941,* vol. 4 (Washington, D.C.: Government Printing Office, 1956), 633–37, 642–43, 661–64.

meeting in regard to a return to the status which prevailed prior to the Japanese move into south Indochina last July, and said that they had anticipated that the Japanese Government might perceive difficulty in moving troops out of Indochina in short order, but that nevertheless the Japanese Government was now prepared to offer a proposal on that basis. He said, however, that the proposal represented an amplification of the Ambassador's suggestion. He then read the proposal to the Secretary which was as follows:

[Here follows the text of the proposal.]

The Secretary said that he would later examine the proposal, and that he would give sympathetic study to the proposal speaking generally, but that the comments which he was about to make were not directed specifically to the proposal but to the general situation. The Secretary said that Japan had it in its power at any moment to put an end to the present situation by deciding upon an all-out peaceful course; that at any moment Japan could bring to an end what Japan chose to call encirclement. He said that we want to have Japan develop public opinion in favor of a peaceful course. Mr. Kurusu said that if we could alleviate the situation by adopting a proposal such as the Japanese Government had just made it would help develop public opinion. The Ambassador said that the Japanese Government was clearly desirous of peace and that it was trying to show this peaceful purpose by relieving the pressure on Thailand which adoption of the proposal would accomplish.

The Secretary asked what the Ambassador thought would be the public reaction in this country if we were to announce tomorrow that we had decided to discontinue aid to Great Britain. He said that in the minds of the American people the purposes underlying our aid to China were the same as the purposes underlying aid to Great Britain; that the American people believed that there was a partnership between Hitler and Japan aimed at enabling Hitler to take charge of one-half of the world and Japan of the other half; and that the fact of the Tripartite Alliance and the continual harping by Japanese leaders upon slogans of the Nazi type such as "new order in East Asia" and "co-prosperity sphere" served to strengthen the public in their belief. What was therefore needed, the Secretary pointed out, was the manifestation by Japan of a clear purpose to pursue peaceful courses.

The Ambassador replied that there was no doubt of Japan's desire for peace, as this was clear from the eagerness of the Japanese Government to reach a settlement of the China affair — and indeed adoption of the Japanese Government's proposal that he had just presented was designed to bring about speedy settlement of the China affair. He said that the Japanese people after four years of fighting were jaded and that the slogans to which the Secretary had made reference were intended to encourage the Japanese people to push on to victory.

The Secretary said that we of course are anxious to help work this matter out for if we should get into trouble everybody was likely to get hurt.

Mr. Kurusu said that if we could go ahead with the present proposal the Japanese idea would be that we could go on working at fundamentals. He said that Japan has never pledged itself to a policy of expansion. The Secretary observed that the Chinese might have an answer to that point. The Secretary said that our people desired to avoid a repetition in east Asia of what Hitler was doing in Europe; that our people oppose the idea of a "new order" under military control. He said also that the public in this country thinks that Japan is chained to Hitler. Mr. Kurusu asked how Japan could eradicate such a belief as Japan could not abrogate the Tripartite Pact. The Secretary said that he did not want to be disagreeable, but he felt he must observe that Japan did not talk that way about the Nine Power Treaty. Mr. Kurusu said something about the Nine Power Treaty being twenty years old and being outmoded. The Secretary said that of course he did not wish to argue the matter. He said that when the Japanese complained about our helping China the public in this country wonders what is underneath the [anti-]Comintern Pact. He emphasized that Japan is doing this country tremendous injury in the Pacific; that Japanese statesmen ought to understand that we are helping China for the same reason that we are helping Britain; that we are afraid of the military elements led by Hitler. He added that the methods adopted by the Japanese military leaders in China were not unlike Hitler's methods. The Ambassador asked how we could save the situation at this juncture. The Secretary replied that he agreed upon the urgent importance of saving it, but he asked whether the Ambassador thought that the Japanese statesmen could tone down the situation in Japan. Mr. Kurusu said, with reference to the fifth point in the Japanese proposal, that he did not know whether his Government would agree but he thought that that point might be interpreted to mean that American aid to China would be discontinued as from the time that negotiations were started. The Secretary made no comment on that point but noted that in the last few days there had been marked subsidence in warlike utterances emanating from Tokyo, and he felt that it was indeed a great tribute to the Ambassador and Mr. Kurusu that so much had been accomplished in this direction within a short space of two days as he felt sure that it was their efforts which had brought this about. He said that if so much had been accomplished within the course of two days, much more could be accomplished in the course of a longer period.

No time was set for the next meeting.

JOSEPH W. BALLANTINE

Memorandum

November 22, 1941

The Japanese Ambassador and Mr. Kurusu called at the Secretary's apartment by appointment made at the request of the Ambassador. The Secretary said that he had called in the representatives of certain other governments concerned in the Pacific area and that there had been a discussion of the question of whether things (meaning Japanese peaceful pledges, et. cetera) could be developed in such a way that there could be a relaxation to some extent of freezing. The Secretary said that these representatives were interested in the suggestion and there was a general feeling that the matter could all be settled if the Japanese could give us some satisfactory evidences that their intentions were peaceful.

The Secretary said that in discussing the situation with the representatives of these other countries he found that there had arisen in their minds the same kind of misgivings that had troubled him in the course of the conversations with the Japanese Ambassador. He referred to the position in which the Japanese Government had left the Ambassador and the Secretary as they were talking of peace when it made its move last July into Indochina. He referred also to the mounting oil purchases by Japan last Spring when the conversations were in progress, to the fact that he had endured public criticism for permitting those shipments because he did not wish to prejudice a successful outcome to the conversations and to the fact that that oil was not used for normal civilian consumption.

The Secretary went on to say that the Japanese press which is adopting a threatening tone gives him no encouragement and that no Japanese statesmen are talking about a peaceful course, whereas in the American press advocacy of a peaceful course can always get a hearing. He asked why was there not some Japanese statesman backing the two Ambassadors by preaching peace. The Secretary pointed out that if the United States and other countries should see Japan coming along a peaceful course there would be no question about Japan's obtaining all the materials she desired; that the Japanese Government knows that.

The Secretary said that while no decisions were reached today in regard to the Japanese proposals he felt that we would consider helping Japan out on oil for civilian requirements only as soon as the Japanese Government could assert control of the situation in Japan as it relates to the policy of force and conquest. He said that if the Ambassador could give him any further assurances in regard to Japan's peaceful intentions it would help the Secretary in talking with senators and other persons in this country.

Mr. Kurusu said it was unfortunate that there had been a special session of the Diet at this time, as the efforts of the Government to obtain public support had brought out in sharp relief the abnormal state of the present temper of the Japanese people who had been affected by four years of war and by our freezing measures.

The Secretary asked to what extent in the Ambassador's opinion did the firebrand attitude prevail in the Japanese army. Mr. Kurusu said that it took a great deal of persuasion to induce the army to abandon a position once taken, but that both he and the Ambassador had been pleasantly surprised when the Japanese army acceded to their suggestion in regard to offering to withdraw the Japanese troops from southern Indochina. He said he thought this was an encouraging sign, but that nevertheless the situation was approaching an explosive point.

The Secretary asked whether it was not possible for a Japanese statesman now to come out and say that Japan wanted peace; that while there was much confusion in the world because of the war situation Japan would like to have a peace which she did not have to fight for to obtain and maintain; that the United States says it stands for such ideas; and that Japan might well ask the United States for a show-down on this question.

The Ambassador said he did not have the slightest doubt that Japan desired peace. He then cited the popular agitation in Japan following the conclusion of the peace settlement with Russia in 1905, as pointing to a difficulty in the way of publicly backing a conciliatory course.

The Secretary asked whether there was any way to get Japanese statesmen to approach the question before us with real appreciation of the situation with which we are dealing including the question of finding a way to encourage the governments of other powers concerned in the

Pacific area to reach some trade arrangement with Japan. He pointed out that Japan's Indochina move, if repeated, would further give a spurt to arming and thus undo all the work that he and the Ambassador had done. He suggested that if the United States and the other countries should supply Japan with goods in moderate amounts at the beginning those countries would be inclined to satisfy Japan more fully later on if and as Japan found ways in actual practice of demonstrating its peaceful intentions. He said that one move on Japan's part might kill dead our peace effort, whereas it would be easy to persuade the other countries to relax their export restrictions if Japan would be satisfied with gradual relaxation.

Mr. Kurusu said that at best it would take some time to get trade moving. The Secretary replied that he understood this but that it would be difficult to get other countries to understand until Japan could convince those countries that it was committed to peaceful ways. Mr. Kurusu said that some immediate relief was necessary and that if the patient needed a thousand dollars to effect a cure an offer of three hundred dollars would not accomplish the purpose. The Secretary commented that if the Japanese Government was as weak as to need all that had been asked for, nothing was likely to save it.

Mr. Kurusu said that Japan's offer to withdraw its forces from southern Indochina would set a reverse movement in motion.

The Secretary said that the Japanese were not helping as they should help in the present situation in which they had got themselves but were expecting us to do the whole thing.

Mr. Kurusu asked what was the idea of the American Government.

The Secretary replied that although the Japanese proposal was addressed to the American Government he had thought it advisable to see whether the other countries would contribute and he found that they would like to move gradually. The effect of an arrangement between these countries and Japan would be electrifying by showing that Japan had committed herself to go along a peaceful course.

Mr. Kurusu asked what Japan could do. The Secretary replied that if, for example, he should say that he agreed to enter into a peaceful settlement provided that there should be occasional exceptions and qualifications he could not expect to find peaceful-minded nations interested.

The Secretary then asked whether his understanding was correct that the Japanese proposal was intended as a temporary step to help organize public opinion in Japan and that it was intended to continue the conversations looking to the conclusion of a comprehensive agreement. Mr. Kurusu said yes.

Mr. Kurusu asked whether the Secretary had any further suggestions. The Secretary replied that he did not have in mind any suggestions and that he did not know what amounts of exports the various countries would be disposed to release to Japan. He said that Japan made the situation very difficult, for if Japan left her forces in Indochina, whether in the north, east, south or west, she would be able to move them over night, and that therefore this would not relieve the apprehensions of neighboring countries. The British, for example, would not be able to move one warship away from Singapore.

The Ambassador argued that it would take many days to move troops from northern Indochina to southern Indochina, and he stated that the Japanese desired the troops in northern Indochina in order to bring about a settlement with China. He said that after the settlement of the China affair Japan promised to bring the troops out of Indochina altogether.

The Secretary emphasized again that he could not consider this, that also uneasiness would prevail as long as the troops remained in Indochina, and commented that Japan wanted the United States to do all the pushing toward bringing about a peaceful settlement; that they should get out of Indochina.

Mr. Kurusu observed that the Japanese Foreign Minister had told Ambassador Grew that we seemed to expect that all the concessions should be made by the Japanese side.

The Secretary rejoined that Mr. Kurusu had overlooked the fact that in July the Japanese had gone into Indochina. He added that the United States had remained from the first in the middle of the road, that it was the Japanese who had strayed away from the course of law and order, and that they should not have to be paid to come back to a lawful course.

Mr. Kurusu said that this country's denunciation of the commercial treaty had caused Japan to be placed in a tight corner.

The Secretary observed that Japan had cornered herself; that we had been preaching for the last nine years that militarism was sapping everybody and that if the world were to be plunged into another war there would not be much left of the people anywhere. He said that in 1934 he had told Ambassador Saitō that Japan was planning an overlordship in East Asia. The Secretary added that he had tried to persuade Hitler that participation by him in a peaceful course would assure him of what he needed. The Secretary said it was a pity that Japan could not do just a few small peaceful things to help tide over the situation.

Mr. Kurusu asked what the Secretary meant. The Secretary replied that the major portion of our fleet was being kept in the Pacific and yet

Japan asked us not to help China. He said we must continue to aid China. He said it was little enough that we were actually doing to help China. The Ambassador commented that our moral influence was enabling Chiang to hold out.

The Secretary said that a peaceful movement could be started in thirty or forty days by moving gradually, and yet Japan pushed everything it wanted all at once into its proposal. The Ambassador explained that Japan needed a quick settlement and that its psychological value would be great.

The Secretary said that he was discouraged, that he felt that he had rendered a real contribution when he had called in the representatives of the other countries, but that he could only go a certain distance. He said he thought nevertheless that if this matter should move in the right way peace would become infectious. He pointed also to the danger arising from blocking progress by injecting the China matter in the proposal, as the carrying out of such a point in the Japanese proposal would effectually prevent the United States from ever successfully extending its good offices in a peace settlement between Japan and China. He said this could not be considered now.

There then ensued some further but inconclusive discussion of the troop situation in Indochina, the Secretary still standing for withdrawal, after which the Ambassador reverted to the desire of the Japanese Government to reach a quick settlement and asked whether we could not say what points in the Japanese proposal we would accept and what points we desired to have modified.

The Secretary emphasized that there was no way in which he could carry the whole burden and suggested that it would be helpful if the Japanese Government could spend a little time preaching peace. He said that if the Japanese could not wait until Monday [November 24, 1941] before having his answer there was nothing he could do about it as he was obliged to confer again with the representatives of the other governments concerned after they had had an opportunity to consult with their governments. He repeated that we were doing our best, but emphasized that unless the Japanese were able to do a little there was no use in talking.

The Ambassador disclaimed any desire to press the Secretary too hard for an answer, agreed that the Secretary had always been most considerate in meeting with the Ambassador whenever an appointment had been requested, and said that the Japanese would be quite ready to wait until Monday.

The Secretary said he had in mind taking up with the Ambassador sometime a general and comprehensive program which we had been engaged in developing and which involved collaboration of other countries.

The Ambassador said that the Japanese had in mind negotiating a bilateral agreement with us to which other powers could subsequently give their adherence.

JOSEPH W. BALLANTINE

Memorandum

November 22, 1941

MR. SECRETARY: With reference to the Japanese proposal of November 20 for a *modus vivendi* and our memorandum containing suggestions for possible comment that might be made orally to the Japanese in regard to their proposal (copy of which is attached), there are given below additional suggestions for possible comment:

With reference to item three in regard to cooperation in obtaining from the Netherlands East Indies materials which our two countries need, it is not clear why the Japanese Government desires to limit this proposal to Netherlands East Indies. It would appear to us that, if the Japanese Government could see its way clear to adopting our proposal in regard to commercial policy, the field for cooperation by the two countries would not be limited to any one area but would extend to the entire world. It would seem to us that the Japanese proposal takes no account of our broad offer which was renewed in very specific terms in the paper which was given to the Japanese Ambassador on November 15. It would seem to us that such a proposal would be open to possible criticism. That is to say that, whereas Japan was insisting on preferential treatment for itself in certain areas, in other areas it was asking for cooperation of the United States in obtaining for Japan the very kind of economic opportunities which Japan was trying to deny to third countries elsewhere. This Government has consistently advocated broadening the basis of world trade not from any selfish point of view but from the point of view of providing stable peace and elimination of chronic political instability and recurrent economic collapse. Such a program would provide means of raising living standards all over the world, thus promoting the well-being of all peoples.

With reference to the provision that the Government of the United States should supply Japan a required quantity of oil, it may be observed that until very recently the United States was supplying Japan with an ever-increasing amount of petroleum products, even to the extent where there was widespread public criticism in the United States of permitting this to continue. The period since 1937 was marked, on the one hand, by a tremendous increase in imports into Japan from the United States of petroleum products and, on the other hand, according to reports reaching us, by a progressive curtailment in the amounts of oil released in that country for normal peacetime consumption. There is no desire in this country to deny to Japan petroleum products needed for its normal economy, but the increased consumption of American petroleum products in Japan for a military purpose brings to the fore a question which we have called to the attention of the Japanese Ambassador, namely, that the Japanese association with the Axis powers is doing the United States tremendous injury.

With regard to the fifth point in the Japanese proposal, you might wish to emphasize again what you said to the Japanese Ambassador on November 20, namely, that, when the Japanese complain about our helping China, the public in this country wonders what is underneath the Anti-Comintern Pact; that Japanese statesmen ought to understand we are helping China for the same reason that we are helping Britain; that we are afraid of the military elements throughout the world led by Hitler; and that the methods adopted by the Japanese military leaders in China are not unlike Hitler's methods. You might then ask what the Ambassador thinks would be the public reaction in this country if we were to announce that we had decided to discontinue aid to Great Britain. You might say that in the minds of American people the purposes underlying our aid to China are the same as the purposes underlying our aid to Great Britain and that the American people believe that there is a partnership between Hitler and Japan aimed at dividing the world between them.

J[OSEPH] W. B[ALLANTINE]

Draft of Proposed Modus Vivendi *with Japan*

November 22, 1941

Strictly Confidential,
Tentative and without
Commitment

Oral

The representatives of the Government of the United States and of the Government of Japan have been carrying on during the past several months informal and exploratory conversations for the purpose of arriving at a settlement if possible of the questions relating to the entire Pacific area based upon the principles of law and order and fair dealing among nations. These principles include the principle of inviolability of territorial integrity and sovereignty of each and all nations; the principle of non-interference in the internal affairs of other countries; the principle of equality, including equality of commercial opportunity and treatment; and the principle of reliance upon international cooperation and conciliation for the prevention and pacific settlement of controversies and for improvement of international conditions by peaceful methods and processes.

On November 20 the Japanese Ambassador indicated that the Government of Japan is desirous of going ahead with such a program; that the domestic political situation within Japan is urgent; and that, in order to give the Japanese Government opportunity to develop and promote public sentiment in Japan in support of a comprehensive and liberal program of peace such as has been under discussion between our two Governments, it would be helpful if there could be taken some initial steps toward resumption of trade and normal intercourse between Japan and the United States. At that time the Japanese Ambassador communicated to the Secretary of State proposals in regard to measures to be taken respectively by the Government of Japan and by the Government of the United States, which measures are understood to have been designed to create an atmosphere favorable to pursuing the conversations which have been taking place. These proposals contain features which from the point of view of the Government of the United States present difficulties in reference to the broad-gauge principles the practical application of which represents the desires of both Governments as manifested in current conversations. In as much as the Government of the United States desires to contribute to the peace of the Pacific area and to afford every opportunity to continue discussions with the Japanese Government directed toward working out a broad-gauge program of peace throughout the Pacific area, the Government of the United States offers for the consideration of the Japanese Government suggestions as follows:

Modus Vivendi

1. The Government of the United States and the Government of Japan, both being solicitous for the peace of the Pacific, affirm that their national policies are directed toward lasting and extensive peace throughout the Pacific area and that they have no territorial designs therein. They undertake reciprocally not to make by force or threat of force, unless they are attacked, any advancement, from points at which they have military establishments, across any international border in the Pacific area.

2. The Japanese Government undertakes forthwith to withdraw its armed forces now stationed in southern French Indochina, not to engage in any further military activities there, including the construction of military facilities, and to limit Japanese military forces in northern French Indochina to the number there on July 26, 1941, which number in any case would not exceed 25,000 and which number would not be subject to replacement.

3. The Government of the United States undertakes forthwith to remove the freezing restrictions which were placed on Japanese assets in the United States on July 26 and the Japanese Government agrees simultaneously to remove the freezing measures which it imposed in regard to American assets in Japan. Exports from each country would thereafter remain subject to the respective export control measures which each country may have in effect for reasons of national defense.

4. The Government of the United States undertakes forthwith to approach the British and the Dutch Governments with a view to their Governments' taking, on a basis of reciprocity with Japan, measures similar to those provided for in paragraph three above.

5. The Government of the United States would not look with disfavor upon the inauguration of conversations between the Government of China and the Government of Japan directed toward a peaceful settlement of their differences nor would the Government of the United States look with disfavor upon an armistice during the period of any such discussions. The fundamental interest of the Government of the United States in reference to any such discussions is simply that they be based

upon and exemplify the fundamental principles of peace which constitute the central spirit of the current conversations between the Government of Japan and the Government of the United States.

In case any such discussions are entered into between the Government of Japan and the Government of China, the Government of the United States is agreeable to such discussions taking place in the Philippine Islands, if so desired by both China and Japan.

6. It is understood that this *modus vivendi* is of a temporary nature and shall not remain in effect for a period longer than three months unless renewed by common agreement.

Revised Draft of Proposed Modus Vivendi *with Japan*

November 24, 1941

... 1. The Government of the United States and the Government of Japan, both being solicitous for the peace of the Pacific, affirm that their national policies are directed toward lasting and extensive peace throughout the Pacific area and that they have no territorial designs therein.

2. They undertake reciprocally not to make from regions in which they have military establishments any advance by force or threat of force into any areas in Southeastern or Northwestern Asia or in the southern or the northern Pacific area.

3. The Japanese Government undertakes forthwith to withdraw its armed forces now stationed in southern French Indochina and not to replace those forces; to reduce the total of its forces in French Indochina to the number there on July 26, 1941, which number in any case shall not exceed 25,000; and not to send additional forces to Indochina for replacements or otherwise.

4. The Government of the United States undertakes forthwith to modify the application of its existing freezing and export restrictions to the extent necessary to permit the following resumption of trade between the United States and Japan in articles for the use and needs of their peoples:

   (*a*) Imports from Japan to be freely permitted and the proceeds of the sale thereof to be paid into a clearing account to be used for the purchase of the exports from the United States listed below, and at Japan's option for the payment of interest and principal of Japanese obligations within the United States, provided that at least two-thirds in value of such imports per month consist of raw silk. It is understood that all American-owned goods now in Japan, the movement of which in transit to the United States has been interrupted following the adoption of freezing measures, shall be forwarded forthwith to the United States.

(b) Exports from the United States to Japan to be permitted as follows:

(i) Bunkers and supplies for vessels engaged in the trade here provided for and for such other vessels engaged in other trades as the two Governments may agree.

(ii) Food and food products from the United States subject to such limitations as the appropriate authorities may prescribe in respect of commodities in short supply in the United States.

(iii) Raw cotton from the United States to the extent of $600,000 in value per month.

(iv) Medical and pharmaceutical supplies subject to such limitations as the appropriate authorities may prescribe in respect of commodities in short supply in the United States.

(v) Petroleum. The United States will permit the export to Japan of petroleum upon a monthly basis for civilian needs, the proportionate amount of petroleum to be exported from the United States for such needs to be determined after consultation with the British and the Dutch Governments. It is understood that by civilian needs in Japan is meant such purposes as the operation of the fishing industry, the transport system, lighting, heating, industrial and agricultural uses, and other civilian uses.

(vi) The above stated amounts of exports may be increased and additional commodities added by agreement between the two governments as it may appear to them that the operation of this agreement is furthering the peaceful and equitable solution of outstanding problems in the Pacific area.

5. The Government of Japan undertakes forthwith to modify the application of its existing freezing and export restrictions to the extent necessary to permit the resumption of trade between Japan and the United States as provided for in paragraph four above.

6. The Government of the United States undertakes forthwith to approach the Australian, British and Dutch Governments with a view to those Governments' taking measures similar to those provided for in paragraph four above.

7. With reference to the current hostilities between Japan and China, the fundamental interest of the Government of the United States in reference to any discussions which may be entered into between the Japanese and the Chinese Governments is simply that these discussions and any settlement reached as a result thereof be based upon and exemplify the fundamental principles of peace, law, order and justice, which constitute the central spirit of the current conversations between the Government of Japan and the Government of the United States and which are applicable uniformly throughout the Pacific area.

8. This *modus vivendi* shall remain in force for a period of three months with the understanding that the two parties shall confer at the instance of either to ascertain whether the prospects of reaching a peaceful settlement covering the entire Pacific area justify an extension of the *modus vivendi* for a further period.

Final Draft of Proposed Modus Vivendi *with Japan*
November 25, 1941

... 1. The Government of the United States and the Government of Japan, both being solicitous for the peace of the Pacific, affirm that their national policies are directed toward lasting and extensive peace throughout the Pacific area and that they have no territorial designs therein.

2. They undertake reciprocally not to make from regions in which they have military establishments any advance by force or threat of force into any areas in Southeastern or Northeastern Asia or in the southern or the northern Pacific area.

3. The Japanese Government undertakes forthwith to withdraw its armed forces now stationed in southern French Indochina and not to replace those forces; to reduce the total of its forces in French Indochina to the number there on July 26, 1941; and not

to send additional naval, land or air forces to Indochina for replacements or otherwise.

The provisions of the foregoing paragraph are without prejudice to the position of the Government of the United States with regard to the presence of foreign troops in that area.

4. The Government of the United States undertakes forthwith to modify the application of its existing freezing and export restrictions to the extent necessary to permit the following resumption of trade between the United States and Japan in articles for the use and needs of their peoples:

(a) Imports from Japan to be freely permitted and the proceeds of the sale thereof to be paid into a clearing account to be used for the purchase of the exports from the United States listed below, and at Japan's option for the payment of interest and principal of Japanese obligations within the United States, provided that at least two-thirds in value of such imports per month consist of raw silk. It is understood that all American-owned goods now in Japan the movement of which in transit to the United States has been interrupted following the adoption of freezing measures shall be forwarded forthwith to the United States.

(b) Exports from the United States to Japan to be permitted as follows:

(i) Bunkers and supplies for vessels engaged in the trade here provided for and for such other vessels engaged in other trades as the two Governments may agree.

(ii) Food and food products from the United States subject to such limitations as the appropriate authorities may prescribe in respect of commodities in short supply in the United States.

(iii) Raw cotton from the United States to the extent of $600,000 in value per month.

(iv) Medical and pharmaceutical supplies subject to such limitations as the appropriate authorities may prescribe in respect of commodities in short supply in the United States.

(v) Petroleum. The United States will permit the export to Japan of petroleum, within the categories permitted general export, upon a monthly basis for civilian needs. The proportionate amount of petroleum to be exported from the United States for such needs will be determined after consultation with the British and the Dutch Governments.

It is understood that by civilian needs in Japan is meant such purposes as the operation of the fishing industry, the transport system, lighting, heating, industrial and agricultural uses, and other civilian uses.

(vi) The above stated amounts of exports may be increased and additional commodities added by agreement between the two governments as it may appear to them that the operation of this agreement is furthering the peaceful and equitable solution of outstanding problems in the Pacific area.

5. The Government of Japan undertakes forthwith to modify the application of its existing freezing and export restrictions to the extent necessary to permit the resumption of trade between Japan and the United States as provided for in paragraph four above.

6. The Government of the United States undertakes forthwith to approach the Australian, British and Dutch Governments with a view to those Governments' taking measures similar to those provided for in paragraph four above.

7. With reference to the current hostilities between Japan and China, the fundamental interest of the Government of the United States in reference to any discussions which may be entered into between the Japanese and the Chinese Governments is simply that these discussions and any settlement reached as a result thereof be based upon and exemplify the fundamental principles of peace, law, order and justice, which constitute the central spirit of the current conversations between the Government of Japan and the Government of the United States and which are applicable uniformly throughout the Pacific area.

8. This *modus vivendi* shall remain in force for a period of three months with the understanding that the two parties shall confer at the instance of either to ascertain whether the prospects of reaching a peaceful settlement covering the entire Pacific area justify an extension of the *modus vivendi* for a further period.

DISCARDING THE *MODUS VIVENDI*

On November 24, President Roosevelt cabled Prime Minister Winston S. Churchill (referred to as the "Former Naval Person" in their exchanges), giving him an outline of a proposed *modus vivendi* with Japan. This counterproposal to Japan's Plan B in effect offered partial resumption of trade with Japan in return for the latter's agreement to withdraw its forces from southern Indochina. The *modus vivendi* thus called for a return to the status quo of July 1941, before the Japanese occupation of southern Indochina. The fact that Roosevelt solicited Churchill's response indicates that the president agreed with his top advisers that a temporary deal with Japan was worth pursuing.

Churchill's response, however, was lukewarm, as revealed in his cable to Roosevelt. The British leader was particularly concerned that the Chinese appeared to be ignored in the pending U.S.-Japanese deal. Sure enough, as the material printed below reveals, China and other nations expressed strong opposition to the *modus vivendi* idea. They were concerned that such an agreement would convey the impression that the U.S. was willing to purchase a temporary truce with Japan at the expense of China, with serious implications for other parts of the world. The upshot was that the proposal was never formally presented to the Japanese negotiators.

Should the U.S. government have gone ahead with the counter-proposal? Why or why not? Were Churchill, Chiang Kai-shek, and other foreign leaders justified in squelching the initiative? Did they play a large role in thwarting the official presentation of the *modus vivendi*? If they did, would it follow that the United States went to war for the sake of China or of the British empire?

FRANKLIN D. ROOSEVELT

Cable to Winston S. Churchill

November 24, 1941

Secret from the President to the Former Naval Person.

On November 20 the Japanese Ambassador communicated to us proposals for a *modus vivendi*. He has represented that the conclusion of such a *modus vivendi* might give the Japanese Government opportunity to develop public sentiment in Japan in support of a liberal and comprehensive program of peace covering the Pacific area and that the domestic political situation in Japan was so acute as to render urgent some re-

The following selections are from *Churchill and Roosevelt: The Complete Correspondence*, vol. 1, ed. Warren F. Kimball (Princeton, N.J.: Princeton University Press, 1984), 275–78.

lief such as was envisaged in the proposal. The proposal calls for a commitment on the part of Japan to transfer to northern Indochina all the Japanese forces now stationed in southern Indochina pending restoration of peace between Japan and China or the establishment of general peace in the Pacific area when Japan would withdraw all its troops from Indochina, commitments on the part of the United States to supply Japan a required quantity of petroleum products and to refrain from measures prejudicial to Japan's efforts to restore peace with China and mutual commitments to make no armed advancement in the southeastern Asiatic and southern Pacific areas (the formula offered would apparently not exclude advancement into China from Indochina), to cooperate toward obtaining goods required by either in the Netherlands East Indies and to restore commercial relations to those prevailing prior to the adoption of freezing measures.

This Government proposes to inform the Japanese Government that in the opinion of this Government the Japanese proposals contain features not in harmony with the fundamental principles which underlie the proposed general settlement and to which each Government has declared that it is committed. It is also proposed to offer to the Japanese Government an alternative proposal for a *modus vivendi* which will contain mutual pledges of peaceful intent, a reciprocal undertaking not to make armed advancement into areas which would include northeastern Asia and the northern Pacific area, southeast Asia and the southern Pacific area, an undertaking by Japan to withdraw its forces from southern French Indochina, not to replace those forces, to limit those in northern Indochina to the number there on July 26, 1941, which number shall not be subject to replacement and shall not in any case exceed 25,000 and not to send additional forces to Indochina. This Government would undertake to modify its freezing orders to the extent to permit exports from the United States to Japan of bunkers and ship supplies, food products and pharmaceuticals with certain qualifications, raw cotton up to $600,000 monthly, petroleum on a monthly basis for civilian needs, the proportionate amount to be exported from this country to be determined after consultation with the British and Dutch Governments. The United States would permit imports in general provided that raw silk constitute at least two-thirds in value of such imports. The proceeds of such imports would be available for the purchase of the designed exports from the United States and for the payment of interest and principal of Japanese obligations within the United States. This Government would undertake to approach the British, Dutch, and Australian Governments on the question of their taking similar economic measures. Provision is made that the *modus vivendi* shall remain in force for three months with the understanding that at the instance of either party the two parties shall confer to determine whether the prospects of reaching a peaceful settlement covering the entire Pacific area warrant extension of the *modus vivendi.*

This seems to me a fair proposition for the Japanese but its acceptance or rejection is really a matter of internal Japanese politics. I am not very hopeful and we must all be prepared for real trouble, possibly soon.

ROOSEVELT

WINSTON S. CHURCHILL

Cable to Franklin D. Roosevelt
November 26, 1941

Most Secret for the President from the Former Naval Person.

Your message about Japan received tonight. Also full accounts from Lord Halifax of discussions and your counter project to Japan on which Foreign Secretary has sent some comments. Of course, it is for you to handle this business and we certainly do not want an additional war. There is only one point that disquiets us. What about Chiang Kai-shek? Is he not having a very thin diet? Our anxiety is about China. If they collapse, our joint dangers would enormously increase. We are sure that the regard of the United States for the Chinese cause will govern your action. We feel that the Japanese are most unsure of themselves.

WINSTON S. CHURCHILL

Cable to Franklin D. Roosevelt
November 30, 1941

Personal and Secret for the President from the Former Naval Person.

It seems to me that one important method remains unused in averting war between Japan and our two countries, namely a plain declaration, secret or public as may be thought best, that any further act of aggression by Japan will lead immediately to the gravest consequences. I realize your constitutional difficulties but it would be tragic if Japan drifted into war by encroachment without having before her fairly and squarely the dire character of a further aggressive step. I beg you to consider whether, at the moment which you judge right which may be very near, you should not say that "any further Japanese aggression would compel you to place the gravest issues before Congress" or words to that effect. We would, of course, make a similar declaration or share in a joint declaration, and in any case arrangements are being made to synchronize our action with yours. Forgive me, my dear friend, for presuming to press such a course upon you, but I am convinced that it might make all the difference and prevent a melancholy extension of the war.

THE HULL NOTE

At a meeting with Ambassadors Nomura and Kurusu on November 26, Secretary of State Hull presented two memorandums, one reiterating the traditional policies of the United States, such as territorial integrity and equal commercial opportunity, and the other offering to resume trade between the two countries if Japan carried out certain terms, the most important of which was the withdrawal of its forces from China and Indochina. Together, these memorandums are known as the "Hull note."

Clearly, the presentation of the Hull note, rather than a *modus vivendi* proposal, meant that the U.S. government had decided against seeking a temporary compromise with Japan. Instead, it would call for a fundamental solution of the Asian-Pacific crisis through a Japanese agreement to go back to the status quo of 1931, before its forces conquered Manchuria. The document, then, reflected the official U.S. view that the crisis between the two countries — "the road to Pearl Harbor," as it would come to be called — began in 1931 and that if the two nations were to live in peace again, it would be necessary to return to the conditions of the 1920s.

The Japanese negotiators, as well as their superiors in Tokyo, were shocked by the Hull note. They had expected a counterproposal to Plan B, not something that read like an ultimatum. (In diplomacy, an *ultimatum* is a notification that unless its recipient accepts certain terms, its sender will resort to some punitive action.) As you will see in the next set of documents, it was after receipt of the Hull note of November 26 that Tokyo decided there was no hope of arriving at a deal with Washington. U.S. officials, including Hull, vehemently denied, both then and after the war, that the two memorandums amounted to an ultimatum. Instead, they insisted, they left room for further talks, if only Japan had been willing to respond. This gap in Japanese and American perceptions of just what was in the Hull note, and what was implied by it, not only exacerbated their relationship but heightened the sense of betrayal the Americans felt when the Japanese struck less than two weeks later.

What is your reading of these documents? If you had been an adviser to Roosevelt and Hull, would you have endorsed handing over these documents to the Japanese? Why or why not? If you had been a Japanese leader, would you have considered the Hull note to be a rejection of all attempts to avoid war — an ultimatum? Did it contain any major concessions by the United States?

CORDELL HULL

Outline of Proposed Basis for Agreement between the United States and Japan

November 26, 1941

Section I

DRAFT MUTUAL DECLARATION OF POLICY

The Government of the United States and the Government of Japan both being solicitous for the peace of the Pacific affirm that their national policies are directed toward lasting and extensive peace throughout the Pacific area, that they have no territorial designs in that area, that they have no intention of threatening other countries or of using military force aggressively against any neighboring nation, and that, accordingly, in their national policies they will actively support and give practical application to the following fundamental principles upon which their relations with each other and with all other governments are based:

   (1) The principle of inviolability of territorial integrity and sovereignty of each and all nations.

The following selections are from *Peace and War: United States Foreign Policy, 1931–1941* (Washington, D.C.: Government Printing Office, 1943), 807–13.

(2) The principle of non-interference in the internal affairs of other countries.
(3) The principle of equality, including equality of commercial opportunity and treatment.
(4) The principle of reliance upon international cooperation and conciliation for the prevention and pacific settlement of controversies and for improvement of international conditions by peaceful methods and processes.

The Government of Japan and the Government of the United States have agreed that toward eliminating chronic political instability, preventing recurrent economic collapse, and providing a basis for peace, they will actively support and practically apply the following principles in their economic relations with each other and with other nations and peoples:

(1) The principles of non-discrimination in international commercial relations.
(2) The principle of international economic cooperation and abolition of extreme nationalism as expressed in excessive trade restrictions.
(3) The principle of non-discriminatory access by all nations to raw material supplies.
(4) The principle of full protection of the interests of consuming countries and populations as regards the operation of international commodity agreements.
(5) The principle of establishment of such institutions and arrangements of international finance as may lend aid to the essential enterprises and the continuous development of all countries and may permit payments through processes of trade consonant with the welfare of all countries.

Section II

STEPS TO BE TAKEN BY THE GOVERNMENT OF THE UNITED STATES
AND BY THE GOVERNMENT OF JAPAN

The Government of the United States and the Government of Japan propose to take steps as follows:

1. The Government of the United States and the Government of Japan will endeavor to conclude a multilateral non-aggression pact

among the British Empire, China, Japan, the Netherlands, the Soviet Union, Thailand and the United States.

2. Both Governments will endeavor to conclude among the American, British, Chinese, Japanese, the Netherland and Thai Governments an agreement whereunder each of the Governments would pledge itself to respect the territorial integrity of French Indochina and, in the event that there should develop a threat to the territorial integrity of Indochina, to enter into immediate consultation with a view to taking such measures as may be deemed necessary and advisable to meet the threat in question. Such agreement would provide also that each of the Governments party to the agreement would not seek or accept preferential treatment in its trade or economic relations with Indochina and would use its influence to obtain for each of the signatories equality of treatment in trade and commerce with French Indochina.

3. The Government of Japan will withdraw all military, naval, air and police forces from China and from Indochina.

4. The Government of the United States and the Government of Japan will not support — militarily, politically, economically — any government or regime in China other than the National Government of the Republic of China with capital temporarily at Chungking.

5. Both Governments will give up all extraterritorial rights in China, including rights and interests in and with regard to international settlements and concessions, and rights under the Boxer Protocol of 1901.

Both Governments will endeavor to obtain the agreement of the British and other governments to give up extraterritorial rights in China, including rights in international settlements and in concessions and under the Boxer Protocol of 1901.

6. The Government of the United States and the Government of Japan will enter into negotiations for the conclusion between the United States and Japan of a trade agreement, based upon reciprocal most-favored-nation treatment and reduction of trade barriers by both countries, including an undertaking by the United States to bind raw silk on the free list.

7. The Government of the United States and the Government of Japan will, respectively, remove the freezing restrictions on Japanese funds in the United States and on American funds in Japan.

8. Both Governments will agree upon a plan for the stabilization of the dollar-yen rate, with the allocation of funds adequate for this purpose, half to be supplied by Japan and half by the United States.

9. Both Governments will agree that no agreement which either has concluded with any third power or powers shall be interpreted by it in

such a way as to conflict with the fundamental purpose of this agreement, the establishment and preservation of peace throughout the Pacific area.

10. Both Governments will use their influence to cause other governments to adhere to and to give practical application to the basic political and economic principles set forth in this agreement.

JOSEPH W. BALLANTINE

Memorandum

November 26, 1941

The Japanese Ambassador and Mr. Kurusu called by appointment at the Department. The Secretary handed each of the Japanese copies of an outline of a proposed basis of an agreement between the United States and Japan and an explanatory oral statement.

After the Japanese had read the documents, Mr. Kurusu asked whether this was our reply to their proposal for a *modus vivendi*. The Secretary replied that we had to treat the proposal as we did, as there was so much turmoil and confusion among the public both in the United States and in Japan. He reminded the Japanese that in the United States we have a political situation to deal with just as does the Japanese Government, and he referred to the fire-eating statements which have been recently coming out of Tokyo, which he said had been causing a natural reaction among the public in this country. He said that our proposed agreement would render possible practical measures of financial cooperation, which, however, were not referred to in the outline for fear that this might give rise to misunderstanding. He also referred to the fact that he had earlier in the conversations acquainted the Ambassador of the ambition that had been his of settling the immigration question but that the situation had so far prevented him from realizing that ambition.

Mr. Kurusu offered various depreciatory comments in regard to the proposed agreement. He noted that in our statement of principles there was a reiteration of the Stimson doctrine. He objected to the proposal for multilateral non-aggression pacts and referred to Japan's bitter experience of international organizations, citing the case of the award against Japan by the Hague tribunal in the Perpetual Leases matter. He went on to say that the Washington Conference Treaties had given a wrong idea to China, that China had taken advantage of them to flaunt Japan's rights. He said he did not see how his Government could consider paragraphs (3) and (4) of the proposed agreement and that if the United States should expect that Japan was to take off its hat to Chiang Kai-shek and propose to recognize him Japan could not agree. He said that if this was the idea of the American Government he did not see how any agreement was possible.

The Secretary asked whether this matter could not be worked out.

Mr. Kurusu said that when they reported our answer to their Government it would be likely to throw up its hands. He noted that this was a tentative proposal without commitment, and suggested that it might be better if they did not refer it to their Government before discussing its contents further informally here.

The Secretary suggested that they might wish to study the documents carefully before discussing them further. He repeated that we were trying to do our best to keep the public from becoming uneasy as a result of their being harangued. He explained that in the light of all that has been said in the press, our proposal was as far as we would go at this time in reference to the Japanese proposal; that there was so much confusion among the public that it was necessary to bring about some clarification; that we have reached a stage when the public has lost its perspective and that it was therefore necessary to draw up a document which would present a complete picture of our position by making provision for each essential point involved.

The Secretary then referred to the oil question. He said that public feeling was so acute on that question that he might almost be lynched if he permitted oil to go freely to Japan. He pointed out that if Japan should fill Indochina with troops our people would not know what lies ahead in the way of a menace to the countries to the south and west. He reminded the Japanese that they did not know what tremendous injury they were doing to us by keeping immobilized so many forces in countries neighboring Indochina. He explained that we are primarily out for our permanent futures, and the question of Japanese troops in Indochina affects our direct interests.

Mr. Kurusu reverted to the difficulty of Japan's renouncing its support of Wang Ching-wei. The Secretary pointed out that Chiang Kai-shek had made an outstanding contribution in bringing out national spirit in China and expressed the view that the Nanking regime had not asserted itself in a way that would impress the world. Mr. Kurusu agreed with what the Secretary had said about Chiang, but observed that the question of the standing of the Nanking regime was a matter of opinion. His arguments on this as well as on various other points were specious, and unconvincing.

The Ambassador took the occasion to observe that sometimes statesmen of firm conviction fail to get sympathizers among the public; that only wise men could see far ahead and sometimes suffered martyrdom; but that life's span was short and one could only do his duty. The Ambassador then asked whether there was no other possibility and whether they could not see the President.

The Secretary replied that he had no doubt that the President would be glad to see them at any time.

Mr. Kurusu said that he felt that our response to their proposal could be interpreted as tantamount to meaning the end, and asked whether we were not interested in a *modus vivendi*.

The Secretary replied that we had explored that. Mr. Kurusu asked whether it was because the other powers would not agree; but the Secretary replied simply that he had done his best in the way of exploration.

The Ambassador when rising to go raised the question of publicity. The Secretary replied that he had it in mind to give the press something of the situation tomorrow, and asked what the Ambassador thought. The Ambassador said that they did not wish to question the Secretary's right to give out what he desired in regard to the American proposal.

JAPAN'S VIEW OF THE HULL NOTE

The receipt of the Hull note drove the Japanese government into a flurry of activity. Considering the note a virtual ultimatum, the leaders in Tokyo began taking steps toward a break in diplomatic relations with Washington — and toward war. Although no final decision for war was made until December 1 (see pages 86–95), the secret cables exchanged between the Foreign Ministry and the embassy in Washington indicate a sense of urgency.

Exactly how urgent was the situation? Some of the decoded messages suggest that the Japanese diplomats in Washington persisted in the hope that further talks could be held with the Americans in an effort to avoid war. The gap between the thinking of the Japanese in Tokyo and in Washington constitutes an important part of the drama, for the embassy diplomats did not really believe — nor were they informed — that Tokyo was about to go to war against the United States.

Did the U.S. leaders share this sense of urgency? Recall that they were reading the same cables you will read below: the intercepted and decrypted PURPLE messages. U.S. policymakers have been aware that the Japanese considered the Hull note a point of no return. Nevertheless, as some of the cables reveal, U.S. officials did not believe that all negotiation would cease just because of the Hull note. How would you have read the messages between Tokyo and Washington if you had been a policymaker in Washington at that time? Some of the cables indicate that the Japanese embassies were being instructed to destroy their code machines. What would that have meant to the United States, whose officials were reading such instructions?

FROM: TOKYO
TO: BERLIN [JAPANESE EMBASSY IN GERMANY]
NOVEMBER 30, 1941
(PURPLE)
#986

The proposal presented by the United States on the 26th made this attitude of theirs clearer than ever. In it there is one insulting clause which says that no matter what treaty either party enters into with a third power it will not be interpreted as having any bearing upon the basic object of this treaty, namely the maintenance of peace in the Pacific. This means specifically the Three-Power Pact. It means that in case the United States enters the European war at any time, the Japanese Empire will not be allowed to give assistance to Germany and Italy. It is clearly a trick. This clause alone, let alone others, makes it impossible to find any basis in the American proposal for negotiations. What is more, before the United States brought forth this plan, they conferred with England, Australia, the Netherlands, and China — they do so repeatedly. Therefore, it is clear that the United States is now in collusion with those nations and has decided to regard Japan, along with Germany and Italy, as an enemy.

FROM: WASHINGTON
TO: TOKYO
DECEMBER 1, 1941
(PURPLE)
#1227

Indications are that the United States desires to continue the negotiations even if it is necessary to go beyond their stands on the so-called ba-

The following selections are from Henry C. Clausen and Bruce Lee, *Pearl Harbor: Final Judgment* (New York: Crown, 1992), 334–41.

sic principles. However, if we keep quibbling on the critical points and continue to get stuck in the middle as we have been in the past, it is impossible to expect any further developments. If it is impossible from the broad political viewpoint, to conduct a leaders' meeting at this time, would it not be possible to arrange a conference between persons in whom the leaders have complete confidence (for example, Vice President Wallace or Hopkins from the United States and the former Premier Konoye, who is on friendly terms with the President, or Adviser to the Imperial Privy Council Ishii). The meeting could be arranged for some midway point, such as Honolulu. High army and navy officers should accompany these representatives. Have them make one final effort to reach some agreement, using as the basis of their discussions the latest proposals submitted by each.

We feel that this last effort may facilitate the final decision as to war or peace.

We realize of course that an attempt to have President Roosevelt and former Premier Konoye meet, failed. Bearing in mind the reaction to that in our nation, it may be to our interest to first ascertain the U.S. attitude regarding this possibility. Moreover, since we have no guarantee either of success or failure of the objectives even if the meeting is held, careful consideration should first be given this matter.

We feel, however, that to surmount the crisis with which we are face to face, it is not wasting our efforts to pursue every path open to us. It is our opinion that it would be most effective to feel out and ascertain the U.S. attitude regarding this matter, in the name of the Japanese Government. However, if this procedure does not seem practical to you in view of some internal conditions, then how would it be if I were to bring up the subject as purely of my own origin and in that manner feel out their attitude. Then, if they seem receptive to it the government could make the official proposal.

Please advise me of your opinions on this matter.

FROM: TOKYO
TO: WASHINGTON
DECEMBER 1, 1941
(PURPLE)
CIRCULAR #2436

When you are faced with the necessity of destroying codes, get in touch with the Naval Attache's office there and make use of chemicals they have on hand for this purpose. The Attache should have been advised by the Navy Ministry regarding this.

FROM: TOKYO
TO: LONDON
DECEMBER 1, 1941
(PURPLE)
CIRCULAR #2443

Please discontinue the use of your code machine and dispose of it immediately.

In regard to the disposition of the machine please be very careful to carry out the instructions you have received regarding this. Pay particular attention to taking apart and breaking up the important parts of the machine.

As soon as you have received this telegram wire the one word SETUJU in plain language and as soon as you have carried out the instructions wire the one word HASSO in plain language.

Also at this time you will of course burn the machine codes and YU GO No. 26 of my telegram. (The rules for the use of the machine between the head office and the Ambassador resident in England.)

(NOTE: THIS MESSAGE CARRIED A NOTATION ON THE BOTTOM AS A RESULT OF MY AFFIDAVIT OF CAPTAIN LAYTON SAYING:

Message not seen but — British reported that Japs had destroyed their purple machine in London, 26 April 1945. [signed] E.J. Layton.)

FROM: TOKYO
TO: WASHINGTON
DECEMBER 1, 1941
(PURPLE-CA)
#865

1. The date set in my message #812 has come and gone, and the situation continues to be increasingly critical. However, to prevent the United States from becoming unduly suspicious we have been advising the press and others that though there are some wide differences between Japan and the United States, the negotiations are continuing. (The above is only for your information.)

2. We have decided to withhold submitting the note to the U.S. Ambassador to Tokyo as suggested by you at the end of your message #1124. Please make the necessary representations at your end only.

3. There are reports here that the President's sudden return to the capital is an effect of Premier Tōjō's statement. We have an idea that the

President did so because of his concern over the critical Far Eastern situation. Please make investigations into this matter.

FROM: WASHINGTON
TO: TOKYO
DECEMBER 2, 1941
(PURPLE)
#1232 (PART 1 OF 2)

Today, the 2nd Ambassador KURUSU and I had an interview with Under-Secretary of State WELLES. At that time, prefacing his statement by saying that it was at the direct instruction of the President of the United States, he turned over to us the substance of my separate wire #1233. Thereupon we said: "Since we haven't been informed even to the slightest degree concerning the troops in French Indo-China, we will transmit the gist of your representations directly to our Home Government. In all probability they never considered that such a thing as this could possibly be an upshot of their proposals of November 20th." The Under-Secretary then said: "I want you to know that the stand the United States takes is that she opposes aggression in any and all parts of the world." Thereupon we replied: "The United States and other countries have pyramided economic pressure upon economic pressure upon us Japanese. (I made the statement that economic warfare was even worse than forceful aggression.) We haven't the time to argue the pros and cons of this question or the rights and wrongs. The people of Japan are faced with economic pressure, and I want you to know that we have but the choice between submission to this pressure or breaking the chains that it invokes. We want you to realize this as well as the situation in which all Japanese find themselves as the result of the four-year incident in China; the President recently expressed cognizance of the latter situation.

FROM: WASHINGTON (NOMURA)
TO: TOKYO
DECEMBER 2, 1941
(PURPLE)
#1232 (PART 2 OF 2)

Furthermore, I would have you know that in replying to the recent American proposals, the Imperial Government is giving the most profound consideration to this important question which had to do with our national destiny.["] Under-Secretary of State WELLES said: "I am well aware of that." I continued: "We cannot overemphasize the fact that, insofar as Japan is concerned, it is virtually impossible for her to accept the new American proposals as they now stand. Our proposals proffered on the 21st of June and the proposals of September 25th, representing our greatest conciliations based on the previous proposal, still stand. In spite of the fact that the agreement of both sides was in the offing, it has come to naught. At this late juncture to give a thoughtful consideration to the new proposals certainly will not make for a smooth and speedy settlement of the negotiations. Recently, we promised to evacuate our troops from French Indo-China in the event of a settlement of the Sino-Japanese Incident and the establishment of a just peace in the Far East. In [the event of] the settlement of fundamental questions, the [kinds] of [problems you mentioned today] would naturally dissolve." The Under-Secretary assiduously heard us out and then said: "The American proposals of the 26th were brought about by the necessity to clarify the position of the United States because of the internal situation here." [2] Then he continued: "In regard to the opinions you have expressed, I will make it a point immediately to confer with the Secretary."

I got the impression from the manner in which he spoke that he hoped Japan in her reply to the American proposals of the 26th would leave this much room.

Judging by my interview with Secretary of State HULL on the 1st and my conversations of today, it is clear that the United States, too, is anxious to peacefully conclude the current difficult situation. I am convinced that they would like to bring about a speedy settlement. Therefore, please bear well in mind this fact in your considerations of our reply to the new American proposals and to my separate wire #1233.

FROM: TOKYO (TOGO)
TO: WASHINGTON
DECEMBER 2, 1941
(PURPLE)
#867 (STRICTLY SECRET)
(CORRECTED TRANSLATION)

1. Among the telegraphic codes with which your office is equipped burn all but those now used with the machine and one copy each of "O" code (Oite) and abbreviating code (L). (Burn also the various other codes which you have in your custody.)

2. Stop at once using one code machine unit and destroy it completely.

3. When you have finished this, wire me back the one word "haruna."

4. At the time and in the manner you deem most proper dispose of all files of messages coming and going and all other secret documents.

5. Burn all the codes which Telegraphic official KOSAKA brought you. . . .

FROM: WASHINGTON
TO: TOKYO
DECEMBER 3, 1941
(PURPLE)
#1223

Judging from all indications, we feel that some joint military action between Great Britain and the United States, with or without a declaration of war, is a definite certainty in the event of an occupation of Thailand.

FROM: WASHINGTON
TO: TOKYO
DECEMBER 5, 1941
(PURPLE)
#1268

From Councillor of Embassy Iguchi to the Chief of the Communication Section:

We have completed destruction of codes, but since the U.S.-Japanese negotiations are still continuing I request your approval of our desire to delay for a while yet the destruction of the one code machine.

FROM: TOKYO
TO: WASHINGTON
DECEMBER 6, 1941
(PURPLE)
#901

1. The Government has deliberated deeply on the American proposal of the 26th of November and as a result we have drawn up a memorandum for the United States contained in my separate message #902 (in English).

2. This separate message is a very long one. I will send it in fourteen parts and I imagine you will receive it tomorrow. However, I am not sure. The situation is extremely delicate, and when you receive it I want you please to keep it secret for the time being.

3. Concerning the time of presenting this memorandum to the United States, I will wire you in a separate message. However, I want you in the meantime to put it in nicely drafted form and make every preparation to present it to the Americans just as soon as you receive instructions.

Imperial Conference
December 1, 1941

We can date Japan's final decision for war to the December 1 conference of its leaders in the presence of the emperor. As you will read in the record of the conference, they agreed that given the failure of the negotiations in Washington to arrive at any settlement by the end of November, the nation would have to proceed with its original plan of action. The navy (the Combined Fleet) was told to prepare for war immediately. Its commander, Admiral Isoroku Yamamoto, ordered the task force that had been assembled to plan the Pearl Harbor attack "to climb Mount Niitaka," a code that had been agreed upon as the go-ahead signal.

That strategy had been devised by Admiral Yamamoto as the only plausible way to fight a war with a nation far richer and mightier than Japan. The idea was to strike the first blow in order to disable U.S. warships in Hawaii (where they had been kept since 1940) long enough for Japanese forces to consolidate their position in Asia (including Southeast Asia, which Japan invaded and occupied simultaneously with the Pearl Harbor attack).

Compare the imperial conferences of November 5 and December 1. The participants were the same, but in December they were more willing to sanction war as the only way out of the impasse. What had changed? Were the Japanese justified in believing the futility of further negotiation with the United States? Even if that were the case, could they have considered other options than a war which, as the document indicates, they knew would be an extremely difficult, even hopeless, undertaking? From these discussions, can you discern that Japanese officials were willing to accept some compromises with the United States? What role did the emperor seem to play in the official decision? Is there any clue as to his attitude?

Nobutaka Ike, *Japan's Decision for War: Records of the 1941 Policy Conferences* (Stanford, Calif.: Stanford University Press, 1967), 263–64, 270–74, 279–83.

Agenda: Failure of Negotiations with the United States Based on the "Essentials for Carrying Out the Empire's Policies" Approved on November 5; Declaration of War on the United States, Great Britain, and the Netherlands.

Statement by Prime Minister Tōjō

With your permission, I will begin the proceedings today.

On the basis of the Imperial Conference decision of November 5, the Army and Navy, on the one hand, devoted themselves to the task of getting everything ready for military operations; while the Government, on the other hand, used every means at its disposal and made every effort to improve diplomatic relations with the United States. The United States not only refused to make even one concession with respect to the position she had maintained in the past, but also stipulated new conditions, after having formed an alliance with Great Britain, the Netherlands, and China. The United States demanded complete and unconditional withdrawal of troops from China, withdrawal of our recognition of the Nanking Government, and the reduction of the Tripartite Pact to a dead letter. This not only belittled the dignity of our Empire and made it impossible for us to harvest the fruits of the China Incident, but also threatened the very existence of our Empire. It became evident that we could not achieve our goals by means of diplomacy.

At the same time, the United States, Great Britain, the Netherlands, and China increased their economic and military pressure against us; and we have now reached the point where we can no longer allow the situation to continue, from the point of view of both our national power and our projected military operations. Moreover, the requirements with respect to military operations will not permit an extension of time. Under the circumstances, our Empire has no alternative but to begin war against the United States, Great Britain, and the Netherlands in order to resolve the present crisis and assure survival.

We have been engaged in the China Incident for more than four years, and now we are going to get involved in a great war. We are indeed dismayed that we have caused His Majesty to worry.

But, on further reflection, I am thoroughly convinced that our military power today is far stronger than it was before the China Incident; that the morale of the officers and men of the Army and Navy is high; that unity in domestic politics is greater; that there is willingness on the part of individuals to make sacrifices for the nation as a whole; and that, as a result, we can anticipate that we will overcome the crisis that confronts the nation.

I should, therefore, like to have you discuss the proposal on the agenda today. I now turn the meeting over to other Ministers and to officers of the Supreme Command, who will make statements about diplomatic negotiations, military affairs, and other matters.

Statement by Foreign Minister Tōgō on Japanese-American Negotiations

... I understand that our two Ambassadors pointed out the unreasonable character of these provisions [the Hull note] and lodged a strong protest; but Secretary Hull indicated no willingness to compromise. It appears that when our two Ambassadors met with the President on the 27th, the President stated that he still hoped that Japanese-American negotiations could be brought to a successful conclusion; but he added that cold water had been dashed on the efforts because Japanese forces had moved into southern Indochina in July while the negotiations were going on, and he felt that negotiations were still hampered, according to recent reports. He said that even if the two countries should attempt to break the deadlock with a *modus vivendi,* such a temporary solution would ultimately be useless as long as the two countries did not agree on basic principles.

There are several provisions in the American proposal that we could accept: the problem of commerce (Provisions 6, 7, and 8) and the abolition of extraterritoriality in China (Provision 5). But our Empire could not agree to those on China and French Indochina (Provisions 2 and 3), withdrawal of recognition of the National Government (Provision 4), non-recognition of the Tripartite Pact (Provision 9), and the multilateral nonaggression pact (Provision 1). Compared to previous American proposals, this one is a conspicuous retrogression; and we had to recognize that it was an unreasonable proposal, which completely disregarded the negotiations that had gone on for half a year.

In short, the United States Government has persistently adhered to its traditional doctrines and principles, ignored realities in East Asia, and tried to force on our Empire principles that she herself could not easily carry out. Despite the fact that we made a number of concessions, she maintained her original position throughout the negotiations, lasting for seven months, and refused to budge even one step. I believe that America's policy toward Japan has consistently been to thwart the establishment of a New Order in East Asia, which is our immutable policy. We must recognize that if we were to accept their present proposal, the international position of our Empire would be reduced to a status lower than it was prior to the Manchurian Incident, and our very survival would inevitably be threatened.

First, China under Chiang's control would increasingly come to rely on Britain and the United States; our Empire would betray its faith toward the National Government of China, and our friendship with China would be marred for a long time to come. We would be forced to retreat completely from the mainland, and as a result our position in Manchuria would necessarily be weakened. Any hope of settling the China Incident would be swept away, root and branch.

Second, Britain and the United States would gain control over these regions. The prestige of our Empire would fall to the ground, and our role as stabilizer would be destroyed. Our great undertaking, the establishment of a New Order in East Asia, would be nipped in the bud.

Third, the Tripartite Pact would be reduced to a dead letter, and the reputation of our Empire abroad would decline.

Fourth, the attempt to control our Empire by including the Soviet Union in a multilateral agreement would magnify our problems along the northern border.

Fifth, the principle of nondiscrimination in trade, and other principles, should not necessarily be rejected out of hand; but the attempt to apply them only to the Pacific area is nothing but a way of carrying out a policy to benefit Britain and the United States, and this limited application would present a great obstacle to our acquiring vital materials.

In short, one must say that it was virtually impossible for us to accept their proposal; and even if we were to continue negotiations on the basis of this proposal in order to get the United States to withdraw it, it would be almost impossible for us to obtain what we seek.

Statement by Navy Chief of Staff Nagano

. . . The United States, Great Britain, and the Netherlands have steadily strengthened their defenses; and they have gradually become better prepared, especially in the South Pacific. However, we judge that their present state of preparedness is not greatly different from what we had anticipated; and hence we are convinced that it will present no hindrance to our launching military and naval operations, and that we will be able to proceed as we have planned.

With regard to the Soviet Union, we are maintaining strict vigilance, along with appropriate diplomatic measures; but at present, judging from the deployment of their forces, we need not feel a sense of insecurity. In this most serious crisis since the founding of our country all of the officers and men in the task forces of the Army and Navy have extremely high morale and are prepared to lay down their lives for their country. Once the Imperial Command is given, they will undertake their assignments. I hope Your Majesty will feel assured on this point.

Statement by Minister for Home Affairs Tōjō

I would like to speak on popular movements relating to Japanese-American problems and on measures for dealing with these movements.

When we take an overall view of popular opinion relating to Japanese-American problems, we conclude that the people in general are aware that our nation, in view of the present world situation, stands at a crossroad, one road leading to glory and the other to decline. They have shown an extraordinary interest in the diplomatic negotiations being carried out by the Government. Even though the Americans have given no indication that they would reconsider, and even though this has led to a rupture in diplomatic negotiations and [will lead] to the outbreak of war, they are prepared to accept this as an inevitable development. They are displaying the spirit characteristic of the Japanese people; and they are truly determined to undergo all manner of hardships, and to overcome adversity by united action.

The so-called nationalistic organizations have advocated a strong foreign policy; and once diplomatic negotiations end in failure, they will very likely demand that we move southward at once. Even the owners of small and medium-sized enterprises, whose livelihood has been much affected by the recent strengthening of economic controls — to say nothing of the laboring and peasant classes — are clearly aware of the position in which our country finds itself, and their spirits are high. It appears that they tend to want the Government to take an unambiguous position in executing a strong policy. There are, however, some within our large nation who would like to avoid war as much as possible at this time; but even these people have made up their minds that as long as the United States refuses to acknowledge our legitimate position, does not remove the economic blockade, and refuses to abandon her policy of oppressing Japan, our moving southward is inevitable; and if this action leads to a clash between Japan and the United States, this also cannot be helped.

To ensure that we will be able to maintain internal security in case an emergency situation arises following the rupture of Japanese-American negotiations, we have begun to make detailed plans for the more stringent measures that will be taken. Preparations for some of these are completed, and we are beginning to implement them:

First, we have especially strengthened our controls over those who are antiwar and antimilitary, such as Communists, rebellious Koreans, certain religious leaders, and others who we fear might be a threat to the public order. We believe that in some cases we might have to subject some of them to preventive arrest.

Second, there are the nationalistic organizations. Some of these tend to be very excitable; they are rash, and they may resort to violence. We believe they should be kept under observation and control; it may be necessary to temporarily detain those who would disturb the public peace. Accordingly, we plan to do everything to provide adequate protection for the Senior Statesmen and those political and financial leaders who are regarded by extremists as being pro-British and pro-American, as well as for foreign diplomats and their staffs, and for law-abiding foreigners.

Third, there is the control of rumors. We must be prepared for many rumors, given the serious nature of the situation. To stabilize the views held by the people, it will be necessary to guide public opinion, and at the same time to exercise rather strict controls over it.

Fourth, as for foreigners of whom there is some suspicion, we have completed all of our investigations; we believe it will be necessary to round them up and detain them when the time comes.

Fifth, with respect to various crimes that will arise in the confusion of war, we have finished conferring with the Minister of Justice. We have given thought to various measures, especially making penalties more stringent, simplifying criminal trial procedure, and so on.

Sixth, we have already completed plans and preparations for the mobilization and deployment of police officials and firemen, who will be responsible for dealing with emergencies.

Seventh, we can anticipate that in a period of emergency the people are bound to be uneasy for a time because of food and monetary problems. We are paying particular attention to trends in attitudes among the people.

We have touched on the main points concerning the maintenance of public peace and security. We officials of the Ministry of Home Affairs are cooperating with other agencies concerned, and we anticipate that all measures for dealing with the emergency will prove to be adequate. . . .

[There followed questions and answers:] . . .

[President of the Privy Council] *Hara:* It appears, according to a radio broadcast, that our two Ambassadors are to confer with Hull today. If this is true, who took the initiative in these negotiations? If I assume that our side sought to confer with Hull, then why did we take this step?

[Foreign Minister] *Tōgō:* They have not told us when the meeting is to take place. Having studied the American proposal, we cannot let it go by without taking further action. I have ordered the two Ambassadors: "Tell the United States that the Japanese proposal of November 25 was a just one; that we find it difficult to understand the position the United States has taken in the past, and that she ought to reexamine her stand."[1] Because of this, I think it is quite conceivable that our Ambassadors might have sought a meeting with Hull.[2]

Hara: I would like to question the Supreme Command. It is indeed gratifying that preparations for commencing hostilities have been completed. According to recent reports from Britain and the United States, those countries are stepping up their military preparedness in the Far East. It appears that they are increasing the number of warships. If this is so, how much of an increase is there? Will it have an adverse effect on our operations?

Nagano, Navy Chief of Staff: The distribution of American strength is still 40 percent in the Atlantic and 60 percent in the Pacific. Recent activity is confined to Great Britain. . . .

Because Germany and Italy have become somewhat less active, and particularly because the Italian Navy has become passive, the British Navy has recently acquired reserve power and is gradually adding to its strength in the Orient. . . .

The purpose of this increase is to protect commerce in the Indian Ocean, to prepare for hostilities against Japan, and to protect the ships from German and Italian submarines. Some people say that the increase in the number of battleships, in particular, was brought about by their transfer to this area in order to avoid damage by German planes. As for the strengthening of land forces, it appears certain that 2,000 Canadian troops were landed in Hong Kong.

---

[1]This must be in error. Tōgō was probably referring to the Japanese note of November 20.

[2]The Japanese Ambassadors met with Secretary Hull that day and discussed the possibility that the United States might reexamine her position; but Hull firmly stated that the American proposal of November 26 must stand.

Thus there has been some strengthening of their forces; but this does not call for changes in the deployment of our forces. It will have no effect on our operations.

Hara: What is the situation with reference to the Army? May I assume that the increase in the number of enemy troops is still within the limits anticipated by the Supreme Command?

Sugiyama, Army Chief of Staff: There has been a 2,000-man reinforcement of Hong Kong, as reported by Navy Chief of Staff Nagano. Since our previous Imperial Conference they have landed about 6,000 to 7,000 men in Singapore; and there are reports of additional troops in Burma. But there appears to have been no large-scale buildup.

We have assumed in our planning to date that something like this would occur. It will have no effect on our operations, since we have set up everything in such a way that an increase of this magnitude will be of no consequence.

Hara: Will Thailand ally herself with Japan or with Great Britain? What is the outlook here? What's going to happen if Thailand opposes us? What are you going to do?

Tōjō: Concerning Thailand, it is our thought, based on the policy approved by the Imperial Conference of November 5, that we will deal with the situation just prior to our sending in troops. It is uncertain which side Thailand will choose. Thailand herself is in a quandary. It is our hope to bring her in on our side by peaceful means; in order to do this, early [aggressive] action is undesirable, but late action will also have harmful effects. Accordingly, we intend to broach the matter just before we begin the war, and to make her agree to our demands. It is our plan to do everything to prevent her from resisting, even though we may have to use force if worse comes to worst.

Hara: The Minister of Home Affairs has just told us in some detail what effect the war will have on the domestic scene. There is one thing I don't understand, and that is what will happen in the event of air raids. It's admirable that you are providing a good deal of training for emergencies, such as air-raid drills, in order to avoid damage as much as possible. But in the event of a conflagration, can we bring it under control, given the kind of buildings in Tokyo, even though we may try to prevent it from spreading? What are we going to do if a large fire should break out in Tokyo? Do you have a plan to cope with it?

Suzuki, Director of the Planning Board: Let me tell you some of the things we currently have in mind. First, we have enough food stored. Next, we hope that some of the people whose homes are burned can seek refuge elsewhere. As for those who must remain, we are planning to put up simple shelters.

Hara: It is not enough merely to have given some thought to the matter. Your plans are inadequate. I hope that you will be fully prepared. I won't ask any more questions.

Now I will give my views.

In negotiating with the United States, our Empire hoped to maintain peace by making one concession after another. But to our surprise, the American position from beginning to end was to say what Chiang Kai-shek wanted her to say, and to emphasize those ideals that she had stated in the past. The United States is being utterly conceited, obstinate, and disrespectful. It is regrettable indeed. We simply cannot tolerate such an attitude.

If we were to give in, we would give up in one stroke not only our gains in the Sino-Japanese and Russo-Japanese wars, but also the benefits of the Manchurian Incident. This we cannot do. We are loath to compel our people to suffer even greater hardships, on top of what they have endured during the four years since the China Incident. But it is clear that the existence of our country is being threatened, that the great achievements of the Emperor Meiji would all come to naught, and that there is nothing else we can do. Therefore, I believe that if negotiations with the United States are hopeless, then the commencement of war, in accordance with the decision of the previous Imperial Conference, is inevitable.

I would like to make a final comment: there is no doubt that initial operations will result in victory for us. In a long-term war, however, it is necessary to win victories on the one hand, while, on the other hand, we keep the people in a tranquil state of mind. This is indeed the greatest undertaking since the opening of our country in the 19th century. We cannot avoid a long-term war this time, but I believe that we must somehow get around this and bring about an early settlement. In order to do this, we will need to start thinking now about how to end the war. Our nation, governed by our magnificent national structure [*kokutai*], is, from a spiritual point of view, certainly unsurpassed in all the world. But in the course of a long-term war, there will be some people who will fall into erroneous ways. Moreover, foreign countries will be actively engaged in trying to undermine the morale of the people. It is conceivable that even patriotic individuals will on occasion attempt to do the same. It will be very difficult to deal with these people. I believe that it is particularly important to pay attention to our psychological solidarity. We must be very concerned about this. Be sure you make no mistakes in handling the inner turmoil of the people.

I believe that the proposal before us cannot be avoided in the light of present circumstances, and I put my trust in officers and men whose loyalty is supreme. I urge you to make every effort to keep the people in a tranquil state of mind, in order to carry on a long-term war.

Tōjō: The Government is fully aware of the importance of your remarks and views, and is doing everything it can along these lines. We are fully prepared for a long war. We would also like to do everything we can in the future to bring the war to an early conclusion. We also intend, in the event of a long war, to do our utmost to keep the people tranquil, and particularly to maintain the social order, prevent social disorganization, and block foreign conspiracies.

We have now completed our questions and remarks. I judge that there are no objections to the proposal before us.

I would now like to make one final comment. At the moment our Empire stands at the threshold of glory or oblivion. We tremble with fear in the presence of His Majesty. We subjects are keenly aware of the great responsibility we must assume from this point on. Once His Majesty reaches a decision to commence hostilities, we will all strive to repay our obligations to him, bring the Government and the military ever closer together, resolve that the nation will go on to victory, make an all-out effort to achieve our war aims, and set His Majesty's mind at ease.

I now adjourn the meeting.

[During today's Conference, His Majesty nodded in agreement with the statements being made, and displayed no signs of uneasiness. He seemed to be in an excellent mood, and we were filled with awe.]

JAPAN'S DECEMBER 7 NOTE

Having decided on war, on December 7 the Japanese government instructed its embassy in Washington to submit to the State Department a lengthy memorandum detailing the reasons why Japan saw no alternative but to terminate bilateral negotiations. The memorandum was not a declaration of war. Japan's official declaration of war was issued at 11 A.M. on December 8, Tokyo time (9 P.M. on December 7, Washington time).

Nor was the Japanese note strictly speaking a formal notification breaking off diplomatic relations, which international law customarily requires of a nation going to war against another. Even so, the fact that this memorandum was delivered to the State Department *after* the Pearl Harbor attack had taken place infuriated the Americans.

This was not a simple case of deception, however. The note was drafted for delivery to the United States because many Japanese, including Admiral Isoroku Yamamoto, who had planned the Pearl Harbor strategy, believed it was important to notify the U.S. government of the termination of negotiations before an actual attack took place. The Foreign Ministry in Tokyo obliged and composed a long message, but it consisted of seven sections and was sent in fourteen separate telegrams. As you will note in this document, there is no inkling until you get to the final section that this is a grave diplomatic note, terminating all negotiations. The embassy had not been notified of the home government's decision for war, but its staff must have realized something serious was going to happen, since they were instructed to decode, translate into English, and retype the message without using secretarial assistance, that is to say, without obtaining the help of American typists. The fourteenth cable, the concluding part of the message, did not arrive until the early morning of December 7, and it was followed by another telegram, reaching the embassy around 11 A.M., instructing the ambassadors to deliver the entire memorandum to the State Department at 1 P.M. (7:30 A.M. Hawaii time).

If the note had been delivered at that time, it would have preceded the Pearl Harbor attack by twenty-five minutes. The attack would still have been considered a surprise, a "sneak" act carried out before a formal declaration of a break in relations, and would have inflamed U.S. opinion, but at least the Japanese diplomats would have been spared the embarrassment of presenting the note after a state of war had come into existence. However, the note was not brought to Secretary Hull until 2:20 P.M., nearly one hour after the first Japanese bombs had been dropped on Pearl Harbor.

There were several reasons for the delay. For one thing, the fourteen-part telegram was too long to be decoded and retyped quickly. The embassy had been instructed to destroy two out of its three decoding machines, so the whole process took time. Besides, Japanese embassy personnel proved to be poor typists, causing additional delay. There were gaps in the telegrams received, and the embassy had to wait for clarification. By the time the fourteenth telegram arrived, past 3 A.M., most of the embassy staff had gone home, and it was not until after

11 A.M. on December 7 that the entire message had been decoded and copied. It was only then that the Japanese diplomats grasped the gravity of the situation. Around 12:30 P.M., the message had finally been retyped, and at 2:05 P.M. Nomura and Kurusu took it to the State Department. Secretary of State Hull was incensed, not only because he knew the Pearl Harbor attack had already taken place, but also because the message he received merely terminated negotiations; it did not declare war.

The picture is complicated because, thanks to the Magic intercepts, the top leaders in Washington knew the contents of the last-minute Japanese message. It had been decoded by 5:30 A.M. — nearly eight hours before the Pearl Harbor attack. Why did President Roosevelt, who received the decoded text by 9 A.M. and is said to have remarked, "This means war," not do anything to alert his military commanders in Hawaii and elsewhere? Such a question inevitably leads to a theory, held by some advocates even today, that there was a conspiracy in Washington to keep these commanders in the dark. The United States needed Japan's surprise attack to incense American citizens so they would eagerly accept a war with Japan and its ally, Germany. This conspiracy theory is not accepted by most authorities, but there is no doubt that a failure of communication took place between Washington and the military leaders elsewhere. A timely forewarning might have prevented the Pearl Harbor disaster. We must recognize, however, that although the leaders in Washington expected an impending war, they had little or no idea that the Japanese would attack Hawaii. Their attention was focused on a possible Japanese offensive in Southeast Asia, against Malaya, for instance, not against Hawaii. Even so, the commander of the U.S. forces in the Philippines, General Douglas MacArthur, was never instructed to disperse aircraft or otherwise prepare for a Japanese attack.

If you had been in the president's position and had the information that he had on the morning of December 7, what might you have done? If you had been one of the Japanese ambassadors and received instructions to deliver this important message to the State Department, could you have done anything to mitigate the impending disaster? Why did the Japanese government fail to foresee that such a sloppy handling of the final memorandum would infuriate the Americans and unite them, like nothing else, in a war of revenge? Finally, to what extent would it be possible to say that the Japanese memorandum and Hull's response indicated a serious gap in U.S. and Japanese perceptions of the situation in Asia and the Pacific in 1941 — such a serious gap that no peaceful solution of their differences would have been possible? Some writers have suggested that at bottom there was a cultural clash between the two countries, a clash between two contrasting belief systems and ways of life. Would you agree? Were there profound differences in the two countries' perceptions of the world, of international affairs, and of themselves so that nothing short of a wholesale transformation in Japanese attitudes would have satisfied the Americans?

KICHISABURŌ NOMURA

Memorandum

December 7, 1941

1. The Government of Japan, prompted by a genuine desire to come to an amicable understanding with the Government of the United States in order that the two countries by their joint efforts may secure the peace of the Pacific Area and thereby contribute toward the realization of world peace, has continued negotiations with the utmost sincerity since April last with the Government of the United States regarding the adjustment and advancement of Japanese-American relations and the stabilization of the Pacific Area.

The Japanese Government has the honor to state frankly its views concerning the claims the American Government has persistently maintained as well as the measures the United States and Great Britain have taken toward Japan during these eight months.

2. It is the immutable policy of the Japanese Government to insure the stability of East Asia and to promote world peace and thereby to enable all nations to find each its proper place in the world.

Ever since the China Affair broke out owing to the failure on the part of China to comprehend Japan's true intentions, the Japanese Government has striven for the restoration of peace and it has consistently exerted its best efforts to prevent the extension of war-like disturbances. It was also to that end that in September last year Japan concluded the Tripartite Pact with Germany and Italy.

However, both the United States and Great Britain have resorted to every possible measure to assist the Chungking régime so as to obstruct

The following selections are from *Peace and War: United States Foreign Policy, 1931–1941* (Washington, D.C.: Government Printing Office, 1943), 832–38.

the establishment of a general peace between Japan and China, interfering with Japan's constructive endeavours toward the stabilization of East Asia. Exerting pressure on the Netherlands East Indies, or menacing French Indo-China, they have attempted to frustrate Japan's aspiration to the ideal of common prosperity in cooperation with these regions. Furthermore, when Japan in accordance with its protocol with France took measures of joint defence of French Indo-China, both [the] American and British Governments, willfully misinterpreted it as a threat to their own possessions, and inducing the Netherlands Government to follow suit, they enforced the assets freezing order, thus severing economic relations with Japan. While manifesting thus an obviously hostile attitude, these countries have strengthened their military preparations perfecting an encirclement of Japan, and have brought about a situation which endangers the very existence of the Empire.

Nevertheless, to facilitate a speedy settlement, the Premier of Japan proposed, in August last, to meet the President of the United States for a discussion of important problems between the two countries covering the entire Pacific area. However, the American Government, while accepting in principle the Japanese proposal, insisted that the meeting should take place after an agreement of view had been reached on fundamental and essential questions.

3. Subsequently, on September 25th the Japanese Government submitted a proposal based on the formula proposed by the American Government, taking fully into consideration past American claims and also incorporating Japanese views. Repeated discussions proved of no avail in producing readily an agreement of view. The present cabinet, therefore, submitted a revised proposal, moderating still further the Japanese claims regarding the principal points of difficulty in the negotiation and endeavoured strenuously to reach a settlement. But the American Government, adhering steadfastly to its original assertions, failed to display in the slightest degree a spirit of conciliation. The negotiation made no progress.

Therefore, the Japanese Government, with a view to doing its utmost for averting a crisis in Japanese-American relations, submitted on November 20th still another proposal in order to arrive at an equitable solution of the more essential and urgent questions which, simplifying its previous proposal, stipulated the following points:

(1) The Governments of Japan and the United States undertake not to dispatch armed forces into any of the regions, excepting French Indo-China, in the Southeastern Asia and the Southern Pacific area.

(2) Both Governments shall cooperate with the view to securing the acquisition in the Netherlands East Indies of those goods and commodities of which the two countries are in need.

(3) Both Governments mutually undertake to restore commercial relations to those prevailing prior to the freezing of assets.

The Government of the United States shall supply Japan the required quantity of oil.

(4) The Government of the United States undertakes not to resort to measures and actions prejudicial to the endeavours for the restoration of general peace between Japan and China.

(5) The Japanese Government undertakes to withdraw troops now stationed in French Indo-China upon either the restoration of peace between Japan and China or the establishment of an equitable peace in the Pacific Area; and it is prepared to remove the Japanese troops in the southern part of French Indo-China to the northern part upon the conclusion of the present agreement.

As regards China, the Japanese Government, while expressing its readiness to accept the offer of the President of the United States to act as "introducer" of peace between Japan and China as was previously suggested, asked for an undertaking on the part of the United States to do nothing prejudicial to the restoration of Sino-Japanese peace when the two parties have commenced direct negotiations.

The American Government not only rejected the above-mentioned new proposal, but made known its intention to continue its aid to Chiang Kai-shek; and in spite of its suggestion mentioned above, withdrew the offer of the President to act as so-called "introducer" of peace between Japan and China, pleading that time was not yet ripe for it. Finally on November 26th, in an attitude to impose upon the Japanese Government those principles it has persistently maintained, the American Government made a proposal totally ignoring Japanese claims, which is a source of profound regret to the Japanese Government.

4. From the beginning of the present negotiation the Japanese Government has always maintained an attitude of fairness and moderation, and did its best to reach a settlement, for which it made all possible concessions often in spite of great difficulties. As for the China question which constituted an important subject of the negotiation, the Japanese Government showed a most conciliatory attitude. As for the principle of non-discrimination in international commerce, advocated by the American Government, the Japanese Government expressed its desire to see the said principle applied throughout the world, and declared that along with the actual practice of this principle in the world, the Japanese Gov-

ernment would endeavour to apply the same in the Pacific Area including China, and made it clear that Japan had no intention of excluding from China economic activities of third powers pursued on an equitable basis. Furthermore, as regards the question of withdrawing troops from French Indo-China, the Japanese Government even volunteered, as mentioned above, to carry out an immediate evacuation of troops from Southern French Indo-China as a measure of easing the situation.

It is presumed that the spirit of conciliation exhibited to the utmost degree by the Japanese Government in all these matters is fully appreciated by the American Government.

On the other hand, the American Government, always holding fast to theories in disregard of realities, and refusing to yield an inch on its impractical principles, caused undue delay in the negotiation. It is difficult to understand this attitude of the American Government and the Japanese Government desires to call the attention of the American Government especially to the following points:

1. The American government advocates in the name of world peace those principles favorable to it and urges upon the Japanese Government the acceptance thereof. The peace of the world may be brought about only by discovering a mutually acceptable formula through recognition of the reality of the situation and mutual appreciation of one another's position. An attitude such as ignores realities and imposes one's selfish views upon others will scarcely serve the purpose of facilitating the consummation of negotiations.

   Of the various principles put forward by the American Government as a basis of the Japanese-American Agreement, there are some which the Japanese Government is ready to accept in principle, but in view of the world's actual conditions, it seems only a utopian ideal on the part of the American Government to attempt to force their immediate adoption.

   Again, the proposal to conclude a multilateral non-aggression pact between Japan, United States, Great Britain, China, the Soviet Union, the Netherlands and Thailand, which is patterned after the old concept of collective security, is far removed from the realities of East Asia.

2. The American proposal contained a stipulation which states — "Both Governments will agree that no agreement, which either has concluded with any third power or powers, shall be interpreted by it in such a way as to conflict with the fundamental purpose of this agreement, the establishment and preservation of

peace throughout the Pacific area." It is presumed that the above provision has been proposed with a view to restrain Japan from fulfilling its obligations under the Tripartite Pact when the United States participates in the War in Europe, and, as such, it cannot be accepted by the Japanese Government.

The American Government, obsessed with its own views and opinions, may be said to be scheming for the extension of the war. While it seeks, on the one hand, to secure its rear by stabilizing the Pacific Area, it is engaged, on the other hand, in aiding Great Britain and preparing to attack, in the name of self-defense, Germany and Italy, two Powers that are striving to establish a new order in Europe. Such a policy is totally at variance with the many principles upon which the American Government proposes to found the stability of the Pacific Area through peaceful means.

3. Whereas the American Government, under the principles it rigidly upholds, objects to settle international issues through military pressure, it is exercising in conjunction with Great Britain and other nations pressure by economic power. Recourse to such pressure as a means of dealing with international relations should be condemned as it is at times more inhumane than military pressure.

4. It is impossible not to reach the conclusion that the American Government desires to maintain and strengthen, in coalition with Great Britain and other Powers, its dominant position it has hitherto occupied not only in China but in other areas of East Asia. It is a fact of history that the countries of East Asia for the past hundred years or more have been compelled to observe the *status quo* under the Anglo-American policy of imperialistic exploitation and to sacrifice themselves to the prosperity of the two nations. The Japanese Government cannot tolerate the perpetuation of such a situation since it directly runs counter to Japan's fundamental policy to enable all nations to enjoy each its proper place in the world.

The stipulation proposed by the American Government relative to French Indo-China is a good exemplification of the above-mentioned American policy. That the six countries,—Japan, the United States, Great Britain, the Netherlands, China and Thailand,— excepting France, should undertake among themselves to respect the territorial integrity and sovereignty of French Indo-China and equality of treatment in trade and commerce would be tantamount to placing that territory under the joint guarantee of the Governments of those six countries. Apart from the fact that such a proposal totally ignores the position of France, it is unacceptable to the Japanese Government in that such an arrangement cannot but be considered as an extension to French Indo-China of a system similar to the Nine Power Treaty structure which is the chief factor responsible for the present predicament of East Asia.

5. All the items demanded of Japan by the American Government regarding China such as wholesale evacuation of troops or unconditional application of the principle of non-discrimination in international commerce ignored the actual conditions of China, and are calculated to destroy Japan's position as the stabilizing factor of East Asia. The attitude of the American Government in demanding Japan not to support militarily, politically or economically any régime other than the régime at Chungking, disregarding thereby the existence of the Nanking Government, shatters the very basis of the present negotiation. This demand of the American Government falling, as it does, in line with its above-mentioned refusal to cease from aiding the Chungking régime, demonstrates clearly the intention of the American Government to obstruct the restoration of normal relations between Japan and China and the return of peace to East Asia.

5. In brief, the American proposal contains certain acceptable items such as those concerning commerce, including the conclusion of a trade agreement, mutual removal of the freezing restrictions, and stabilization of yen and dollar exchange, or the abolition of extra-territorial rights in China. On the other hand, however, the proposal in question ignores Japan's sacrifices in the four years of the China Affair, menaces the Empire's existence itself and disparages its honour and prestige. Therefore, viewed in its entirety, the Japanese Government regrets that it cannot accept the proposal as a basis of negotiation.

6. The Japanese Government, in its desire for an early conclusion of the negotiation, proposed simultaneously with the conclusion of the Japanese-American negotiation, agreements to be signed with Great Britain and other interested countries. The proposal was accepted by the American Government. However, since the American Government has made the proposal of November 26th as a result of frequent consultation with Great Britain, Australia, the Netherlands and Chungking, and presumably by catering to the wishes of the Chungking régime in the

questions of China, it must be concluded that all these countries are at one with the United States in ignoring Japan's position.

7. Obviously it is the intention of the American Government to conspire with Great Britain and other countries to obstruct Japan's efforts toward the establishment of peace through the creation of a new order in East Asia, and especially to preserve Anglo-American rights and interests by keeping Japan and China at war. This intention has been revealed clearly during the course of the present negotiation. Thus, the earnest hope of the Japanese Government to adjust Japanese-American relations and to preserve and promote the peace of the Pacific through cooperation with the American Government has finally been lost.

The Japanese Government regrets to have to notify hereby the American Government that in view of the attitude of the American Government it cannot but consider that it is impossible to reach an agreement through further negotiations.

[WASHINGTON.] *December 7, 1941.*

JOSEPH W. BALLANTINE

Memorandum

December 7, 1941

The Japanese Ambassador asked for an appointment to see the Secretary at 1:00 P.M., but later telephoned and asked that the appointment be postponed to 1:45 as the Ambassador was not quite ready. The Ambassador and Mr. Kurusu arrived at the Department at 2:05 P.M. and were received by the Secretary at 2:20.

The Japanese Ambassador stated that he had been instructed to deliver at 1:00 P.M. the document which he handed the Secretary, but that he was sorry that he had been delayed owing to the need of more time to decode the message. The Secretary asked why he had specified one o'clock. The Ambassador replied that he did not know but that was his instruction.

The Secretary said that anyway he was receiving the message at two o'clock.

After the Secretary had read two or three pages he asked the Ambassador whether this document was presented under instructions of the

Japanese Government. The Ambassador replied that it was. The Secretary as soon as he had finished reading the document turned to the Japanese Ambassador and said,

"I must say that in all my conversations with you [the Japanese Ambassador] during the last nine months I have never uttered one word of untruth. This is borne out absolutely by the record. In all my fifty years of public service I have never seen a document that was more crowded with infamous falsehoods and distortions — infamous falsehoods and distortions on a scale so huge that I never imagined until today that any Government on this planet was capable of uttering them."

The Ambassador and Mr. Kurusu then took their leave without making any comment.

A copy of the paper which was handed to the Secretary by the Japanese Ambassador is attached.

A Declaration of War That Was Never Sent

December __th, 1941

Shortly before the Pearl Harbor bombing, the Japanese Foreign Ministry drafted a declaration of war for possible delivery to the U.S. embassy in Tokyo prior to the attack. The document was drafted in English and thus contains some awkward expressions. This declaration was, however, never presented to the U.S. embassy. If it had, some scholars argue, it would have spared Japan from the opprobrium of having perpetrated a treacherous attack. Do you agree?

Your Excellency:

I have the honour, under instructions from my Government, to inform Your Excellency that as the hostile measures taken by the United States have seriously jeopardized the security, and therefore existence, of Japan, they have been constrained to resort to measures of self-defense and **consequently there now exists a state of war between the two countries.**

This Is Yomiuri (Tokyo: Yomiuri Shimbunsha, March 1998), 220–21.

I am also directed to leave with Your Excellency a copy of the Statement of my Government which sets forth their views concerning the rupture of our relations.

I avail myself of this opportunity to renew to Your Excellency the assurances of my highest consideration.

Statement of the Japanese Government

Being earnestly desirous of the peace of the Pacific, the Japanese Government have consistently pursued a policy of promoting friendly relations with Great Britain and the United States. These relations, however, have suffered a progressive deterioration in recent years largely through the unresponsive attitude of these Powers who have failed to understand the realities of the situation prevailing in our part of the world.

Our cardinal policy aims at inaugurating a new order in Greater East Asia throughout which we are striving to ensure and enhance a common prosperity. It is essentially a policy of peace designed to cultivate the friendship among, and increase the welfare of, the peoples of this vast region. It is thus a policy calculated to serve the interests of these peoples, redounding ultimately to the benefit of the whole mankind.

Great Britain and the United States, however, have willfully misunderstood our aims and aspirations and, in collusion with other hostile countries, have endeavoured, openly and covertly, to oppose and obstruct the peaceful execution of our constructive policy. The Anglo-Saxon Powers have not scrupled to render active assistances to the Chungking régime, a mere pawn in their game of Imperialist politics, prolonging the latter's futile struggle to the untold misery of China's teeming millions who are becoming increasingly anxious for peace with Japan. By aiding the Chungking régime these Powers have greatly impeded the restoration of tranquility in China and by thus opposing our efforts for a speedy settlement of the China Affair, they have more than forfeited the good will of our people. Anxious, however, to maintain amicable relations with them, Japan has, displaying utmost patience, persevered in the face of provocations hoping that they will reconsider and repair their attitude. It is highly regrettable that these Powers should have failed to respond to our policy and should have, on the contrary, resorted to unfriendly measures, some of them very severe and stringent, vis-à-vis this country.

In these circumstances, Japan concluded the Tripartite Pact with Germany and Italy, two leading Powers of Europe who, fully sharing our views, have pledged their willing cooperation in establishing a new order in Greater East Asia. But our association with the Axis Powers has added yet another cause of alienation in our relations with the so-called Democratic Powers who have begun to entertain unwarranted misapprehensions regarding our policy and purposes, despite our repeated assurances that we seek no quarrel with them. Far from harbouring any aggressive design, Japan was, as stated above, bent upon the peaceful initiation of an era of common prosperity throughout the Greater East Asia.

It will be recalled that in August last year Japanese forces were dispatched to Northern French Indo-China in connection with the prosecution of the China Affair. Later on, in summer this year, our forces made a peaceful entry into the Southern region in virtue of the Protocols for the Joint Defense of French Indo-China in order to cope with the grave situation developing in the South-western Pacific, due to the rapid augmentation of military measures by the United States, Great Britain and her allies and associates. These Powers chose to regard our peaceful advance into Southern French Indo-China as a menace to their territories and froze our assets in their respective countries, a measure tantamount to a wholesale rupture of economic relations. They have since even gone the length of establishing encircling positions against Japan which, creating an unprecedented tension in the Pacific, has greatly exacerbated their relations with us. The increasing pressure they have brought to bear upon Japan has as its aim no other than our economic strangulation. Sometimes, economic warfare is admittedly more cruel and disastrous than an open resort to arms. Thus the ruthless measures of economic attrition now directed against us constitute a really serious threat, affecting as they deeply do, the very existence of our Empire. In other words, we, as a nation, are faced with the question of life and death. We could not acquiesce in these hostile measures, as it would spell the decline and downfall of our nation.

Finding ourselves in such a predicament, we still patiently endeavoured to seek a peaceful way out of it. The negotiations at Washington are a case in point.

Our Government have, since April last, conducted protracted negotiations with the American Government with a view to bringing about a friendly and fundamental adjustment of the Japanese-American relations. We were afraid that the steady deterioration of our relations would, if left without a timely check, drift toward an inevitable catastrophe, an awful eventuality entailing immense suffering not only on the countries in the Pacific basin but on the entire mankind as well. We were convinced that, good will animating both sides, there should be no question that is not amenable to amicable settlement. We, therefore, exercised utmost patience and, in the spirit of compromise, proposed many a formula, often involving great sacrifices on our part, to meet the desires of the American Government which were, we much regret to say, not always reasonable nor practicable. In fact, we went to the last possible limit of concessions, short of compromising the honour and prestige as a great Power, in order to satisfy the United States. But the latter has persistently maintained a very rigid attitude, making not the slightest gesture to respond to our sincere efforts to reach a friendly settlement. In short, the American Government were singularly lacking in the spirit of mutual accommodation which is indispensable to a successful conclusion of any international negotiations. They maintained, throughout the course of negotiations lasting more than seven months, their original position from which they stubbornly refused to withdraw even an inch. Thus, it has finally come to the present pass where it can no longer serve any useful purpose by continuing further negotiations. Our untiring and unsparing efforts have been frustrated through the uncompromising attitude of the American Government and we have now been forced, although with great reluctance, to abandon the negotiations and, with that, renounce our cherished desire to come to a friendly understanding with the United States.

With the breakdown of the negotiations, we have thus been led to give up, at last and finally, the hope to find an escape, through peaceful means, from our predicament. At the same time, the hostile ring encircling our Empire is being steadily strengthened day after day, gravely threatening our safety and security. The economic warfare, in its most relentless form, is also being prosecuted with renewed energy against this country. In short, the concerted pressure of the hostile Powers is such that our national existence is now in serious jeopardy. Standing at the cross-roads of her destiny, Japan decided to defend her prime right of existence, a course that offered the only possible way of survival. Our patience finally exhausted and our destiny at stake, the nation has risen, as one man, to meet the challenge. Steeped in the conviction that right always will triumph, our hundred million peoples have girt on the sword of justice, anxious to defend the fatherland and eager to vindicate our glorious cause.

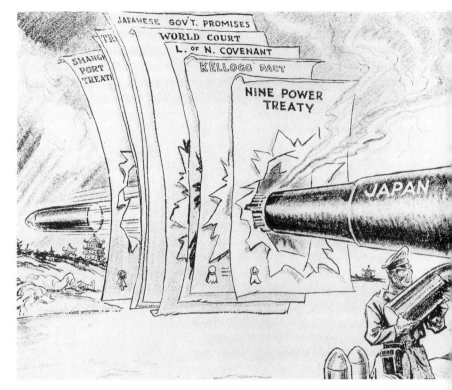

Figure 1. The Japanese take Manchuria, despite treaty pledges — a U.S. press view of Japanese aggression in China.
The Granger Collection, New York.

On the next two pages

Figure 2. *Left page:* Japanese and German officials celebrate the conclusion of the Tripartite Pact, October 1940 (Army Minister Tōjō in uniform at the center, Foreign Minister Matsuoka raising his glass, fourth from the right).
UPI/Corbis-Bettmann.

Figure 3. *Right page, top:* Roosevelt and Churchill at the Atlantic Conference, August 1941.
The National Archives/Corbis.

Figure 4. *Right page, bottom:* Ambassadors Nomura and Kurusu after a meeting with Secretary of State Hull, November 1941.
UPI/Corbis-Bettmann.

Figure 5. *Above:*
Japanese bombers warming up on deck before leaving for their mission to attack Pearl Harbor, December 7, 1941.
The National Archives/Corbis.

Figure 6. *Right:*
Rising as one man — a U.S. press response to the Pearl Harbor attack.
© *Copyrighted Chicago Tribune Company.*

RISING AS ONE MAN

PART TWO

Introduction: Pearl Harbor in Global Context

The documents you examined in Part One put the Pearl Harbor affair in a binational framework and discuss how and why Japan came to the decision to attack the United States. Some of the essays in this section give additional details on the two countries' policies and strategies. As these essays make clear, however, the Pacific conflict cannot be fully understood unless we put it in a broader global context. After all, by the fall of 1941, Japan and China had not been fighting one another for more than four years in isolation; each had been assisted from the outside in various ways. In addition, German forces, having conquered most countries in Europe, were trying to bring both Britain and the Soviet Union to their knees. A crisis in U.S.-Japanese relations would have immediate repercussions on these other countries' destinies. It is only by examining these repercussions, and the ways in which the unfolding U.S.-Japanese drama affected events elsewhere, that we gain more than a superficial understanding of the crucial weeks leading up to Pearl Harbor.

The essays contained in this section examine the perspectives, interests, and experiences of several countries with a stake in the U.S.-Japanese drama. It will be useful to summarize briefly the positions of these and other countries in the fall of 1941. In considering each country's involvement in the Pearl Harbor story, try putting yourself in the position of a leader of that country, and ask yourself how you might have responded to the deepening crisis across the Pacific. What might you have done to affect the course of events? What factors — geopolitical, economic, ideological — would have motivated your decisions? What would you have sought to gain from the U.S.-Japanese crisis? On December 7, 1941, what were the implications for your country of Japan's waging war against the United States?

CHINA

China had been at war with Japan since July 1937, when skirmishes outside of Beijing (called Peiping then) developed into a full-scale conflict. (If we go back to 1931, when Japan used force to detach Manchuria from the rest of the country, the Chinese-Japanese war can be said to have been going on for more than ten years.) There was no end in sight, and China had been divided loosely into three segments: the areas occupied by the Japanese forces (Manchuria, north China, the coastal areas all the way to the south, and railway stations and some urban centers elsewhere), "Free China" in the interior of the country under the Nationalist regime in Chongqing (Chungking) led by Chiang Kai-shek, and the Communist-controlled region in the northwest, with Yan'an (Yenan) as its capital. The latter two were nominally combined in their resistance against Japan, but already in the spring of 1941 Nationalist and Communist forces had clashed, each seeking to diminish the power of the other. Of course, all factions in China wanted ultimately to expel the Japanese forces, but they were not confident that they could do so without external assistance. The Soviet Union had provided military assistance to keep the Japanese forces tied down in China and, even more important, to prevent them from attacking Siberia. However, after April 1941, when the Soviet Union signed a neutrality treaty with Japan, China could no longer count on that help. That left the United States as the only outside power whose policy could check Japan. Washington had, since the end of 1938, extended loans to China and imposed embargoes on shipments of arms, iron and steel, and aviation fuel to Japan. By the summer of 1941, the list of embargoed items had come to include virtually all goods — except for petroleum.

Official Chinese policy, then, was quite obviously to ensure continued U.S. assistance. How exactly to achieve this objective, however, was a problem. If the Chinese forces showed strong confidence in their ability to resist Japan, U.S. authorities might consider that any involvement on their part would be superfluous or less critical than involvement in Europe. On the other hand, too passive a stance against Japan would dismay the United States, which might decide to accept the status quo and enter into a temporary compromise with Japan. To obtain U.S. support, Chiang tried many tactics: having his American-educated wife contact her friends in the United States to step up pressure on Washington for a more forceful strategy in East Asia; working closely with the British in order to bring about U.S. involvement in the war both in Asia and in Europe; and even encouraging fear in the United States that China might capitulate and accept Japanese domination in the hope that the United States would try to prevent this development.

In November 1941, Chiang and his aides were particularly concerned over what appeared to be intensive negotiations in Washington between Japanese and U.S. officials. He was aware of the rough outline of these negotiations, thanks to intelligence gathering by Chinese officials and to information conveyed by the British embassy in Chungking. Any improvement in U.S.-Japanese relations boded ill for China; conversely, a crisis leading to war in the Pacific would be welcome, for then the United States would finally tie itself to China's side, thus ensuring China's survival and ultimate victory.

THE SOVIET UNION

As mentioned previously, the Soviet Union signed a treaty of neutrality with Japan in April 1941. The idea behind it was straightforward geopolitics: to prevent a possible combination of German and Japanese forces against the Soviet Union. Soviet leader Joseph Stalin and his officials suspected, from intelligence sources in Japan and elsewhere, that Germany would sooner or later attack the Soviet Union despite the nonaggression treaty that the two countries had signed in August 1939. Soviet and Japanese forces had clashed in the Mongolian-Manchurian border on several occasions in the late 1930s, and therefore such risks had to be minimized if the Soviet Union were to become involved in a war with Germany. Because Moscow had been a major supporter of China's war against Japan, a neutrality treaty with Tokyo would be a rapprochement with Japan at the expense of China. The Chinese, both Nationalists and Communists, were sorely disappointed when the treaty was signed. They considered it Stalin's betrayal, although officially they continued to profess Chinese-Soviet friendship.

With Germany's invasion of Soviet territory on June 22, Stalin had all the more reason to adhere to the terms of the neutrality treaty with

Japan. According to the treaty, Japan would refrain from joining forces with Germany against the Soviet Union, and the latter would not lend a hand in the event that Japan went to war against the United States and other nations. Stalin stuck to this bargain throughout the fall of 1941. With the fate of his regime and his country at stake, this was the only choice he had. At the same time, he welcomed the growing crisis in U.S.-Japanese relations—as long as the crisis centered on Southeast Asia. In this situation, Japan would be less likely to adopt aggressive action against Soviet territory. Through its spies—the most famous being Richard Sorge, a German journalist who had become a confidant of Germany's ambassador in Tokyo and operated as head of the Soviet spy ring in Tokyo—the Communist International (Comintern) had a good idea of developments in U.S.-Japanese relations. These agents, including some Japanese close to government leaders, encouraged the Japanese government to push for a "southward advance" policy to establish a Great East Asian Coprosperity Sphere, embracing all of East and Southeast Asia under Japanese leadership. Thus Soviet policy was well defined in a self-centered way, with Moscow playing only an indirect role in the Pearl Harbor story.

GREAT BRITAIN

By the fall of 1941, Britain had developed a close working relationship with the United States in dealing with the war in Europe and the crisis in the Pacific. At their meeting off the coast of Newfoundland in August, President Roosevelt and Prime Minister Churchill confirmed the two nations' de facto alliance and asserted their shared war aims, known as the Atlantic Charter. Britain expected that sooner or later—although the precise timing could not be determined—the United States would enter the war on its side. Assuming that there would be a global war, the two powers developed a basic strategy (the so-called ABC-1), which emphasized the priority of the European theater, with the implication that in the Asian-Pacific theater they would at first adopt a defensive posture. Even so, the United States and Britain, together with China and the Dutch East Indies, sought to coordinate their policies toward Japan. Referred to as the ABCD powers, these four exchanged information and kept in close touch with one another as the Japanese crisis deepened in the summer and fall of 1941. U.S. and British strategists worked out joint plans in case of Japan's attack southward.

As far as British leaders were concerned, the prospect of a war between the United States and Japan was not unwelcome. Indeed, Churchill expressed his satisfaction and delight at the news of Japan's attack on Pearl Harbor; with the U.S. entry into the Asian war now assured, he was certain that Britain would ultimately win the war, not just against Japan, but against Germany as well. It cannot be said, however, that Churchill's cabinet engaged in a conspiracy to drag the United States into the war. Britain was essentially a bystander in the U.S.-Japanese crisis, although Churchill did warn Roosevelt against seeking a *modus vivendi* with Japan. He was convinced that any weakening of the U.S. stand in China would have negative repercussions in Europe. Churchill was even willing to mount a coordinated campaign with Chiang Kai-shek to persuade the Americans to desist from working out a compromise settlement with the Japanese. By doing so, of course, Britain had to consider the likelihood that Japan would attack its imperial possessions in Southeast Asia. Anticipating a war with Japan, London dispatched two battleships, the *Repulse* and the *Prince of Wales,* to Singapore and in the meantime sought an explicit commitment from Washington that a Japanese attack on British territory would bring about U.S. intervention. On December 1, Roosevelt told Lord Halifax, the British ambassador in Washington, that should Japanese forces engage in military action against British possessions, "then, of course, we will be in it together." This was as close to a clear-cut commitment as Churchill could have received, and henceforth he could proceed on the assumption that in the very near future there would be an Asian war pitting the United States and Britain against Japan — a war that would, he believed, lead to a world conflict between the Allies and the Axis.

THE BRITISH COMMONWEALTH

British territory in Asia was huge: Hong Kong, Singapore, Malaya, Burma, India, and Ceylon. The larger British empire also included Australia and New Zealand. The imperial conference of 1926 established a commonwealth, and these countries and territories became members. They were united through their allegiance to the king, but otherwise they differed a great deal from one another.

Hong Kong, for instance, was a tiny crown colony. In the event of a war, there was no way it could be defended against a formidable Japanese invading force. The majority of the inhabitants were Chinese who were hostile to Japan, but they could not be counted on to resist a Japanese invasion in cooperation with the British. This matter of indigenous cooperation was a sensitive issue, not just in Hong Kong, but elsewhere in Britain's vast Asian empire. In Malaya, Burma, India, and Ceylon, nationalist movements had developed against British rule. Would the leaders of these movements, as well as the rest of the indigenous population, remain loyal to the king, or would they welcome the Japanese invaders as liberators? Little had been done before 1941 to prepare the colonial people for such a war; for instance, they had not been organized into militias with their own weapons, for the simple reason that such armament could be turned against the colonial masters. Nor had there been much political or ideological indoctrination about the Japanese menace. The majority of the indigenous people may or may not have been aware of the Atlantic Charter, with its lofty proclamation of national self-determination, but Prime Minister Churchill explicitly excepted the British empire from this principle. Some nationalists looked to the Soviet Union for inspiration and support; the Comintern had, since its creation in 1919, preached the doctrine of anti-imperialism and often, though not always, supported indigenous Communists and nationalists in their struggle against colonial regimes. In the fall of 1941, however, the Soviets were not in a position to help much, due to their own trouble at home. China offered an alternative source of support; both the Nationalists and the Communists had long identified themselves with the cause of anti-imperialism. Here again, though, the situation in late 1941 was not very encouraging, given China's unceasing war with Japan.

India presented a particularly vexing problem for the British government. It was the one colony where a well-organized, clearly articulated liberation movement under the leadership of Mohandas Gandhi and Jawaharlal Nehru had developed. They rejected compromise in their quest for freedom and withheld support for Britain's war effort until Britain granted at least autonomy to the subcontinent. The situation was ripe for international intrigue, for both Germany and Japan were interested in dealing a blow to Britain by provoking a massive anticolonial movement in South Asia. If India dropped out of the British empire with German and Japanese support, it would be of real strategic advantage to the Axis powers. Thus some Japanese military officers and civilians sought clandestine contact with Indian nationalists.

Although little was accomplished before Pearl Harbor, a functioning underground movement was organized in the neighboring colony of Burma. A group of Japanese army officers and Burmese intellectuals were making plans for proclaiming Burma's liberation from British rule. It should be pointed out, however, that once war came, this movement was suppressed by Japanese occupation forces that showed little interest in indigenous nationalism.

In sharp contrast to the Asian colonies were Australia and New Zealand, "European" countries in the South Pacific whose inhabitants retained their loyalty to the motherland. They sent troops and ships to help Britain in its war against Germany, but it was becoming evident that Britain would not be able to reciprocate by defending them against Japanese assault. By 1941, communication was tenuous as Germany controlled the vast region from Western Europe to North Africa, and the German army in Libya and western Egypt threatened Suez. London admitted to its inability to defend Australia and New Zealand when it decided to reinforce Singapore rather than deploy forces to these countries. The idea was that holding Singapore would protect Australia and New Zealand, but all the same they remained in a precarious situation — unless the United States could help. It was indeed the United States that was steadily assuming the role as ally and protector. Such a stance made sense in view of the grave situation in Europe, but also because the United States had to defend the Philippines, its colony, an archipelago that lay near Australia. By the fall of 1941, the U.S. military reinforced Philippine defenses by sending them warplanes. With the increasing military power of the United States in the southwestern Pacific, it was natural that Australia and New Zealand would come to identify themselves more as a part of the strategic picture of the United States than of Britain.

Nevertheless, this development was creating a psychological crisis, especially among Australians. Many of them were working in other parts of the British empire, some in the Dutch East Indies, and their orientation was still toward Europe. It seemed strange to embrace the United States as the principal defender of their interests. Because Australian troops were called on to contribute to the defenses of the mother country, it was difficult to be told, by Prime Minister Churchill no less, to fend for themselves and not to count on further help.

THE DUTCH EAST INDIES

The Netherlands' colonies in the Pacific, comprising most of today's Indonesia, lay just north of Australia. They were, however, far less "European," with the Dutch colonial administrators, military forces, businessmen, and other civilians comprising only a tiny percentage of the whole population. Even after the fall of the Netherlands to Germany in the spring of 1940, the colonial government continued to function, free from German interference, and it was determined to prevent Germany's Japanese ally from controlling the region's rich natural resources. Throughout 1941, Dutch colonial authorities worked closely with U.S. and British officials to resist Japanese pressure for more oil and to plan for the defense of the islands in the event of a Japanese attack.

The indigenous population was engaged mostly in agriculture, many of them living on plantations producing rubber, oil, and other resources, as well as working in mines extracting tin, tungsten, and other materials. A large number worked for the colonial administration as minor officials and for Dutch families, restaurants, golf courses, and the like, as servants.

Since the late 1920s, there had been a movement among Indonesians clamoring for liberation from Dutch colonial rule. Far from fully developed or well organized, the movement nevertheless survived the arrest and imprisonment of its leaders, and in the late 1930s and the early 1940s, it had attracted the attention of the Japanese military, which was planning for a possible assault on the Dutch colony. Clandestine contact was established between some Japanese officers and Indonesian nationalists, among whom the most prominent were Mohammed Hatta and Sukarno, men who were to play crucial roles in Indonesian politics after the war. The Japanese sought to turn the movement for independence into an anti-Dutch offensive, but as of December 1941, few concrete gains had been achieved because Japan's primary interest in the Dutch East Indies lay in their rich natural resources, not in their political future. If the Dutch authorities on the islands could be persuaded to provide Japan with sufficient quantities of petroleum, so much the better. If not, the Japanese would contemplate a forceful seizure of the oil fields. In either case, the well-being of the indigenous population was of secondary consideration.

THE PHILIPPINES

In 1934, the U.S. Congress passed a law — the Tydings-McDuffie Act — promising independence to the Philippines in 1946. (The act was a response both to a persistent sentiment for independence among the Filipinos and to the growing conviction in the United States that the archipelago, a U.S. colony since 1898, had brought much more trouble than tangible benefits to the nation.) In the meantime, both Filipinos and Americans were deeply concerned over the defense of the islands in the event of a war with Japan. U.S. war plans were giving top priority to the European theater, relegating the southwestern Pacific to a position of only secondary importance. In the summer of 1941, however, U.S. military strategists revised their defensive posture and adopted a more aggressive policy. They sent an increasing number of bombers and fighter aircraft and appointed General Douglas MacArthur as commander of U.S. and Philippine forces. (MacArthur had served in the U.S. army of occupation in the Philippines. He retired from active duty in the mid-1930s as the highest-ranking army general.) This shift was a result of the general hardening of U.S. policy toward Japan that was intent on deterring aggressive Japanese action in Southeast Asia as well as against the Soviet Union.

Unlike the situation in the British and Dutch empires, the Filipinos were generally cooperative with U.S. authorities. For one thing, the United States had given them a measure of autonomy over the last thirty years and had cooperated with them in establishing their own legislative bodies and governmental agencies. They would certainly have preferred to see their country become independent in 1946 rather than be overrun by Japanese forces. Nevertheless, they had to consider the possibility that the archipelago might turn into a vast battlefield, with devastating consequences for the civilian population. What should the Filipinos do if Japanese invaders succeeded in driving out the Americans? Should they persist in resisting the Japanese, or should they think about ways to collaborate with Japan? Before any definite solution was arrived at, the Filipinos woke up on the morning of December 8, 1941, to learn of the Pearl Harbor bombing, which was soon followed by a Japanese attack on Clark Airfield in Manila.

FRENCH INDOCHINA

Curiously, the French empire in Asia proved to be the last European colony to succumb to Japanese rule despite the fact that France had been occupied by German forces since June 1940. This was largely because the Japanese considered it more expedient to deal with the Vichy (i.e., "collaborationist") government in Indochina rather than expel it and replace it with their own regime. After all, in the summer of 1940, the French authorities in Hanoi agreed to the stationing of some Japanese forces in northern Indochina, sealing off land communication and preventing arms shipments between the peninsula and "Free China" to the north. In July 1941, Japan put pressure once again on the French authorities to occupy the whole country — to occupy it, but not to govern it. The French would continue to exercise colonial control over the indigenous population, while Japanese forces would determine Indochina's military affairs. This turned the colony into Japan's de facto protectorate, but the Vichy regime in France, as well as in Indochina, accepted the situation as preferable to an outright end to French colonial rule in Asia. (At that time, it should be noted, the United States maintained diplomatic relations with Vichy France, which were broken off when the whole of France was occupied by German forces in 1942. The French colonial regime in Hanoi played no role in the U.S.-Japanese drama leading up to Pearl Harbor.)

Among the Vietnamese population, a well-organized nationalist movement had been in existence for more than twenty years. Led by Ho Chi Minh and other radicals, the nationalists showed no interest in collaborating with Japan and were determined to expel both French *and* Japanese forces from the peninsula. Ho and his colleagues were mostly Communists, influenced by Soviet anti-imperialism, but like their Chinese counterparts, they found Soviet support to be fleeting. Instead, they realized it was more expedient to work clandestinely with Chinese Communists and then with U.S. officials, believing that the United States was far more sympathetic to their cause than either Japan or France. As of December 1941, however, there was no well-coordinated strategy of liberation on the basis of U.S.-Vietnamese cooperation.

GERMANY

Germany, Italy, and Japan concluded a triple alliance, the Tripartite (Axis) Pact, in 1940. Unlike Britain and the United States, however, the Axis allies did not work out a system for coordinating their strategies. Although they shared their hostility toward the Anglo-American democracies, too much separated Germany and Japan — racially, culturally, and historically — to turn the alliance into anything more than a marriage of convenience. Even after Pearl Harbor, Germany and Japan never organized a combined force or established combined chiefs of staff, unlike their enemies. Nevertheless, Adolf Hitler and his officials were keenly interested in the developments in the Asian-Pacific region throughout 1941. As U.S.-Japanese relations deteriorated, Hitler urged Japan to take a firm stand. He reasoned that such a position would force the United States to pay increasing attention to the Pacific and would in effect weaken its resolve in the Atlantic. German leaders were explicit in trying to persuade the Japanese to attack Hong Kong, Singapore, and other British possessions in Asia, irrespective of the outcome of the negotiations in Washington. Such action, it was believed, would deal a crushing blow to the British empire and thus to Britain. Hitler also wanted Japan to join him in invading the Soviet Union, but here the Japanese proved less obliging; they would not accept the drain on resources and men that a pincers attack on Soviet territory would require when they were planning a war against the United States and Britain.

Germany did not play a direct role in the last-minute negotiations in Washington. Indirectly, however, it remained a factor inasmuch as U.S. officials remained adamant to the end that Japan liberate itself from the Axis partnership if it wanted to live in peace with the Western democracies. The Japanese were never willing to denounce the alliance explicitly, although in the end it was the question of China, not Germany, that proved the most intractable.

The Essays

There are literally thousands of studies on the coming of the war in the Pacific of which the ten essays you are going to read are only a tiny fraction. However, they are all based on research in archival material and add fresh, and often conflicting, perspectives. History is both record and interpretation. Having examined some of the crucial documents on the road to Pearl Harbor, you are now in a position to explore how identical events can suggest contrasting meanings, depending on what questions you ask, what themes you think are important, and in what larger frameworks you want to place the record.

SUMIO HATANO AND SADAO ASADA

Japan's Decision to "Go South"

As the documents in Part One reveal, Japan's decision in July 1941 to occupy southern Indochina set in motion a chain of events that sparked the U.S.-Japanese crisis and ultimately resulted in war. However, the strategy of "southward advance" did not begin in the summer of 1941. Japan had long been fascinated with the resource-rich region of Southeast Asia and the southwestern Pacific, and in the late 1930s and the early 1940s, many in the army and the navy eyed the region, all the more eagerly as the war in

Sumio Hatano and Sadao Asada, "The Japanese Decision to Move South," in Robert Boyce and Esmonde M. Robertson, eds., *Paths to War: New Essays on the Origins of the Second World War* (New York: St. Martin's Press, 1989), 391–400.

China steadily bogged down. At the same time, this was the very area in which the European colonial powers — in particular Britain and the Netherlands — were determined to uphold their existing rights and interests. The United States supported them.

To understand the circumstances in which Japan moved southward, it is necessary to study the thinking of the Japanese military regarding their southern strategy. Two leading historians of Japanese foreign and military affairs provide essential information in the following essay. What does the essay indicate about the nature of strategic decision making in Japan in 1940 and 1941, especially concerning the role and attitude of the Japanese navy?

. . . Japanese troops began marching into northern Indochina on 22 September 1940. The United States responded with a new loan to China, and on 26 September President Franklin D. Roosevelt signed an executive order placing aviation gasoline, high-grade iron and steel scrap under export licensing. To keep in step with United States policy, the British soon reopened the Burma Road. Having survived the Battle of Britain, they were moving closer to an alliance with the United States.

Soon after the Japanese thrust into northern Indochina and conclusion of the Tripartite Pact (signed on 27 September), the Kiri Project (peace negotiations with Chungking) collapsed, leaving Japan no choice but to abandon a bilateral settlement of the China war and recognize the Wang Ching-wei regime. From this time onwards the army became convinced that the only positive means left for terminating the China war had to be sought in the European war. The army draft memorandum (4 November) stated that to conclude the China war and overcome economic dependence on the Anglo-American powers, Japan must "seize an opportunity to take military actions (*sic*) in southern areas."[1] Settlement of the China war was to depend on an armed southern advance.

In late 1940 army planners began to spell out the circumstances under which Japan would undertake military operations in the south. The program of southward advance was still predicated on an early German invasion of Britain, which would become the signal for Japanese attacks on Britain's Far Eastern colonies. According to the army general staff's estimate in September–October 1940, Hitler's delay in attacking Britain was merely "tactical" and did "not mean any change in determination to invade." The cross-Channel invasion would take place by the

---

[1] Navy general staff, "Shōwa 15-nen Shina jihen shori yōkō tsuzuri" (Files relating to settlement of the China Incident, 1940), Part I, JDA (Japanese Defense Agency) Archives.

spring of 1941 at the latest.[2] Such wishful thinking was belied by the fact that in mid-September Hitler issued an order indefinitely postponing — in effect, abandoning — the cross-Channel operation. Such a development undermined Japan's program for a southward advance. The premise underlying the army's opportunistic policy (as set out in the "Outline of the Main Principles") was becoming increasingly untenable.

Meanwhile army planners made rapid progress in working out the southern strategy. By mid-July they had prepared an operational program, according to which construction of air bases in southern Indochina was the pre-requisite for attacks on the British colonies and the Dutch East Indies.

Before the strategists could make much more headway, the border dispute between Indochina and Thailand intensified. With the collapse of Thai-Indochinese negotiations in October, the Japanese army became anxious to intervene. As the condition for its mediating efforts, the army demanded military agreements whereby Japan would obtain the right to construct air bases in southern Indochina and supply bases in Thailand.

When in January 1941 this border dispute escalated into an armed conflict, the Japanese government feared that Thailand might seek British support. The liaison conference decided to prepare for coercive action — the army by reinforcing troops in northern Indochina and the navy by maneuvers off the Indochina peninsula.

It is worth noting that in inter-service deliberations the navy, hitherto content with a passive stance, was beginning to take the initiative in a hardline southern policy. Especially important in this process, from a bureaucratic viewpoint, was the establishment of the First Committee in December 1940.[3] This was part of a broader institutional reorganization in the navy designed to gain a greater voice in national policy. Composed

---

[2]Army general staff, "Kokusai jōhō geppō" (Monthly report on the international situation), no. 20 (25 September 1940); no. 21 (25 October 1940).

[3]The first study to emphasize the role of the First Committee is Jun Tsunoda, "Nihon no tai Bei kaisen, 1940–1941" (Japan's decision for war with the United States, 1940–41) in *Taiheiyō sensō e no michi* (The road to the Pacific War, Tokyo, 1962), vol. 7. According to Tsunoda, it was the pro-Axis, anti-American members of the First Committee who pressed for an armed southern advance with the realization that it would lead to war with the United States. See also Sadao Asada, "The Japanese Navy and the United States," in Dorothy Borg and Shumpei Okamoto (eds.), *Pearl Harbor as History: Japanese-American Relations, 1931–1941* (New York, 1973), pp. 233–34. Official naval historians, most notably Minoru Nomura, minimize the influence of the First Committee on the navy's decision-making process. Nomura regards this committee merely as a niche for Captain Shingo Ishikawa who led it with his bellicose self-assertions. Bōeichō Senshishitsu, *Senshi sōsho, Daihen'ei kaigunbu: Rengō kantai, I: kaisen made* (War History Series: Imperial Headquarters, Navy: The Combined Fleet, vol. I: Up to the outbreak of the war) (Tokyo, 1976), pp. 495–96. See also Kiyoshi Ikeda, "The Japanese View of the Royal Navy," in Ian Nish (ed.), *International Studies 1985/3: Anglo-Japanese Naval Relations*, pp. 1–9.

of energetic strategists at the section-chief level, the First Committee was led by the chief of the operations division of the naval general staff and the chief of the newly established second section of the naval affairs bureau, whose duty it was to specialize in foreign and defense policy and conduct liaison with the army. Members of the First Committee, impatient with the "passive" and "vacillating" stand of senior officers, showed willingness to risk war with the United States.

Although some Japanese historians have questioned the importance of this committee, there is no doubt that its members were determined to assert their leadership over the navy's policy toward South-East Asia. In January 1941 the navy suddenly began to take an extremely tough position. The navy's policy towards the Thai-Indochina dispute was so bellicose that it surprised even the army general staff.

One possible reason for the navy's sudden militancy at this time may have been a recently revealed incident in intelligence warfare — the "*Automedon* affair" of December 1940.[4] Under extraordinary circumstances the Japanese navy had come into possession of a copy of the British war cabinet minutes of 8 August 1940, portraying an extremely pessimistic outlook on the Far Eastern situation. The top secret chiefs of staff report attached to the minutes emphasized that since Britain was "unable to send the fleet to the Far East," it "must avoid [an] open clash" with Japan:

> In current situation, we would put up with Japanese attack on Siam or Indochina without going to war. In [the] event of Japanese attack on the Dutch, and they offered no resistance, no war between us and Japan. But if the Dutch resist, then they would have our full military support.[5]

Upon receiving this information from the German naval *attaché,* Paul Wennecker, vice-admiral Nobutake Kondō, vice-chief of the navy general staff, remarked that "such a significant weakening of the British Empire could not have been identified by outside appearances."

[4] On 11 November 1940 the British steamer *Automedon* was intercepted by the German raider *Atlantis* off the Nicobar Islands in the Indian Ocean. Among the 60 packages of mail seized was a copy of the War Cabinet minutes for 8 August 1940, including the highly secret chiefs of staff report, which was being sent to the commander-in-chief Far East, Robert Brooke-Popham. After having sunk the *Automedon,* the *Atlantis* reached Kobe on 4 December. James Rusbridger, "The Sinking of the 'Automedon,' the Capture of 'Nankin,'" *Encounter* LIV (May 1985), p. 10. For the background of the War Cabinet minutes, see Peter Lowe, *Great Britain and the Origins of the Pacific War: A Study of British Policy in East Asia 1937–1941* (Oxford, 1977), pp. 160–65.

[5] John W. M. Chapman, edited and translated, *The Price of Admiralty: The War Diary of the German Naval Attaché in Japan, 1939–1943,* vols. II & III (East Sussex, 1984), pp. 333–34.

There is some evidence that Japanese naval leaders regarded this information as confirming not only Britain's capabilities but also its intentions. At the liaison conference of 27 December 1940, navy minister Koshirō Oikawa stated: "According to our intelligence document, it is estimated that Britain would not go to war as long as Japan confines itself to advancing into French Indochina, but war would become inevitable if Japan should advance into the Dutch East Indies."[6] Given such an estimate, the Japanese naval leaders must have been all the more emboldened to launch military operations in southern Indochina.

On 30 January the liaison conference approved the "Outline of Policy toward French Indochina and Thailand," which envisioned strengthening Japan's control over French Indochina and Thailand.[7] However, Foreign Minister [Yōsuke] Matsuoka opposed the demands of the navy and the army for military action on the grounds that it would lead to war with Britain and the United States. Instead, he succeeded in mediating the Thai-Indochinese dispute. As a navy general staff officer complained, the mediation was virtually "an unremunerated labor," since Japan's military demands in southern Indochina were "simply shelved."[8]

The navy had been engaged in maneuvers off Saigon and Bangkok, and was keenly aware of the alarmist reactions of the British who were vociferous about "a crisis in the Far East."[9] Commander Shigeru Fujii, a member of the First Committee, wrote in his diary that navy maneuvers had triggered a crisis fraught with danger of war with the U.S. He held that these actions strengthened "the oppressive anti-Japanese front" led by the United States. "As long as such a drift toward mutual provocations goes unchecked," he wrote, "a Japanese-American war is conceived to be inevitable."[10]

Such a view again showed the navy's conviction that Britain and the United States were inseparable, and that a further armed advance southward would lead directly to war with the United States. The judgment of senior navy leaders was that even if Germany should defeat Britain, this would not provide an opportunity for southward expansion.

[6]The first Japanese scholar to write on the *"Automedon* affair" and its impact on Japan's southern policy is Kiyoshi Ikeda, "Aru jōhōsen: Wennekā senji nisshi o yonde" (An episode in intelligence warfare: On the wartime journal of Paul Wennecker), Nihon Bunka Kaigi (ed.), *Bunka kaigi* (March 1986), pp. 14–19. Sanbō Honbu (ed.), *Sugiyama memo* (Tokyo, 1967), vol. 1, p. 157.

[7]James W. Morley (ed.), *The Fateful Choice: Japan's Advance into Southeast Asia, 1939– 1941* (New York, 1980), pp. 277–32; Arthur J. Marder, *Old Friends, New Enemies: The Royal Navy and the Imperial Japanese Navy, 1936–1941* (Oxford, 1981), pp. 156–57.

[8]Diary of Shigeru Fujii, 25 June 1941, p. 127, JDA.

[9]Marder, pp. 185–87.

[10]Diary of Fujii, p. 180.

In late March 1941 the navy presented a scenario of southern policy that supposed war with the United States.

1. For the moment Japan should continue negotiations to construct bases in Indochina and Thailand.

2. Japan must resort to force only when the United States, alone or in co-operation with Britain and the Netherlands, imposed total embargoes, or when the United States applied military pressures on Japan.

3. Resources in the Dutch East Indies must be obtained only by diplomatic negotiations.[11] In short, unless Japan was prepared and determined to fight the United States, military action in Thailand and Indochina would be impossible.

By the end of March the army, struck by the hostile reactions of the Anglo-American powers to Japanese mediation of the Thai-Indochina dispute, had come to agree with the navy that Britain and the United States were "inseparable." From January to March the army had made a reappraisal of Japan's national strength, especially strategic resources, in case of war. The conclusion was that shortage of liquid fuel made protracted war impossible; for the moment Japan should avoid further provocation, attempting to secure strategic resources through negotiations with the Dutch East Indies.

As a result of these basic reconsiderations it became necessary to scrap the opportunistic southern policy of July 1940 (the "Outline of the Main Principles") and to formulate a new policy in accord with the international situation. Adopted by the army and navy on 17 April 1941, the new policy paper (the "Outline of Policy towards the South")[12] stated that Japan should expand southward by diplomatic means, unless resort to military measures became imperative for "the empire's self-existence and self-defense."

A disgruntled Commander Fujii wrote in his diary that the new policy could be interpreted as "avoidance of the use of force in the southern regions."[13] Looked at the other way, however, it could also be argued that the navy had determined to take action in the south and open hostilities

---

[11] Sanbō Honbu Sensō Shidōhan (war guidance section, the army general staff), "Kimitsu sensō nisshi" (Secret war journal), 5 April 1941, JDA.

[12] The English translation is printed in Morley (ed.), *Fateful Choice*, pp. 303–304. For a good analysis, see James Crowley, "Japan's Military Foreign Policies," in James W. Morley (ed.), *Japan's Foreign Policy, 1868–1941: A Research Guide* (New York, 1974), pp. 91–93.

[13] Diary of Fujii, p. 125.

with the United States if and when Japan faced an all-out US embargo. For this reason, some Japanese historians argue that this policy constituted a further step toward Japan's military advance southward.

On 18 April, the day on which the army and navy agreed on a new southern policy, Tokyo received from Ambassador Kichisaburō Nomura in Washington the draft understanding between the United States and Japan, which had been informally worked out by the unofficial American advisers on foreign policy, the John Doe Associates.[14] This draft understanding, although demanding that Japan not enter the war on the side of the Axis, contained conditions favourable to Japan: normalization of US-Japanese commercial relations; US co-operation for procurement of resources in South-East Asia; and mediation of the Sino-Japanese War. Such conditions led the Japanese government to see the possibility of further concessions from the United States.

In sending the draft understanding, Ambassador Nomura took care to emphasize that "not to use military means for southern expansion is the very foundation of this entire draft understanding."[15] Contrary to such caution, however, an optimistic view prevailed among middle-rank army and navy officers who believed that an armed southern advance was compatible with adjustment of relations with the United States. Such optimism was shared by Japanese leaders. It stemmed from the feeling that the southward advance would not bring a war because the United States did not possess vital interests in southern regions, with the exception of the Philippines.

Japanese-American negotiations, commenced through informal channels, met with strong objection from the foreign minister, Matsuoka, who had just returned from a tour of Europe. He suspected that the US aims in these negotiations were to restrain Japanese advances to the south and gain time to extend all-out assistance to Britain. Besides, Japanese-American negotiations were incompatible with his policy of what a later generation would call "brinkmanship." Having lived in the United States in his formative years, he was convinced that a position of strength was necessary in dealing with the United States.[16]

[14] Robert J. C. Butow, *The John Doe Associates: Backdoor Diplomacy for Peace, 1941* (Stanford, 1974).

[15] Gaimushō (Japanese Foreign Ministry) (ed.), *Nichi-Bei kōshō shiryō* (Documents on Japanese-American Negotiations, 1941) (Tokyo, 1979), p. 26; Diary of Fujii, pp. 71–73.

[16] The best treatment of the way in which Matsuoka's attitude toward the United States was shaped by his personal experiences in Oregon is Chihiro Hosoya, "Matsuoka Yōsuke,"

Matsuoka had been planning a four-power pact that would bring the Soviet Union into the existing Tripartite Pact. He wished to start negotiations with the United States, but had counted on browbeating them by confronting them with a Japanese-German-Italian-Soviet pact. However, Matsuoka's proposal to expand the Tripartite Pact to a "four-power alliance" was rejected by Hitler, who had decided to attack the Soviet Union. In Moscow Matsuoka succeeded in concluding a neutrality pact on 13 April. During his tour of Europe and Russia, he had obtained information about the aggravation of German-Soviet relations, although there is no evidence that he took it seriously.[17]

Another expectation that Matsuoka held in concluding the neutrality pact with the Soviet Union was that it would expedite the settlement of problems in the south. The issue that confronted Matsuoka upon his return was economic negotiations with the Netherlands. The Dutch authorities, backed by Britain and the United States, resisted Japanese demands; in late May the negotiations with the Dutch were suspended and in early June the Japanese government decided to call them off. The failure of the Dutch-Japanese negotiations did much to renew the clamor for a military advance into southern Indochina.

Middle-rank navy officers in particular had become increasingly dissatisfied with what they saw as weak leadership on the matter of a southern advance. Echoing this discontent, on 5 June the First Committee presented a notable paper which urged that the navy "immediately make clear its determination for war" with the United States and Britain, and "lead" the higher echelons in the government and the army in this direction. Japan must carry out "without a day's delay" an armed advance into Indochina and Thailand — the key to a strategic position in the Far East. Such expansion was justified by the need to secure strategic resources upon which the "self-existence of the Japanese Empire" was said to depend.[18]

Commander Fujii, who drafted this paper, noted in his diary that it "seems to have greatly shocked the top leadership from the navy minis-

---

in Hayashi Shigeru (ed.), *Jinbutsu Nihon no rekishi* (Japanese history through personalities), vol. 14 (Tokyo, 1966), pp. 176–211; see also Hosoya, "The Tripartite Pact," in James W. Morley (ed.), *Deterrent Diplomacy: Japan, Germany, and the USSR, 1935–1940* (New York, 1976), pp. 191–257, *passim*.

[17] The most detailed treatment of Matsuoka's "grand design" for a four-power pact is contained in Hosoya, "The Japanese-Soviet Neutrality Pact," in Morley (ed.), *The Fateful Choice*, pp. 3–114, *passim*.

[18] Asada, "The Japanese Navy," p. 253.

ter down; it has had a considerable effect in crystallizing the determination for war."[19]

About this time, 5 June, Tokyo received information from Ambassador Hiroshi Ōshima in Berlin that a German-Soviet war was imminent. Since April the rumors of German-Soviet hostilities had been conveyed by *attachés* in European capitals, but could not be substantiated. On 3 June, Ōshima was told about Operation Barbarossa directly by Hitler and his foreign minister, Joachim von Ribbentrop.[20] The First Committee at once demanded a policy of non-intervention. It also redoubled its demand for the construction of bases and stationing of troops in southern Indochina and Thailand. The navy's high echelon leaders were reluctant to station troops there, but were forced to fall in line because of the collapse of economic negotiations with the Dutch East Indies.

The army general staff was also prompted by the rupture of these negotiations to take a stiffer policy on southern expansion, and news of the outbreak of the German-Soviet war supported this move. On 10 July the joint conference of the army and navy bureau chiefs and Operations Division chiefs reached an agreement that the stationing of troops and construction of air bases in southern Indochina must be carried out as soon as possible.

On the basis of this agreement the First Committee drafted a new policy paper, presented by chief of the naval general staff Osami Nagano to the liaison conference on 12 June. It stipulated that Japan should demand bases and the stationing of troops, and if this demand should meet resistance, it should use force. Despite Matsuoka's strenuous opposition, the policy was approved by the liaison conference on 25 June.

The great obstacle here was Matsuoka: Soviet-German hostilities being imminent, he reversed his earlier stand and now opposed a southern advance, insisting on an attack on the Soviet Union even at the cost of shelving the southern policy. Army and navy leaders, who had regarded Matsuoka as a proponent of a southern advance, were at a loss to understand his intentions. Years after the Pacific War, Matsuoka testified that he had objected to armed action in Indochina for fear of provoking war with the United States and Britain, but this explanation remains to be confirmed. Evidently he also attached great importance to the Tripartite Pact, in the conclusion of which he had played a crucial role.

---

[19] Diary of Fujii, p. 188.
[20] Ambassador Ōshima to Foreign Minister Matsuoka, no. 636 (sent on 4 June 1941); nos. 638, 639 (sent on 5 June). (Contained in the papers of Fumimaro Konoe, at Yōmei Bunko, Kyoto).

Whatever the case, the army and navy repeatedly attempted to persuade Matsuoka to drop his opposition. Captain Shingo Ishikawa, a leading member of the First Committee and personally close to Matsuoka, appealed to him in a letter on 19 June.[21] He emphasized that the liaison conference decision of 12 June had unequivocally turned national policy towards southward advance, and time was ripe for striking southward since the threat from the north would lessen with German-Soviet hostilities. Finally Matsuoka came around to endorsing an advance into southern Indochina.

Meanwhile, the army and the navy had drafted a paper explaining the need in detail. Japan's influence in South-East Asia — its "lifeline" — was being eroded because of the ABCD (American-British-Chinese-Dutch) encirclement. Japan must set itself free and consolidate its strategic position in French Indochina against the Anglo-American powers. Stationing troops in southern Indochina would be a great shock to the Chungking government, contributing to a settlement of the China war; it would also help reopen Japanese-Dutch negotiations.[22]

It is to be noted that the Japanese government and the military made no serious study of how the "ABCD powers" would react to Japan's entry into southern Indochina, nor was any thought given to the threat that Japan's military actions in the south would pose to Britain and the United States.

The German attack on the Soviet Union of 22 June shattered Matsuoka's grand design for a four-power pact and drove the Soviet Union into the arms of Britain and the United States. Yet this development did not tempt the Japanese leaders to demand abrogation of the Tripartite Pact; they chose to continue supporting the pact. They predicted that the Soviet-German war would end in an overwhelming German victory and believed it would provide a chance to remove the threat from the north, not to mention an opportunity to strike south. Ever since it received Ambassador Ōshima's dispatch of 5 June, the army had been formulating a new policy; its conclusion was that Japan should station troops in southern Indochina, while preparing for war against the north (the Soviet Union) in case the situation should turn out to be "extremely advantageous." The navy opposed a war against the Soviet Union, but it acquiesced in the army policy on condition that "preparations against the

---

[21]The content of this letter to Matsuoka is confirmed by the diary of Shingo Ishikawa, 19 June 1941, JDA.
[22]Asada, "The Japanese Navy," p. 253.

United States and Britain would not be compromised." This new agreement was sanctioned at the Imperial Conference of 2 July 1941,[23] and on the following day orders were issued to mobilize. The army and the navy prepared for both peaceful and armed advances, and on 28 July 40,000 Japanese troops marched "peacefully" into southern Indochina.

The United States was already aware of Japanese actions through "MAGIC," the technique for decoding secret Japanese telegrams, and a presidential order froze all Japanese assets in the United States on 25 July. The British government immediately followed suit and enforced a complete embargo against Japan. Although the British had contemplated a more limited form of economic retaliation, the war cabinet decided to give whole-hearted support to the United States in order to sustain the development of Anglo-American co-operation.[24] This decision placed the initiative and leadership of policy in the hands of the United States. What had worried London was that it could not obtain a commitment from the United States to give military support in the event of a Japanese attack on British or Dutch possessions, and British leaders now hoped this weakness could be solved by closer co-operation. On 1 August a total oil embargo went into effect, and this confronted Japan with a shortage of petroleum — the lifeblood of its fleet.[25]

Had Japanese leaders calculated the risk of such a sharp reprisal? Already in August 1940 the operations section of the naval general staff had drawn a scenario of mutual escalation leading to hostilities. It was characterized by peculiarly circular reasoning: to prepare for hostilities with the Anglo-American powers, Japan would have to march into Indochina to obtain raw materials; the United States would counter by imposing an economic embargo; this in turn would compel Japan to seize the Dutch

[23] Nobutaka Ike (translated, edited, with an introduction), *Japan's Decision for War: Records of the 1941 Policy Conferences* (Stanford, 1967), pp. 77–90.

[24] "Documents Relating to the Outbreak of War with Japan," p. 46, Foreign Office Archives, Public Record Office; Peter Lowe, *Great Britain and the Origins of the Pacific War: A Study of British Policy in East Asia, 1937–1941* (Oxford, 1971), pp. 236–40; Lowe, "Great Britain and the Coming of the Pacific War," *Transactions of the Royal Historical Society,* 5th Series, vol. 24, 1974, p. 57.

[25] "From the Burma Road Crisis to Pearl Harbor," memorandum by the Far Eastern Department, FO 371/35957, F 26–21 S21/G, p. 46, PRO. A recent study reveals that President Roosevelt had not intended the freeze to result in a total embargo, because he was aware that it might compel Japan to attack the Dutch East Indies or even United States territories. It was the "hawks" in the foreign policy bureaucracy who converted a rather limited measure into an all-out oil embargo. Jonathan G. Utley, *Going to War with Japan* (Knoxville, Tennessee, 1985) pp. 151–56. See also: Irvine H. Anderson, Jr., *The Standard Vacuum Oil Company and United States East Asian Policy, 1933–1941* (Princeton, 1975), pp. 158–200.

East Indies to secure essential oil, a step that would lead to hostilities with the United States.[26]

However, most Japanese leaders held to an optimistic belief that the southward drive would not invite a full embargo. Some members of the First Committee did not expect Washington to respond in such a drastic way because they felt American leaders would surely wish to avoid provoking Japan into war at a time when the United States was not prepared for a two-ocean war. From this perspective, it is not surprising that when the embargo did materialize, Japanese strategists took it as an unmistakable proof that the United States was ready to go to war.[27] . . .

[26] Asada, "The Japanese Navy," p. 253.
[27] Ibid., p. 154.

MINORU NOMURA

The Petroleum Question

In preparing for possible war with the United States, the Japanese navy, which would bear the brunt of what was expected to be an oceanic war, was particularly concerned with the supply of petroleum to fuel its ships and aircraft. In this essay, a former naval officer and one of the leading historians of the Pacific War provides an intimate glimpse into the Japanese navy's thinking on the petroleum question. How does the author characterize the Japanese government and its thinking in 1941? How does his view compare to that of Sumio Hatano and Sadao Asada?

Japan's participation in World War II can, in a sense, be said to have contributed to the post-war emancipation of former colonial nations from the yoke of their suzerain states. Again Japan certainly seems to have been caught in a trap plotted by U.S. President Franklin D. Roosevelt to provide justification for U.S. participation in the war against Germany. Apart from such viewpoints, Japan's participation in the war was by no means based on what the majority verdict at the International Military Tribunal for the Far East described as "a long planned conspiracy."

Minoru Nomura, "Japan's Plans for World War II," *Revue Internationale d'Histoire Militaire,* no. 38 (1978): 201–17.

What prodded Japan into the war were mainly a fear over the uncertainty of future national defense and a miscalculation that it was capable of carrying out a long-term war. In this article, I shall review the process of decision making, with insufficient foresight, regarding Japan's war plans as well as the background and main points of miscalculation.

The Military Oriented State Structure

Government by political parties under a parliamentary system, based on modern democratic principles of the West, was fully established for the first time in Japan only after the proclamation of the Constitution of Japan (generally referred to as the New Constitution in Japan) [1] following World War II.

Under the Imperial Constitution (generally called either the Meiji Constitution or the Former Constitution), [2] in force until the end of World War II, the Japanese government usually operated under a bureaucratic cabinet system, and parliamentary power was limited. The Cabinet was based not on parliamentary power but on the Emperor's decrees.

Though it is true that the Japanese government had been more or less operated under the political party cabinet system from the late 1890's to the early 1930's, [3] the political party system at that time could not gain full public confidence because of the frequent changes of alignment among political parties, their internal strifes, and their lack of competency in international affairs due to their concentrating efforts on internal affairs. With the Manchurian Incident as a turning point, the political party government system gradually declined, and following the February 26 Military Rebellion, [4] the system ceased to give its influence.

There were a variety of discussions concerning the interpretation of the Meiji Constitution in connection with the military field. However, the most generally accepted interpretation in this respect comprised three points, which virtually became the framework for government after the

---

[1] The New Constitution was promulgated on November 3, 1946, and came into effect on May 3, 1947.

[2] The Former Constitution was promulgated on February 11, 1889, and came into effect on November 29, 1890.

[3] The first Shigenobu Ōkuma Cabinet (Kensei-tō— Constitutional Government Party), which was formed on June 30, 1898, was the first Cabinet ever organized with the head of a political party as Prime Minister in Japan. The last Cabinet of this type was the Takeshi Inukai Cabinet (Rikken Seiyū-kai— Constitutional Political Friends Party) which was formed on December 13, 1931.

[4] The largest unsuccessful coup by Army soldiers in the history of modern Japan, which occurred on February 26, 1936.

1930's. The three points were: One, the Cabinet has no power over the command and operations of the Armed Forces,[5] these being the concern of the Military High Command[6] in its role of advisor to the Emperor. Two, the building up, maintenance, and control of the Armed Forces are the responsibility of the Minister of Army and the Minister of Navy, in their roles of advisors to the Emperor.[7] Third, the Diet can intervene in military affairs to the extent necessary for its approval of the annual budget program.[8]

Generally speaking, it is not unusual that well-gifted individuals opt for military careers, in developing countries, which later pave the way into politics along with a rise in military prestige. Japan was no exception. Japan's victories in the wars against China and Russia in the Meiji Era raised prestige and influence of the military, thus opening the way, under the Meiji Constitution, for it to increase its voice in political affairs step by step.

What basically determined the course of Japan's national defense during the period from the Russo-Japanese War to World War II were the "National Defense Policy of the Japanese Empire," the "Force of Arms Necessary for National Defense," and the "Principle for Operations of the Imperial Armed Forces." All were decided upon in 1907 and revised, respectively, three times before World War II.[9] The "National Defense Policy of the Japanese Empire," based on an assessment of the world situation, theoretically assumed certain countries to be enemies of Japan and indicated the basic armament policy. The "Force of Arms Necessary for National Defense" indicated the force of arms necessary to materialize decisions on national defense policy, thus offering targets for national defense arrangements. In addition, the "Principle for Operations of the Imperial Armed Forces" outlined operation plans of the ground and naval forces against imaginary individual enemy countries.

Needless to say, since a war in the first half of the 20th century required all-out efforts on the part of the nations involved, it was necessary

[5] This was based on Article 11 of the Meiji Constitution, which read, "The Emperor commands the Armed Forces."

[6] The Army General Staff and the Naval General Staff.

[7] This was based on Article 12 of the Meiji Constitution, which read, "The Emperor decides on the formation and the strength of the regular armed forces."

[8] This was based on Article 64 of the Meiji Constitution. In accordance with Article 71 of the same Constitution, the Government was empowered to exercise the same budget program as that for the previous fiscal year in the event the National Diet rejected the Government-proposed draft budget program.

[9] The original plan was decided on April 4, 1907. The first revision was dated June 29, 1918, the second February 28, 1923, and the third June 3, 1936.

for Japan to determine its national defense policy on the basis of a comprehensive and integrated study of all the political, economic, social and military factors concerned. The same approach also was indispensable in determining the force of arms necessary for national defense. It also goes without saying that the military plans were subject to the preceding national defense policy and war plan.

The "National Defense Policy of the Japanese Empire" and two other documents were legally subject to sanction by the Emperor. It is self-evident that such documents should be compiled and comprehensively studied with the Cabinet participating as central authority, since it was responsible for political decision making. Notwithstanding, these were, in fact, compiled with the Military High Command as central authority due to the military-oriented state structure of Japan at that time. What lay behind this was doubt regarding the consistency of a national defense policy under a political party cabinet, since it would be subject to changes within relatively short spans of time.

Although the "National Defense Policy of the Japanese Empire" had been submitted to the Prime Minister for approval by the Cabinet prior to the Emperor's sanction, the "Force of Arms Necessary for National Defense" was only referred to the Prime Minister for review, and it was believed that the Cabinet should have no power to revise the policy as compiled by the military. What was more, the "Principle for Operations of the Imperial Armed Forces" was confined within the Military High Command of the Armed Forces and was kept strictly secret even from the Cabinet.[10]

The above-mentioned military-oriented state structure of Japan was the most basic factor in the background of Japan's participation in World War II in addition to the compilation and performance of its war plans.

Operation Plans

The most advanced of the Japanese war plans for World War II were its operation plans. The aforementioned "Principle for Operations of the Imperial Armed Forces" provided that based on the respective "Principle for Operations of the Imperial Armed Forces," the Chief of the Army

[10] Concerning the process of decision making on the "National Defense Policy of the Japanese Empire" and the two other documents, refer to Military History Series, "Conduct of Navy Operations by Imperial Headquarters and Combined Fleet Headquarters (I): Before Outbreak of Pacific War," by the Military History Office of National Defense College of the Defense Agency and published by Asagumo Shimbun-sha, 1975, pp. 100–124, 156–173, 195–204, and 305–332.

General Staff and the Chief of the Naval General Staff (called Chief of the Naval Staff up until 1933) annually compile operation plans for the Army and the Navy, respectively, mutually consult on the plans, and submit these to the Emperor for sanction.

These annual operation plans covered a one-year period from April 1 to March 31. Needless to say, the armed forces of any nation have such annual plans, and the fact that it has such a plan does not necessarily mean that it will translate the plan into action.

The Annual Plan for Operations of the Imperial Army for fiscal 1941 was sanctioned on December 24, 1940.[11] The Annual Plan for Operations of the Imperial Navy for the same fiscal year was sanctioned on December 17, 1940.[12]

Though the Army and the Navy at that time compiled their fiscal operation plans separately, they coordinated their plan categories, the contents of which also were adjusted to a considerable degree. . . .

According to the third revised version of the "National Defense Policy of the Japanese Empire," which was in effect in 1941, the hypothetical enemy countries of Japan at that time were the United States, the Soviet Union, Britain, and China. In principle, the categorical classifications in the annual operation plans were in harmony with the imaginary enemy countries involved in the "National Defense Policy of the Japanese Empire." The Netherlands was suddenly included in the annual operation plans for fiscal 1941 though it had not been earlier included among the imaginary enemy countries. . . .

Out of the prescribed categories in the operation plans, Japan adopted 5-(1) — "Operations in case of a war with the United States, Britain, and the Netherlands during operations against China" — in entering World War II. Each annual plan for operations indicated the respective operations policy, the force of arms to be mobilized (including its formation), and the procedure for operations.

Fiscal 1941 operation plans provided, in case of a war with the United States, Britain, and the Netherlands, for attacks on and occupation of Philippines, Guam, Hong Kong, British Malaysia, British Borneo, and

[11] In Military History Series, "Conduct of Army Operations by Imperial Headquarters (II)," by the Military History Office of National Defense College of the Defense Agency and published by Asagumo Shimbun-sha, 1968, p. 153.

[12] According to the diary of Navy Captain Eiichirō Jō, who was an aide to his Majesty, Admiral Prince Hiroyasu Fushimi, Chief of the Naval General Staff was received by the Emperor on this date, and he recommended the fiscal 1941 Operations Plan of the Navy which was sanctioned on the same date. [Refer to p. 500, Military History Series, "Conduct of Navy Operations by Imperial Headquarters and Combined Fleet Headquarters (I)," as in (10)].

the Dutch East Indies with cooperation between the Army and the Navy, as well as for a surprise naval attack on and occupation of Wake Island at the initial stage of the war.[13]

Along with a rise in tension between Japan and the three countries in 1941, the Army and the Navy advanced consultations further on their operational plans to make them more specific, and finalized their operation plans against the United States, Britain, and the Netherlands. . . .

The Basis of War Plans

The translation into action of operation plans needs the force of arms. The Ministry of the Army and the Ministry of the Navy were responsible for preparing the force of arms required for the operation plans of the Offices of the General Staffs of the Army and the Navy. The Ministry of the Army had a well-detailed annual "mobilization program," and the Ministry of the Navy also prepared an annual "fleet preparation program" centering on the mobilization of naval fleets.

Although adjustments between these two programs were not complete, both the Army and the Navy had obtained large annual military budget appropriations (including the extraordinary military appropriations) due to the escalation of the China Incident since 1937 and had been financially capable of strengthening their power and organization aside from their costly operations in and around China.[14] In addition, the Navy began "Preparations for Fleet Mobilization" in August 1940 against the United States, and the Army also began full-scale "mobilization" in August 1941, thus preparing a sufficient force of arms prior to the declaration of war.[15]

The biggest problem for Japan in World War II was how to bring about an end to the war after taking over the resources-rich southern area and the peripheral positions necessary to defend this area in accordance with the requirements of the operation plans against the United States, Britain, and the Netherlands.

[13]Though the original copy of the Fiscal 1941 Operations Plan of the Army is still available, that of the Fiscal 1941 Operations Plan of the Navy is not. However, the original copy of the Fiscal 1940 Operations Plan of the Navy with partial revisions for fiscal 1941 is still available. (These are kept as reference materials at the Military History Department, National Defense College, the Defense Agency.)

[14]Refer to Minoru Nomura, "State and the Fiscal Operation Plans of the Army and the Navy" (contained in the combined issues 1–2, Vol. 10, "Military History," edited by the Institute of Military History in Japan, 1974).

[15]Concerning the Navy's "Preparations for Fleet Mobilization," refer to pp. 479–489, 509–518, 542–551, Military History Series, "Conduct of Navy Operations by Imperial Headquarters and Combined Fleet Headquarters (I)," as in (10).

The decision on this comprehensive war plan should have been made by the "Daihonei (Imperial Headquarters) Cabinet Liaison Council"[16] which was a consultative body of the "Daihonei"[17] — which comprised the staffs of the Army and the Navy High Commands — and the Cabinet. Though the Emperor, under the Meiji Constitution, was above all these organizations, it was the common practice at that time that his Majesty normally would not veto decisions of the "Liaison Council." It goes without saying that Japan entered the war without any expectations of a defeat. What Japan hoped for was, if possible, "victory" or, at least, a "draw." The "Liaison Council" on November 15, 1941, decided on the "Draft Plan for Expediting an End to a War with the United States, Britain, and the Netherlands," which read as follows:

". . . while overthrowing the U.S., British and Dutch strongholds in the Far East as soon as possible, take further positive measures to force the Chiang Regime into a surrender, and cooperate with Germany and Italy for forcing, first, Britain to surrender, thus discouraging U.S. resolve to continue the war."

In other words, what Japan expected was, on the premise that Germany would win the on-going war with the Soviet Union, to defeat Chiang Kai-shek's government for herself and lead Britain into a surrender mainly brought about by the strength of Germany and Italy and, next, to move toward an end of the war by holding peace talks with the United States as the main adversary at a time when the United States was discouraged amid growing disadvantages in untoward development of the war.[18]

Japan hoped to end the war as soon as feasible because of its limited war potential. However, as it lacked direct means to overpower the United States, it had to think that the war would inevitably become protracted. The basic concept of Japan's war plans was to fight a protracted war by relying on its original war potential, which Japan had boosted

[16]Together with the Imperial Headquarters, the Imperial Headquarters–Cabinet Liaison Council was founded under the first Konoe Cabinet, but did not meet under the Hiranuma, Abe, or Yonai Cabinets. It was revived under the second Konoe Cabinet and continued to exist under the third Konoe Cabinet, and the Tōjō, Koiso, and Suzuki Cabinets until the end of the war. Though its name was changed to the "Supreme War Guidance Council" under and after the Koiso Cabinet, there were no changes in function.

[17]The Imperial Headquarters was established at the time of the Japan-China War and the Japan-Russia War, and it also was established on November 20, 1937, to cope with the China Incident. It was closed on September 13, 1945, following the end of World War II.

[18]Refer to pages 642–644, Military History Series, "Conduct of Army Operations by Imperial Headquarters (II)"; pp. 565–566, Military History Series, "Conduct of Navy Operations by Imperial Headquarters and Combined Fleet Headquarters (I)"; pp. 344–348, Military History Series, "Army Department of Imperial Headquarters: Transition of Circumstances as to Outbreak of Pacific War (V)."

with painstaking efforts over a long period, plus the expected additional potential which Japan would be able to derive from its industrial potential and exploitation of the resources-rich southern area coming under Japanese control following the opening of the war, while expecting that Germany and Italy would win the ultimate victory.

The most important elements for Japan to fight the protracted war were to secure energy sources necessary for carrying out her military operations and sustaining her war industry and to have necessary marine transport capacity for bringing plentiful resources of the southern countries to Japan and enabling Japan to move and provision her land and sea forces.

Other essential elements were food for members of the armed forces as well as people on the home front and important strategic materials for war industry including iron ore, rubber, tin, nickel, molybdenum and cobalt.

However, almost no study was made on these essential elements from a national point of view until 1940. It is known that the Japanese army, navy and the Planning Agency [19] carried out respective studies on these elements. But in the general view of the times, Japan could not fight an all-out, protracted war as far as the resources are concerned.

Japan more or less suddenly began studying these basic factors in 1941 to prepare for entry into World War II and, finally, reached a conclusion with no solid foundation that it would be capable of fighting a protracted war.

Energy Plans

The most vital of all energy resources for Japan at that time was petroleum, the source of power for aircraft, vessels and tanks. Japan had a considerable coal output which was sufficient to run the war industries, but insufficient to substitute for the role of petroleum. Utilization of natural gas in Japan at that time was insignificant.

Of course, Japan had made extraordinary efforts to stockpile petroleum. The Navy was outstanding in this connection, and in the early 1910's began increasing the petroleum stockpile which grew to 6,500,000 kl immediately before the war.[20] Though the army had made no effort to

[19]This Agency was organized on October 25, 1937, to use and develop the composite national power under direct control of the prime minister.

[20]Refer to pp. 381–389, 533–534, Military History Series, "Conduct of Navy Operations by Imperial Headquarters and Combined Fleet Headquarters (I)"; pp. 685–702, **Military History Series**, "War Preparations of Imperial Navy (I)," by the Military History Office of

stockpile petroleum prior to the China Incident, it took over the function of Kyōdō Enterprise Company, Ltd.,[21] which was founded by the Government specifically for the purpose of stockpiling petroleum after the outbreak of the China Incident, and its petroleum stockpile reached 3,200,000 kl immediately before the war. The private petroleum companies were obligated under the Petroleum Industry Law[22] to stockpile a quantity equivalent to half of their gross petroleum imports in the preceding year, and the petroleum stockpile in the private sector was 700,000 kl immediately before the war.[23]

The First Naval Defense Policy Committee, the administrative authority of the Ministry of Navy and the Office of the Naval General Staff, in its research analysis[24] of June 5, 1941, for the first time made a study of petroleum demand and supply in case of a war from the aspect of the national economy. Based on premises that the war would break out in September 1941 and that Japan would occupy the Dutch East Indies in the initial stage of the war, this analysis studied petroleum demand and supply in the first three years of the war. . . .

According to this analysis, Japan could sufficiently fight a war for two full years but would be short 700,000 kl of petroleum in the third year even if there were no major sea battle, or short 1,200,000 kl if a single major sea battle had occurred. The fact that only one major sea battle was presupposed in this analysis indicates that the administrative authorities of Navy Headquarters had in mind a traditionally planned showdown

---

National Defense College, the Defense Agency, and published by Asagumo Shimbun-sha, 1969.

[21] Kyōdō Enterprise Company, Ltd., was founded on November 10, 1937, and was dissolved with the transfer of its business to the Army in October 1939. The quantity of stockpiled petroleum at the time of transfer was 710,000 kl, pp. 164–168, Military History Series, "Army's Industrial Mobilization for War Supply Production (II)," by the Military History Office of National Defense College and published by Asagumo Shimbun-sha, 1970, pp. 707–708, Military History Series, "War Preparations of Imperial Navy (I)," as in (20).

[22] This was enacted on March 28, 1934 (Law No. 26).

[23] The figures of 1,200,000 kl for the Army, 6,500,000 kl for the Navy, and 700,000 kl for the Private Sector are based on Governor-General of the Planning Agency Teiichi Suzuki's statement at the November 5, 1941, meeting of the Imperial Conference.

[24] This was entitled, "The Imperial Navy's Position in the Current Situation," the full text of which is in Military History Series, "Army Department of Imperial Headquarters: Transition of Circumstances as to Outbreak of Pacific War (IV)," by the Military History Office of National Defense College and published by Asagumo Shimbun-sha, 1974, pp. 61–75. The central figure at the First Naval Defense Policy Committee was Captain Shingo Ishikawa, who was then Chief of the Second Section, Military Administrative Affairs Bureau, Ministry of the Navy (Military History Series, "Conduct of Navy Operations by Imperial Headquarters and Combined Fleet Headquarters (I)," pp. 493–500).

with the U.S. Navy but gave no thought to the possibility of such naval war operations as actually occurred.

Despite these figures, the naval authorities concluded from this research that Japan "will certainly be capable of carrying out the required operations" from the aspect of petroleum. In this connection, they maintained that the petroleum shortage expected in the third year would be covered by an expected increase of about 2,200,000 kl in petroleum supply a year due to (1) increases in synthetic petroleum output, (2) rapid improvement in petroleum exploitation machinery, (3) increases in petroleum supplies from the Dutch East Indies, and (4) increases in petroleum purchases from the USSR.[25]

As the result of its failure to secure a necessary quantity of petroleum imports peacefully from the Dutch East Indies through talks, which had begun in September 1940, Japan sent military forces to the southern part of French Indo-China with a view to exerting pressure on the Dutch East Indies. However, contrary to the general expectations and hopes of the Japanese authorities concerned, Japan had to face a full-scale economic embargo by the United States, Britain and the Netherlands.[26]

Upon realizing the impossibility of petroleum imports under such circumstances, the Administrative Affairs Bureau (with Rear Admiral Takazumi Oka as Director) of the Ministry of the Navy immediately began reviewing the earlier analysis of petroleum demand and supply. . . .

Such research indicated that the largest petroleum crisis would occur at the end of the second year of the war. Because it was believed at that time that the petroleum stockpile would decrease by about 400,000 kl monthly,[27] the Navy Ministry authorities judged that Japan could not compensate for the petroleum crisis at the end of the second year unless it started the war in October 1941. This judgement contributed to strengthening the view that Japan "should begin war as soon as feasible if it is inevitable," which finally prodded Japan into war. . . .

In the actual process of the war, Japan continued its offensive operations even after taking over the resources-rich southern area, and consumed petroleum beyond the limits of this estimate. In fact, Japan at that

[25] Based on the Minutes to the Basic Japan-USSR Treaty, which was signed in Peking on January 20, 1925, Japan held concessions to petroleum interests in Sakhalin.

[26] Pages 323–395, Series of the Military History, "Army Department of Imperial Headquarters: Transition of Circumstances as to Outbreak of Pacific War (IV)"; pp. 526–528, Military History Series, "Conduct of Navy Operations by Imperial Headquarters and Combined Fleet Headquarters (I)."

[27] This is the difference between the total of 400,000 kl of indigenous petroleum output and 300,000 kl of synthetic petroleum production a year (about 58,000 kl per month) and the monthly average consumption of approximately 450,000 to 460,000 kl at that time.

stage was able to continue its offensive because it imported southern petroleum faster and in larger quantities than had been estimated. However, it grew more difficult for Japan to transport petroleum of southern origin to its home islands because of increasing losses of oil tankers from around the beginning of the third year. For this reason, the main fleets of the Japanese Navy had no choice but to sail from southern bases when they fought the Battle of the Philippine Sea and the Battle for Leyte Gulf, thus raising obstacles to drafting of the operation plans. More important was the fact that the training of aircraft pilots became impossible in Japan due to the fuel shortage. It can be said that the major reason for adopting the KAMIKAZE dives in the final stage of the war was the fuel shortage. . . .

Neither research analyses nor any war plans before the war had taken into account the possibility of a direct supply of southern output petroleum for military operations without first transporting it to the Japan Archipelago. . . .

It is often said that petroleum meant everything to Japan in "beginning and ending World War II." . . . Petroleum was the major cause for Japan beginning and ending the war, thus attesting to the pertinence of the above saying. The main cause of the petroleum shortage in Japan can be attributed to the unanticipated great losses of vessels. The actual loss of 7,900,000 gross tons of shipping and the 3,350,000 gross tons of new shipping built during the war years were a far cry from the estimated loss of 800,000 to 1,000,000 gross tons of shipping a year and the estimated average of 600,000 gross tons of new shipping a year.[28]

All in all, it can be said that the defeat of Germany and the shipping losses were fatal to Japan. From the aspect of war potential, there was no hope at all of Japan attaining victory. Notwithstanding, Japan entered the war, because the military-oriented hallucination that the United States would come to attack Japan if Japan's petroleum stockpile were exhausted led it to do so. Japan also could not align the other Asian nations with its policy. It was no longer the time for a nation to rule other nations.

---

[28] Pages 539–541, Military History Series, "Conduct of Navy Operations by Imperial Headquarters and Combined Fleet Headquarters (I)," as in (10). The primary cause of shipping losses was enemy submarine operations, and the secondary cause was enemy air attacks following the failure of the major operations against the United States. The failure of the major operations against the United States led to a shift in the main fighting force from battle ship to aircraft.

WALDO H. HEINRICHS

Ambassador Joseph C. Grew
and the U.S.-Japanese Crisis

The United States was represented in Japan by Joseph C. Grew, a career diplomat who had served as ambassador in Tokyo since 1932. Like his Japanese counterpart in Washington, Grew desperately tried to save the peace. To prevent war between the two nations, he thought both sides needed to make concessions. He also strongly believed that President Roosevelt should meet personally with Prime Minister Fumimaro Konoe (before he was replaced by Hideki Tōjō in October) to work out a mutually acceptable compromise. Such a scheme was not accepted by Grew's superiors in the State Department, and in the fall of 1941 the ambassador saw his role diminish steadily. We may speculate whether a different outcome might have resulted if the last-minute negotiations had been carried out in Tokyo instead of Washington. In this selection, Waldo H. Heinrichs, a leading student of President Roosevelt's foreign policy and a biographer of Grew, recapitulates the final days before Pearl Harbor as seen from the ambassador's perspective. Should Roosevelt have agreed to meet with Konoe? How perceptive was Grew in judging trends in Japan in 1941? Why were his views often ignored by the U.S. government?

Perhaps a leaders' meeting would have averted war. F. C. Jones in his authoritative study of Japanese expansion suggests that a partial agreement was possible. Roosevelt might have undertaken to relax sanctions in return for Konoe giving up the Southward Advance and making a dead letter of the Axis alliance. The two of them might have agreed to disagree about their respective sets of principles and left the China problem aside until a decisive turn in the European war made conclusive decisions on the future of the Far East possible. Perhaps so, but that was not the kind of leaders' meeting Grew had in mind. In August, when the Konoe project was fresh and unencumbered, he believed that Konoe would "appeal for American cooperation in bringing the China affair to a close and would probably be prepared to give far-reaching undertakings in that connection, involving also the eventual withdrawal of Japanese

Waldo H. Heinrichs, *American Ambassador: Joseph C. Grew and the Development of the United States Diplomatic Tradition* (Boston: Little, Brown, 1966), 351–61.

forces from Indo-China." In other words, Grew had in mind a settlement restricted as to detail, but not as to issue. He looked for a comprehensive understanding not a *modus vivendi*. He did not consider the details of a China settlement crucially important because he believed that once the conciliation process began, the details would take care of themselves. Konoe seemed to have reversed the Japanese course so fundamentally, in ways so obviously in the American interest, that American conditions were bound to be satisfied in the long run if the impetus of the trend were maintained. Whereas he did not grapple with the China problem in September because it seemed too forbidding, he ignored it in August because it did not seem a major obstacle.[1]

Grew tended to a more hopeful view of things than circumstances warranted and his optimism of August was reinforced by his habit of viewing Japanese developments in terms of swings between moderation and extremism represented by the pendulum image. This way of describing internal power arrangements in Japan and predicting armed expansion or peaceful diplomacy had proved unhelpful during the early years of his mission because the pendulum was always stuck at the extremist-expansionist terminal and he had dropped it by 1937. However, the struggle over the German alliance in the spring of 1939 seemed to restore the internal dynamic. Following the Nazi-Soviet Pact came a moderate period under the Abe and Yonai Cabinets, succeeded by an extremist period under the Second Konoe Cabinet and Matsuoka. In the spring of 1941, with Matsuoka's failures and signs of strain in the Tripartite relationship, the trend turned once more toward moderation, wobbled a moment with the advance in southern Indo-China, and then went forward with increasing momentum under the Third Konoe Cabinet. The values attached in Grew's mind to a moderate swing were very substantial. It meant that men dedicated to peaceful, humane conduct in international relations were in ascendant power. Credibility and honor, the essentials of diplomacy, existed once more. Therefore, in his mind, a pronounced moderate swing culminating in Konoe's unprecedented gesture placed the intractable problems of Japanese-American discussions in an entirely new light and rendered them capable of solution.

As before, the pendulum image was misleading. Japan was indeed hypersensitive to world developments, but reacted less by internal shifts of power or by changing her requirements than by changing her methods

---

[1] *Papers Relating to the Foreign Relations of the United States, 1941,* vol. 4 (Washington, D.C.: Government Printing Office, 1956). F. C. Jones, *Japan's New Order in East Asia: Its Rise and Fall, 1937–1945* (Oxford, 1954).

of satisfying her requirements. The Army was no less influential and no less determined to achieve its basic objectives in China. The Navy, which Grew persisted in seeing as an influence for moderation, had become quite the reverse. Staff officers urged the Southward Advance as the only way to secure a guaranteed source of fuel for the fleet, accepted the inevitability of war with the United States as a result, and were swinging their superiors to the same view.[2] Retired officers in senior statesman or diplomatic roles like [Mitsumasa] Yonai, [Kichisaburō] Nomura, and [Teijirō] Toyoda were not representative of their service. The Army and Navy conceived Japan's role as a great power to mean preponderance in the Far East with control of an inner strategic zone on the mainland comprising North China, Inner Mongolia and Manchuria, dominance of the Western Pacific, and access to resources in the area to assure imperial self-sufficiency. To retain that position they would fight the United States.

The moderates of August and September 1941, no less than the Army and Navy, desired economic invulnerability and East Asian leadership for Japan. However, they were more subtle, flexible, patient, and wary. The Greater East Asian sphere as they saw it did not necessarily require political domination, and the Nine-Power Treaty order just might be negotiable. They would say to the military, "If we could end the China war while keeping what Japan really wanted, a preferred economic position, and gain access to American and Southeast Asian resources while avoiding a suicidal war with the United States, Japan would forfeit nothing that time and toil could not eventually secure." To the Americans they would say: "We believe in the *status quo* and territorial integrity, but a nation must act when its very existence is threatened, as is ours by want of resources. The German alliance need not stand in the way of peace in the Pacific. We need peace in China, need your help in securing it, and need your cooperation in the reconstruction and development of China. We believe in equality of economic opportunity but China bulks larger in our world than in yours and we cannot be blind to what occurs there." So they argued and would argue. The moderates were not wielders of power or representatives of a contradictory point of view. Their methods were radically different from Matsuoka's but not their aims. They were not a force in their own right as Grew thought they were. They were essentially brokers of power and ideas.

---

[2] Akira Iriye, "Japanese Imperialism and Aggression: Reconsiderations. II," *The Journal of Asian Studies,* XXIII (November 1963), 110; David Lu, *From Marco Polo Bridge to Pearl Harbor: Japan's Entry into World War II* (Washington, D.C., 1961).

Konoe gained approval to try for a leaders' meeting, but with a time limit and without authority to promise total evacuation of China. Some idea of the amount of oil the armed forces expected in case of a settlement can be gained from the fact that the Liaison Conference of November 22 decided that if the United States accepted Japan's conditions, Japan would require that the United States guarantee an annual quota of 3,500,000 tons from the United States and 2,000,000 tons from the Dutch East Indies, or the same amount Japan imported during the year of immense stockpiling before the embargo.[3] Japan was prepared to make concessions but it is doubtful that Grew appreciated their limitation or the extent of the concessions Japan expected in return.

The United States was not in a mood for concessions. American public opinion, sentimental about China, hostile to Japan, determined to stand firm against aggressors, is one reason. The importance of keeping faith with friendly powers, evidence of Japanese preparations for further expansion, staggering resource and production requirements as set by the Victory Program,* and the tendency to underrate the danger of war with Japan are others.[4] Most obvious to Grew was the reason of principle. From nearly a decade in Japan he knew as well as anyone the importance attached to equality of commercial opportunity, nondisturbance of the *status quo,* non-interference in internal affairs, and territorial integrity. The United States had tolerated much and acquiesced in much since 1931 but never, year after year, note after note, had it in the slightest degree formally approved Japanese action in derogation of the policies established and nurtured by Secretaries Hay, Bryan, Hughes, Stimson, and Hull. By 1941 the burden of the clean record was overpoweringly against any settlement short of Japanese capitulation.

The probability of success for a broad-front approach to Japanese-American problems was very small by August 1941 and less than Grew

---

[3] Lu, *From Marco Polo Bridge,* 225. Japan imported 37,960,000 barrels of crude and refined oil in the year ending March 31, 1941, a figure equal to 5,516,524 tons. Samuel Eliot Morison, *The Rising Sun in the Pacific, 1931–April, 1942* (Boston, 1950).

* Refers to a study undertaken in the summer of 1941 by the War and the Navy departments, as well as by various other civilian agencies and the military high command, who were charged by President Roosevelt to explore "the over-all production requirements required to defeat our potential enemies." The study was completed by September and established the basic priorities for arms production.

[4] Memoranda by Hornbeck, August 27, 30, September 2, 5, 1941, *FR, 1941,* IV, 398–99, 412–16, 419, 425–28; Memoranda by Ballantine, September 23, 25, *ibid.,* 470–75, 478–80; William L. Langer and S. Everett Gleason, *The Undeclared War, 1940–1941: The World Crisis and American Foreign Policy* (New York, 1953). Herbert Feis, *The Road to Pearl Harbor* (Princeton, 1950). Paul W. Schroeder, *The Axis Alliance and Japanese-American Relations* (Ithaca, 1958).

supposed it to be. Whether or not he would have done better to use his influence for a stopgap agreement that avoided China problems or a broader agreement that temporarily accepted Japanese control of part of China are matters of speculation. In any case, his concern was less with the kind of solution than arriving at a solution. He believed that the process of conciliation afforded an honorable and realistic approach to peace, that war would be senseless and dangerous, and that his function as a diplomat was to try for reconciliation so long as peace existed, however irreconcilable the differences appeared to be.

The argument for "constructive conciliation" was neither proved nor disproved during Grew's mission to Japan. If the prospect for success was small by the time of the Third Konoe Cabinet, it was greater at the time of the Grew-Nomura talks in 1939. A mediated settlement in China was by no means hopeless in 1937. Opportunities arose time and again for the United States to lend a hand for peace in the Far East and to reach limited, practical agreements with Japan establishing confidence and the habit of negotiation and settlement. Certainly Grew's approach seems more imaginative, positive, and resilient than that of his government. In that decade and earlier the United States might have at least manifested a greater awareness of the very real problems of Japanese security and economic well-being, might have provided profitable, reasonable, honorable alternatives to the use of force and to Imperial isolation, might have above all indicated the very great importance to the United States and the Western world of a nation with the drive and skill and culture and extraordinary sensitivity to the world environment of Japan. That respect Grew never failed to show. His mission was a failure, but not a failure of his own making or of professional diplomacy as he conceived it.

The collapse of the Konoe project did not necessarily spell war, at least not immediately. Prince Konoe urged Grew not to be discouraged and not to discourage his government. Japanese friends tried to wear away the boots-and-spurs image of the new Cabinet of General Hideki Tōjō. They ticked off the moderating factors and related the Emperor's concern for peace. It all seemed familiar, but Grew admitted he had been wrong about a military dictatorship taking over if Konoe failed and agreed that Tōjō was the man to make the Army accept a settlement. The Washington conversations resumed and while they lasted time was gained. "Why on earth rush headlong into war?" he asked October 19. The Japanese problem would solve itself when Hitler was defeated. So he passed on to Washington as encouraging a picture as he could, if only to counteract the assumption of American press and radio that the Tōjō

Cabinet meant new aggression. But he was discouraged. Reaching an agreement now would be "little short of miraculous," hard to imagine in the near future "if ever," "in the lap of the gods." He could not avoid the conviction that with the passing of Konoe the outlook for peace was "far less favorable than it was before."[5]

Grew had borne constantly in mind the danger of war in case peace efforts failed but he had taken it as a hypothetical danger so long as conversations continued. From the end of October he began to worry that not the fact of conversations but their progress was decisive. On October 29 he heard reliable reports of elaborate plans for an army-navy attack on Thailand. On October 30 he had his first conversation with the new Foreign Minister Shigenori Tōgō. The grim and "ultrareserved" Tōgō warned that the deterioration in Japanese-American relations was "fraught with the gravest dangers" and that the Washington talks must be brought to a successful conclusion without delay. The Foreign Minister was even more chilling in his talks with the British Ambassador. [Sir Robert] Craigie reported Tōgō as saying that time was now a very important factor and that further deterioration in the situation "might necessitate an extension of Japan's military measures." Craigie felt that there might be less time left than he thought for solutions. Determined not to let his government "get into war with Japan through any possible misconception of what the Japanese, especially the Japanese army, are capable of doing, contrary to all logic and sanity," Grew composed a war warning.[6]

The purpose of Grew's telegram of November 3 was to warn Washington against assuming that continuance of economic pressure would force the collapse of Japan as a militaristic power without war and without resolution of the peace talks. Again he pointed out that the Japanese temper could not be measured by American standards of logic. The Japanese would not yield to foreign pressure. Japan's "capacity to rush headlong into a suicidal struggle with the United States" must not be underestimated, nor her "obvious preparations to implement a program of war if her peace program fails." If that program failed, the pendulum would

---

[5] Diary, October [n.d.], October 17, 19, 25, 1941; Grew to SecState, October 20, 26, 1941, *FR, 1941,* IV, 541–43, 553–54; Memorandum by Dooman, October 17, 1941, and Konoe to Grew, October 16, 1941, *Papers Relating to the Foreign Relations of the United States: Japan, 1931–1941,* vol. 2 (Washington, D.C.: Government Printing Office, 1942); Joseph C. Grew, *Ten Years in Japan: A Contemporary Record Drawn from the Diaries and Private and Official Papers of Joseph C. Grew, United States Ambassador to Japan, 1932–1942* (New York, 1944), hereafter cited as TY.

[6] Diary, October 29–November 3, 1941; Memorandum by Grew, October 30, 1941, *FR, Japan, 1931–1941,* II, 699–700; Grew to SecState, November 1, 1941, *FR, 1941,* IV, 563–64; TY, 465–66.

reverse and swing even further toward extremism than before. In that event he foresaw an "all-out, do or die attempt, actually risking national hara-kiri, to make Japan impervious to economic embargoes abroad." Those who felt the Japanese temper and psychology from day to day recognized that such an attempt was not only possible but probable. "Action by Japan which might render unavoidable an armed conflict with the United States may come with dangerous and dramatic suddenness." He did not mean to imply that the Administration was pursuing an undeliberated policy or to recommend "for a single moment" any compromise of principle, but the United States government must decide whether war with Japan was justified by American national objectives, policies, and needs. In short, the emerging alternative to settlement was war, the United States must make a positive decision whether it wanted war, and it must decide quickly if it had not decided already because "the sands are running fast."[7]

The succeeding two weeks only confirmed Grew's sense of urgency. As the Embassy Commercial Attaché reported, the Ambassador concurring, Japan's economic plight made a choice between war or agreement with the United States necessary "in the very near future." [Shigeru] Yoshida confessed his fear that a breakdown of the conversations would bring "drastic and fateful results." A pessimistic Tōgō was understood to be shocked at the failure of Washington to understand the need for speed. In the Foreign Minister's view the conversations were already negotiations and these were in the final stage. Craigie reported him as saying that a conclusion was necessary in a week or ten days. Grew warned the Department November 12 that dragging out the talks indefinitely might accelerate the all-out reaction discussed in his November 3 telegram. He could not be sure that Japan had presented her final terms and he was at a loss to say when and where an attack might occur. Rumors of troop concentrations and dates and directions of attack abounded. The best indicator of potential Japanese military action, he pointed out, was the state of progress of the Washington conversations. November 17 he directed the Department's attention to the great importance of guarding against sudden Japanese military and naval action outside the China theater, exploiting the advantage of surprise. He warned his government not to count on the Embassy to provide prior information since strict security precautions made it impossible for his officers including the military attachés to gather reliable intelligence. He concluded: "Therefore, the United States Government is advised, from an abundance of caution, to discount as much as possible the likelihood of

[7] Grew to SecState, November 3, 1941, *FR, Japan, 1931–1941,* II, 701–4.

the Embassy's ability to give substantial warning." There was little more
he could say, either about peace or about war. When this telegram went
off the last echelons of the Pearl Harbor Striking Force were slipping out
of Kure naval base on the Inland Sea and making for a final rendezvous
at Tankan Bay in the Kuriles.[8]

Actually the Japanese had accepted the alternatives as being war or
settlement since the Imperial Conference September 6, the day Grew
dined with Konoe. The difficulty lay in establishing a consensus on fighting or compromising. Typically they decided to keep working for a settlement while preparing for war and set a deadline for final decision. As
long as the impasse continued the final decision was postponable, but
the lateness of the season for attack, the relentless economic squeeze,
and the lack of progress in discussions steadily hardened a decision for
war. Tōjō's deadline was November 25, extended to November 29. The
Japanese knew they were in the final round and so by November 20 did
the Americans, thanks to "Magic." Both sides turned to consideration of
partial, stopgap proposals, the Japanese presenting one and the Americans drafting several. Even on that basis crucial differences remained:
the question of stopping American aid to China while Sino-Japanese
peace talks were under way; the amount of oil the United States would
supply; the timing of Japan's withdrawal from Indo-China. At the last moment, the Administration backed away from the *modus vivendi* idea in
the face of violent Chinese objections, tepid British approval, and mounting evidence of Japanese aggressive purpose furnished by "Magic." Instead, Hull presented a proposal November 26 that was comprehensive, uncompromising, and entirely unresponsive to all Japanese drafts.
Though providing for an unfreezing of assets and negotiation of a trade
agreement, it called for the evacuation by Japan of Indo-China and
China, presumably including Manchuria, in other words a reversal to the
status quo of 1931. The document served to clear the record for the
Americans and to convince the Japanese beyond all doubt that settlement was impossible. On December 1 an Imperial Conference ratified
the decision for war and the following day Admiral Yamamoto confirmed
the order to attack Pearl Harbor.[9]

[8] Diary, November 15, 1941; Memoranda by Grew, November 7, 10, 12 (two), *FR, Japan,
1931–1941,* II, 705–6, 710–14, 719–22; Grew to SecState, November 17, 1941, ibid., 743–
44; Grew to SecState, November 6, 13 (two), 1941, *FR, 1941,* IV, 570–72, 587–88, 589–91;
Morison, *Rising Sun in the Pacific,* 88.

[9] Draft Proposal (Plan B) Handed by Nomura to Hull, November 20, 1941, Document
Handed by Hull to Nomura, November 26, 1941, *FR, Japan, 1931–1941,* II, 755–56, 768–
70; Americans *modus vivendi* drafts and draft suggestions, *FR, 1941,* IV, 626, 627, 635–37,

For Grew the last days of peace were ritualistic. The Tokyo Embassy played no part in the Japanese-American diplomacy of late November. His advice was neither asked nor given. He was not informed of the various *modus vivendi* proposals until after the Hull note of November 26, and he did not comment on them. He assumed the United States was on the verge of war with Germany. On October 27, after the torpedoing of the destroyer *Kearny* in the Atlantic, the President had warned "the shooting has started," and Grew had commented, "There we go, and I'm all for it." He knew his Japanese friends were dismayed by Hull's proposal of November 26, but, in a burst of sheer wishful thinking, he registered support of it. He described it as "a broad-gauge objective proposal of the highest statesmanship, offering to Japan in effect the very desiderata for which she has ostensibly been fighting and a reasonable and peaceful way of achieving her constantly publicized needs." He argued fervently in support of the proposal at the Tokyo Club, one of the few places he could meet Japanese any more. Lacking means of practical assistance and rational hope, lacking even a desire to compromise, he seemed to be trying to resuscitate diplomacy by an act of will. Vague warnings of a break came from Washington, but he packed nothing. On November 29 he wrote in his diary that his mission had survived many critical days and would surmount this crisis, "I still firmly believe." On December 5 he wrote a friend in the State Department, "I am still hopeful that we may be successful."[10]

Late in the evening of December 7, Tokyo time, the Embassy received a message from President Roosevelt for communication to the Emperor. It contained a polite but pointed warning against hostile action in Southeast Asia and an offer for the neutralization of Indo-China. Grew urgently arranged a midnight meeting with Tōgō, at which he requested an audience with the Emperor at the earliest possible moment. Tōgō said he would present the request to the Throne and Grew returned to the Embassy and went to bed. The message was delivered to the Emperor at 3 A.M., about twenty minutes before the attack on Pearl Harbor began. At 7 A.M. Grew awakened to a request for him to come and see the Foreign Minister at once. He dressed hurriedly and reached the Foreign

642–44, 661–64; Langer and Gleason, *Undeclared War,* Chaps. 26, 27; Jones, *Japan's New Order,* Chaps. 9, 10; Lu, *From Marco Polo Bridge,* Chaps. 13, 14.

[10] Diary, October 28, November 29, 1941; Grew to James C. Dunn, December 5, 1941; SecState to Grew, November 28, 1941 (two telegrams), Grew to SecState, December 1, 5, 1941, *FR, 1941,* IV, 682, 683–84, 707, 720–21; SecState to Grew, November 22, 1941, ibid., V, 443; TY, 483–85.

Ministry at seven-thirty. The imperturbable Tōgō received him at once in formal attire, slapped a document on the table with a gesture of finality, and made a short oral statement as a reply from the Emperor to the President. The document, which served as the Emperor's written reply, was Japan's notice breaking off conversations. Nomura had already delivered it to Hull, but, on account of another muddle, not before the attack was launched. The Minister side-stepped Grew's argument for an Imperial audience, thanked him for his efforts in behalf of Japanese-American friendship, and saw him down to his car. Grew returned to the Embassy intending to change clothes for a game of golf, only to hear first news that Japan and his country were in armed conflict. He would not believe it until it was confirmed. Soon police locked the Embassy gates and at 11 A.M. an official of the Foreign Ministry delivered notice that a state of war existed.[11] . . .

Time passed "not unpleasantly" for Grew, with a little work, a lot of reading, regular exercise and poker. Yet he had an ashen feeling. On Memorial Day he told his fellow internees that he had been at leisure to "survey the ruins of a life's work, as an architect might regard, after earthquake and fire, the ruins of a great building which he had conceived and had endeavored to erect, pier by pier and stone by stone. . . ." Bataan, Corregidor, Singapore: each black month brought fresh Japanese conquests. The Greater East Asia Sphere became a reality, from Assam to Wake and Kiska to the Coral Sea. He had "not an iota of doubt" of eventual victory. That was a matter of "fundamental instinctive conviction." But the cost of rolling back the Japanese Empire and destroying Japanese militarism was terrible to contemplate. Had it all been necessary? What if the leaders had met? The questions itched and festered during the months of waiting. Why had the President encouraged a leaders' meeting August 28, a month after the Indo-China advance, and then given no further encouragement? Because of "quibbling over formulas"? "Was the transcendent importance to our country of preserving peace to depend on the utterly futile effort to find satisfactory formulas?" Why hadn't the President made that speech telling the Japanese about the concrete benefits of a settlement? Why had the November 26 note, with

[11] All times are Tokyo time. The attack took place at 3:30 A.M., December 8, Tokyo time, 7:50 A.M., December 7, Honolulu time, and 1:20 P.M., December 7, Washington time. The telegram containing the message for the Emperor was held up ten and a half hours in Tokyo, apparently as a result of an Army-inspired slow-up on delivery of telegrams (Robert J. C. Butow, *Tojo and the Coming of War* [Princeton, 1961]). It is difficult to see how prompt delivery could have made any difference. Diary, December 8, 1941; President Roosevelt to Emperor Hirohito, December 6, 1941, *FR, Japan, 1931–1941*, II, 784–86; TY, 486–93; TE, II, 1249–53; Butow, *Tojo*, 378–96.

"an egregious error of timing," been delivered too late to do any good? Why not in August or September? These questions were all subsidiary to the central one, "whether, compatible with our national interests and without sacrificing any point of principle, war with Japan could have been avoided." He was certain it could have been.[12]

He decided to answer the question in the form of a final political report on his mission. That way he could go on record with a confirmation and justification of his position. That way, life being a school for progress, his experience might provide guidance for the future through the medium of history. That way put the days of internment to constructive use. He quoted George Meredith: "And if I drink oblivion for a day, so shorten I the stature of my soul." So he gathered the memoranda and telegrams of the period of the Third Konoe Cabinet and recapitulated the arguments for a leaders' meeting: the plight of Japan at the time, the choice of peace or war, Konoe's recognition of the danger, his attempt to reverse course, his support in the Army, Navy, Cabinet, and Palace, the new opening for diplomacy, the need for prompt action, the value of a dramatic gesture, the American interest in a settlement. The main thrust of his case was the same, but it derived force and cogency from being collected in one place and from being removed from the uncertainties of pre-Pearl Harbor days. In other words, retrospectively his argument was more convincing than it had been in August and September 1941.[13]

Now, after Pearl Harbor, he gave the China problem positive treatment. He argued that what China needed most was peace. According to the Japanese terms, she would have obtained most of her desiderata immediately and all later. The retention of Japanese garrisons in North China and Inner Mongolia would have been only a "face-saving expedient." In fact, foreign garrisons had only been international practice, he

---

[12] Grew to F. D. Roosevelt, August 14, 1942 (not sent); TY, 528–32.

[13] Grew to F. D. Roosevelt, August 14, 1942 (not sent). In two instances Grew's letter to Roosevelt of 1942 differed from the record of August–September 1941. First, he said, "Prince Konoe . . . told me with unquestionable sincerity that he was prepared at that meeting to accept the American terms whatever they might be." Possibly the Prince did use these words to convince Grew of his sincerity but did not allow him to report them. In any case, Grew did not report them in his memorandum of the September 6 conversation (*FR, Japan, 1931–1941*, II, 604–6). Second, Grew said in the letter to the President of August 1942 that the Emperor "actually instructed the chiefs of the Army and Navy that they were to avoid war with the United States." This is putting somewhat more bluntly a report of October 26, 1941, which, regardless of its validity, could not have influenced American deliberations on the Konoe project, he having resigned October 16 (Grew to SecState, October 26, 1941, *FR, 1941*, IV, 553–54). Neither of these pieces of evidence is included in Grew's final presentation of the case for a leaders' meeting ("Pearl Harbor from the Perspective of Ten Years," Joseph C. Grew, *Turbulent Era: A Diplomatic Record of Forty Years, 1904–1945* [Boston, 1952], hereafter cited as TE, II, Chap. 34).

added, adopting Toyoda's argument. He contended that any commitment on interrupting aid to China would have been contingent on Japan's proving beyond doubt her intention and ability to implement her commitments. How Japan was to give the necessary proof before China was brought around to accepting peace he did not say. In any case, the argument that agreement with Japan would not involve "selling China down the river" was easier to make now than in September 1941.[14]

The "lessons of history" taught by his experience of a decade in Japan were significant nonetheless. A nation could no longer isolate itself from world affairs and the United States had rightly and inevitably shown concern in situations where war threatened. However, he contended, the right to intervene morally or physically carried with it an obligation to show equal concern for the root causes of conflict. As long as the United States manifested indifference to the conditions giving rise to wars and followed policies exclusively for the protection and furtherance of its own interests — he had in mind the whole range of diplomatic, political, and legislative policies and actions — just so long would it fail to employ its limitless strength toward the development of civilization and its own welfare and avoid the "dissipation of lives and wealth in useless wars." History, experience well learned, might still recover value from the "lost opportunities of the past."[15] . . .

[14]Grew to F. D. Roosevelt, August 14, 1942 (not sent); Memorandum by Grew, September 22, 1941, *FR, Japan, 1931–1941,* II, 632.
[15]TY, 516–17; TE, II, 1371–72.

DAVID KAHN

Pearl Harbor as an Intelligence Failure

As is well known — and as you have read in some of the documents in Part One — the U.S. Army succeeded in cracking one of the most secret of Japanese codes, one that was used in communication between the Foreign Ministry in Tokyo and its embassies in Washington and Berlin, among other places. The intercepted and decoded messages were immediately made

David Kahn, "The Intelligence Failure of Pearl Harbor," *Foreign Affairs,* vol. 70, no. 5 (Winter 1991–1992): 138–50.

available to President Roosevelt and a very select group of U.S. leaders. U.S. policy toward Japan, therefore, was developed as a response to Japanese diplomatic moves that were revealed beforehand to the top officials in Washington. Because the last-minute negotiations took place in Washington, rather than Tokyo, we may say that the U.S. government had an advantage over the Japanese. Despite this, however, there was a failure to foresee, let alone prevent, the attack on Pearl Harbor.

What went wrong? Was there a failure in the intelligence system, or was the failure less in the information and more in the use (or lack of use) that was made of it? These questions, which arose immediately after the Pearl Harbor attack, have continued to fascinate students of the Pacific War. In the following essay, a noted writer on wartime intelligence operations offers his thoughts.

On a late summer morning in 1940, Frank B. Rowlett, a 32-year-old civilian employee of the U.S. Army, climbed into his Ford sedan in Arlington, Virginia, and drove to his job in Washington, D.C. Though his work was all but obsessive and tempted him to revert to it during his commute, Rowlett was disciplined and kept his mind on the traffic. He parked in a lot behind the Munitions Building, the army's offices on Constitution Avenue, arriving at 7 A.M., an hour early, as was his custom. He walked down one of the wings that stretched out the back of the building like teeth on a comb. A steel gate and an armed guard blocked the entrance to Rooms 3416 and 3418. They were among the most secure in the entire structure, and the work that went on in them among the most secret in the U.S. government.

Rowlett was a codebreaker; he had charge of the team trying to crack the most secret diplomatic cipher of the Empire of Japan, a machine that American cryptanalysts called PURPLE, and within hours on that day, Friday, September 20, he would be celebrating one of the greatest moments in American cryptology.

Tension with Japan had begun when the United States seized the Philippines in 1898. Within the Imperial Japanese Navy a vocal faction saw the westward march of the United States as squeezing and poisoning Japan. Friction intensified at the Washington disarmament conference of 1922, when the United States forced Japan to accept a lower warship ratio than it would have liked. This American diplomatic victory was achieved with the help of the charismatic cryptanalyst Herbert O. Yardley and his assistants, whose solution of coded Japanese diplomatic messages told American negotiators just how far they could push the Japanese.

But in 1929 Secretary of State Henry L. Stimson, believing that mutual trust worked best in international affairs and that therefore "gentlemen do not read each other's mail," refused to expend State Department funds for cryptanalysis. When Yardley, out of work in the Depression, wrote an indiscreet book in 1931 revealing the inside story, Japanese officials lost face, the Japanese press fulminated, relations with the United States deteriorated — and Japan improved its diplomatic cryptosystems. Tokyo adopted machine ciphers more complex than the system employing simultaneous use of multiple codebooks that Yardley and his team had cracked.

But the dissolution of Yardley's agency had not killed American codebreaking. Both the army and the navy had their own units. The navy's began almost by accident, after naval intelligence, having rifled the trunk of a Japanese naval officer in New York in 1923, found itself with a codebook but without means to exploit it. In January 1924 the navy established a four-man unit to gain information from Japanese communications. Its head was Lieutenant Laurance F. Safford, ranked fifteenth in the Annapolis class of 1916. Since the codebook was Japanese, and since the navy regarded Japan as its most likely enemy, Safford started setting up listening posts in the Pacific.

Safford also hired a brilliant, 32-year-old woman who proved to be an outstanding cryptanalyst. Agnes Meyer Driscoll, who had taught mathematics and music and had worked for Yardley, attacked the messages in the photographed code. The book listed Japanese words, syllables and phrases opposite five-digit codegroups, such as 48771, which replaced them. The codegroups were not used plain, however. They were themselves enciphered. It was the job of "Miss Aggie" to break through this armor and recover the original codegroups. Incessantly turning the pages of the photographed book with the rubber tip of her eraser, she eventually succeeded. The codegroups then yielded Japanese text, which a husband-and-wife team translated.

But in December 1930 the code, which by then was 12 years old, was replaced by a new one. The hardest part of breaking a code is getting started. As one of the naval codebreakers explained: "It first off involved what I call the staring process. You look at all of these messages that you have; you line them up in various ways; you write them one below the other; you'd write them in various forms and you'd stare at them. Pretty soon you'd notice a pattern; you'd notice a definite pattern between these messages. This was the first clue."

Miss Aggie, who by then had learned the ships' names, the communications patterns and the frequently used phrases of the Japanese fleet, no doubt utilized a form of this process first to dissolve the codeword encipherment and then to reconstruct the new 85,000-group code. For years it gave the U.S. Navy insight into Japanese forces and tactics, as expressed during fleet exercises.

And it was only one source of communications intelligence. During the 1930s, the navy attacked and often solved other Japanese naval codes — for administration, merchant ships, logistics, intelligence — and several cipher machines. When codebreaking failed, traffic analysis provided much information. Traffic analysis infers an organization's structure and operation from message routing, message volume, call signs and operators' chatter. A prime tool, direction-finding, locates a radio transmitter. Much as a portable radio can be rotated to bring in a station most strongly, a sensitive antenna can find the direction from which a signal is coming. If two antennas take bearings on the source of a signal, a control center can draw the lines of direction on a map; their intersection marks the position of the transmitter. Such a fix can tell where, for example, a ship is. Successive fixes can plot its course and speed. A study of call signs, combined with direction-finding, can show which stations are talking to which and which of those are communications centers and, therefore, presumably headquarters. Finally, increased volume in one area may suggest increased activity. The intercept and direction-finding stations that Safford swung in a vast arc across the central Pacific furnished both the intercepts that the cryptanalysts solved and the data for the traffic analysts. All of these sources gave the U.S. Navy a fairly complete picture of the Imperial Japanese Navy's forces, organization and movements throughout the 1930s and into 1941.

While the navy was expanding its communications intelligence organization, so was the army. The Signal Corps had hired in 1921 a 29-year-old who was even then one of the world's great cryptanalysts. William F. Friedman had written some theoretical treatises of landmark importance and had solved German codes in France during World War I. Friedman's job now was to improve the army's cryptosystems. With the closing of Yardley's agency, the Signal Corps added foreign codebreaking to its responsibilities, and Friedman became the head of a new Signal Intelligence Service. The first new hire was Rowlett, who was 21 at the time. After a couple of years of training in cryptanalysis under Friedman, Rowlett and two colleagues began attacking Japanese diplomatic cryptosystems, mainly because diplomatic intercepts were available and Japanese army intercepts were not. The three cracked a simple code that served for personnel matters and expenses of Japanese diplomats. Then they turned their attention to what appeared to be a machine system that seemed to protect the more important messages. The army cryptanalysts reconstructed the machine and named it RED.

That solution made codebreaking the nation's premier source of secret intelligence. It easily surpassed espionage: except for a few local agents who provided observations to naval attachés, the United States had no spies anywhere in the world. And codebreaking outperformed the diplomats, gaining information long before they did and in a highly specific form, namely, word-for-word instructions and reports. In March 1937, for example, the intercepts revealed advance information about Italy's possible adherence to the German-Japanese anti-Comintern pact — six months before American diplomats began reporting on it. Later the intercepts revealed part of the text of the treaty. In 1937, for the first time, solutions of intercepted foreign messages began flowing to the White House.

Then, on March 20, 1939, three messages in a new cryptosystem were intercepted. Within three months, the new system had displaced RED, whose mechanisms were wearing out. Japan's major diplomatic messages had become unreadable. Faced with the loss of the nation's paramount intelligence, the Signal Intelligence Service mounted a concentrated attack on Japan's new machine. Friedman put Rowlett in charge. The Americans called the new machine PURPLE.

Rowlett's team was assigned to two rooms of the Munitions Building. Rowlett worked in Room 3416, his mind focused. He never hummed or chewed his pencil or muttered to himself; he looked out the window onto the neighboring wing only when something distracted him; he never drank coffee, but he did puff on a pipe. Most mornings he held a conference with the other cryptanalysts. Afterwards they collectively scrutinized the intercepts. Most of these had been teletyped in from army intercept stations that monitored the commercial radio circuits used by the Japanese Foreign Ministry for most of its messages. The cryptanalysts' work consisted of matching proposed plaintext — a guess as to the text of the original message — against the text of the cryptograms. The proposed plaintext came from circular telegrams sent simultaneously in the readable RED and in PURPLE during the three months that both systems served, from formulaic diplomatic language, and in a few cases from the State Department's supplying of the text of notes to or from the Japanese ambassadors.

Friedman, who had assembled the team, supervised. He did not engage in any of the actual cryptanalysis but made sure the unit had all the support it needed. Determination pervaded Rowlett's co-workers, who remained confident that they would break PURPLE the way RED had been broken. The summer of 1940 arrived. Rowlett drove his Ford to work. Belgium, the Netherlands, France fell. England braced for invasion. Japan, persisting in its three-year-old aggression in China, seemed now to cast a covetous eye on orphaned French Indochina and the Dutch East Indies. In July President Franklin D. Roosevelt embargoed the export of aviation fuel and high-grade scrap metal to Japan.

Though the cryptanalysts followed these developments in the newspapers, their inspiration came less from the pressure of events than from fascination with the cryptologic problem. They struggled to envision what kind of electromechanical device could produce these groups of incoherent letters from Japanese plain language. A hypothesis emerged. As they sought to test it, construction workers began to build an additional floor above them. Hammers pounded; men shouted. If the cryptanalysts closed the windows to reduce the noise, they sweltered in the non-air-conditioned offices; if they opened them, they could barely think. Still they persisted. Just as the new structure was finished, a fire destroyed it — and it had to be built all over again.

Then on September 20, cryptanalyst Genevieve Grotjan spotted a particular pattern among the letters she was scrutinizing. The 26-year-old codebreaker looked for another. Soon another member of the PURPLE team noticed that she seemed to be concentrating extremely intently. He spoke to Grotjan about it and then he, Rowlett and another cryptanalyst came to her desk. At once they grasped the significance of what Grotjan was showing them: the pattern confirmed the team's theory of how the PURPLE machine worked. One of the team members dashed around the room; another shouted "Hooray!" Rowlett jumped up and down, crying: "That's it! That's it!" Grotjan's discovery capped one of the greatest cryptanalyses of all time: enciphered Japanese diplomatic cables were now comprehensible. And how did the codebreakers celebrate? They sent out for Cokes!

A week later, the day the Tripartite Pact established the Rome-Berlin-Tokyo axis and a day after Roosevelt prohibited the export of all iron and steel scrap to Japan, the Signal Intelligence Service handed in its first two solved PURPLE messages. These two drops of intelligence marked the trickling start of what, a year later, would grow into a stream. By late 1941 solutions of messages in PURPLE and in lower-level Japanese diplomatic cryptosystems soared to 50 to 75 messages a day. The most important of these, selected by army and navy intelligence officers, went to the president, the secretaries of state, war and the navy, the chief of staff, the chief of naval operations and a handful of top-level officials. (The secretary of war was Stimson, who had closed Yardley's unit in 1929 but now welcomed the intercepts. He was not inconsistent: he believed that codebreaking was a legitimate function of a military service but not of a diplomatic one.) These intercepts provided insight into the thoughts and activities of Japan's Foreign Office and corroborated the evidence from negotiations and events, such as Japan's occupation of French Indochina, that matters were approaching a crisis.

For example a PURPLE message on July 31, 1941, from the foreign minister in Tokyo to the ambassador in Washington declared: "There is more reason than ever before for us to arm ourselves to the teeth for all-out war." The occasional instruction to seek a peaceful solution, such as one on November 15, was overwhelmed by belligerent indications. On November 19, the Foreign Office arranged with its embassies and legations that "in case of emergency (danger of cutting off diplomatic relations), and the cutting off of international communications," the phrase "east wind rain" would be added in the middle of the daily Japanese language shortwave newscast to indicate Japanese-American relations were threatened. "When this is heard please destroy all code papers," the Foreign Office instructed. On November 30, Tokyo told its ambassador in Berlin to "say very secretly to them [Adolf Hitler and Foreign Minister Joachim von Ribbentrop] that there is extreme danger that war may suddenly break out between the Anglo-Saxon nations and Japan through some clash of arms and add that the time of the breaking-out of this war may come quicker than anyone dreams."

But the Japanese diplomatic PURPLE and other intercepts did not reveal military or naval plans. The army had not solved any Japanese army codes because it could not intercept enough messages. The navy had made scant progress on the main Japanese operations code, JN25, whose second, enlarged edition, JN25b, had been introduced on December 1, 1940. With Miss Aggie and reserve Lieutenant Prescott Currier leading the attack, the navy had stripped off most of the additive groups that concealed the underlying codegroups, but had recovered only a small number of these, so that by December 1941 only about 10 percent of the text of an average JN25b message could be read. This was due less to Japanese cryptographic superiority than to the navy's insufficiency of cryptanalysts, in part because it was helping the army decipher PURPLE messages (once the machine had been solved) while also helping the British break U-boat messages in the German navy's Enigma cipher machine.

Nor did other sources provide much insight into the specifics of Japanese military or naval planning. U.S. military attachés furnished 90-page reports on weapons, tactics, personalities and organization but had no solid information on the intentions of the Japanese armed forces. The diplomats concentrated on the political situation and, likewise, had little hard information on military developments. In January 1941 Ambassador Joseph Grew duly reported that a Peruvian colleague had heard that Japan was planning an attack on Pearl Harbor. The rumor was false, for at the time no attack was being planned. Washington, in any event, filed the report and forgot about it. William J. Donovan, named in July 1941 to head what became the Office of Strategic Services, had no secret agents and thus no independent source with which to make predictions.

Only one form of intelligence appeared to offer relatively solid information about Japanese naval matters: traffic analysis. For years traffic analysts watched with precision the ships and squadrons of the Japanese fleet and their maneuvers. Two tense situations in 1941 reconfirmed their ability. During the war scare of February, when Japan was moving on French Indochina with the apparent intention of attacking Singapore (which might have brought the United States into the war), various forms of intelligence observed the southward movements of Japanese warships. Traffic analysis added to this. When its monitors picked up no communications either to or from the aircraft carriers, its analysts concluded that these vital units were standing by in home waters as a covering force in case of an attack on Japan's main islands. Later intelligence confirmed this analysis. In July, when Japan occupied French Indochina, carrier communications again went dead. Again traffic analysis decided that the carriers had been in home waters. Twice, then, a complete blank of communications with the carriers, together with indications of a strong southward thrust, had meant the presence of the carriers in Empire waters. A pattern seemed to have emerged.

Throughout the fall tension between Japan and the United States escalated. Negotiations all but ended after an American démarche on November 26, the acceptance of whose demands would have required Japan to pull out of China and in other ways to reverse its foreign policy. Japan then finalized its decisions for war with a nation whose population was twice as large and whose industrial output nine times as great as its own. Why did Tokyo make this apparently irrational move? Premier Hideki Tōjō told the Privy Council on December 1 that, if Japan were to submit to American demands, "Japan's existence itself would be endangered. . . . Japan has now no other way than to wage war against the United States." Japan had never intended to invade the United States. It planned only to cripple the main American instrument of war — the U.S. Pacific Fleet — and then wait behind a ring of impregnable defenses until the Americans wearied of the struggle and quit, leaving Japan to wax fat on its conquests and to reign as master of East Asia.

American officials did not think Japan would attack their country. To start war with so superior a power would be to commit national hara-kiri [suicide]. To Western modes of thought, it made no sense. This rationalism was paralleled by a racism that led Americans to underrate Japanese abilities and will. Such views were held not only by common bigots but by opinion-makers as well. These preconceptions blocked out of American minds the possibility that Japan would attack an American possession.

Yet on December 3, 1941, an intercept revealed Tokyo instructing its Washington embassy to burn codes and destroy cipher machines. How else could it be interpreted but as a preparation for war? On the evening of Saturday, December 6, Roosevelt, who had excused himself from a large dinner party, and his aide Harry Hopkins read an intercept in his lamplit White House study as the naval lieutenant who had delivered it watched. "This means war," the lieutenant remembered the president saying in effect. What could he have meant? Perhaps eventual or accidental hostilities, perhaps hostilities following a Japanese conflict with Britain through a move against the Malay Peninsula, at whose tip lay Singapore.

An attack on Pearl Harbor was seen as all but excluded. Though senior army and navy officers knew that Japan had often started wars with surprise attacks, and though the naval air defense plan for Hawaii warned of a dawn assault, officials also knew that the base was the nation's best defended and that the fleet had been stationed that far west not to attract, but to deter, Japan.

The evidence available early in December seemed to confirm American preconceptions. Reports from consuls, attachés, and ships' masters told of Japanese forces moving southward. American reconnaissance airplanes saw Japanese submarines, cruisers, transports and destroyers in Camranh Bay and elsewhere along the French Indochina coast. On December 5, British aircraft spotted three Japanese convoys rounding Cambodia Point and entering the Gulf of Siam. American traffic analysis further indicated an advance to the south. Many Japanese units were heard as they headed that way. Yet no communications went to or came from the carriers. As in February and July, the carriers were apparently in home waters. So certain were American officials of this southward move that, in a staff meeting on the morning of December 7, as Chief of

Staff General George C. Marshall was about to warn Pacific commands that Japan was breaking off negotiations at 1 P.M. Washington time, one general shouted out to the communications officer that if there were a question about priority, the first message should go to the Philippines.

As he was saying this, six of the carriers thought by traffic analysis to be lying in home waters were in fact plowing the seas north of Hawaii. They had launched airplanes for a Sunday morning attack on the Pacific Fleet at Pearl Harbor. Japan's strategic plan would prove unsuccessful. The attack so enraged and unified the American people that they would never tire of the struggle but would battle on to total victory. Yet Japan's tactical plan worked to perfection: the raid achieved complete surprise.

American intelligence had failed. Evidence warning of an attack could have overcome American preconceptions, but intelligence — which relied almost solely on the *diplomatic* transmissions via PURPLE — had found no such evidence. Japan had sealed all possible leaks. The ambassadors in Washington were not told of the attack. Knowledge of it was limited in Tokyo to as tight a circle as possible. Plans for it were distributed by hand to the ships of the task force. No reference to a raid on Pearl Harbor ever went on the air, even coded. The February and July situations misled traffic analysts. JN25b messages intercepted before the attack, but solved after the war, show that even if that naval code had been fully solved and those messages read before December 7, they would not have foretold the attack. And though war with Japan was indeed expected, that expectation did not — could not — imply knowledge of an attack on Pearl Harbor, for it is impossible in logic to leap from a general belief to a specific prediction.

Some historians, pointing out that officials saw the intercepts only day by day, claim that had someone sat down and looked through them all at one time, he or she would have seen a pattern indicating the attack. This is extremely unlikely. There was nothing in either the diplomatic or the naval intercepts about an attack on Pearl Harbor. Indeed such a collation might have pointed *away* from Hawaii. Of solved messages reporting ship movements between August 1 and December 6, 1941, 59 dealt with the Philippines, 23 with the Panama Canal and only 20 with Pearl Harbor.

In her 1962 study, *Pearl Harbor: Warning and Decision,* Roberta Wohlstetter argues, "We failed to anticipate Pearl Harbor not for want of the relevant materials, but because of a plethora of irrelevant ones." In the terms of information theory that Wohlstetter uses, this means that the noise was too great for the signal to be picked out. But she errs. There was a dearth of intelligence materials. Not one intercept, not one datum of intelligence ever said a thing about an attack on Pearl Harbor. There was, in Wohlstetter's terms, no signal to be detected. Intelligence officers could perhaps have foreseen the attack if the United States, years before, had insinuated spies into high-level Japanese military and naval circles, flown regular aerial reconnaissance of the Japanese navy, put intercept units aboard ships sailing close to Japan to pick up naval messages that a greatly expanded codebreaking unit might have cracked, or recruited a network of marine observers to report on ship movements. The intelligence failure at Pearl Harbor was one not of analysis, as Wohlstetter implies, but of collection.

For many people, Pearl Harbor remains an enigma. "We were breaking the codes," they cry. "Roosevelt must have known!" Or, as Congress's Joint Committee on the Investigation of the Pearl Harbor Attack put it: "Why, with some of the finest intelligence available in our history, with the almost certain knowledge that war was at hand, with plans that contemplated the precise type of attack that was executed by Japan on the morning of December 7—Why was it possible for a Pearl Harbor to occur?" The simple answer is that the intelligence, good though it was in certain areas, was not good enough.

To some people the intelligence failure was deliberate. They contend that President Roosevelt provoked the attack by his intransigence toward Japan and ensured its success by suppressing intelligence and withholding information from the commanders at Pearl Harbor. His purpose, the theory goes, was to trick a reluctant United States into the war. After the war, when the cryptologic details became public, the conspiracy theories blossomed.

The naval commander at Pearl, Admiral Husband Kimmel, complained that he was taken by surprise in part because he had not been allowed to receive the diplomatic intelligence obtained from PURPLE. But its additional details of the deteriorating situation could not have alerted him more than the November 27 message of the chief of naval operations, which began, "This dispatch is to be considered a war warning."

Safford, who was head of the naval codebreaking and codemaking unit on December 7, insisted that the "winds" code had been executed and that evidence of it had been suppressed. On December 3 or 4, he said, Japan had broadcast "East wind rain," meaning war was imminent with the United States. The intercept with the serial number JD-1:7001 was not in the files; this was obviously the "winds" execute, Safford charged, and it was missing because higher authority had ordered the removal of this evidence. The first problem with this theory, which incriminates Roosevelt and his aides, is that interception of such an order would not have told anybody anything more than he or she already knew. The second problem is that it raises the incredible picture of Admiral Harold Stark, the chief of naval operations, rummaging through file drawers in an office with which he was unfamiliar to find and abstract a piece of paper. No one ever reported his presence in the office or said they had received orders from him to destroy a government record. Finally, naval officers reported that serial numbers were sometimes canceled for legitimate reasons, such as duplication.

More recently a book by intelligence writer James Rusbridger and former Australian codebreaker Eric Nave, *Betrayal at Pearl Harbor,* claims that a British codebreaking unit at Singapore, where Nave worked, solved JN25 before the Pearl Harbor attack. This revealed the forthcoming Japanese strike to Prime Minister Winston Churchill, who said nothing about it to Roosevelt because, according to the authors, he wanted the United States in the war with him. A massive coverup, they assert, has kept this information from coming out.

Several flaws destroy this theory. Churchill wanted the United States in the war against Germany, not Japan. A British codebreaker's diary states that the prime minister was surprised by the attack. The code in use from December 1, 1940, was not JN25, but the quite different JN25b. The British and the Americans exchanged codegroup recoveries in this system, so the Americans would have been able to discover the same things the British had. Finally, none of the presumed JN25b solutions the authors cite even mention Pearl Harbor.

Upon similar close examination, the other anti-Roosevelt conspiracy theories likewise fall apart. Most spring from a wish to defend Kimmel or the army commander at Pearl, General Walter Short, or from a hatred of Roosevelt. They demonstrate their fundamental illogic by forgetting, for example, that had the army lieutenant who headed a radar unit at Pearl Harbor, which had spotted the incoming flight of Japanese bombers, not told the radar operators to "forget it," the Roosevelt plot would have been frustrated. They ignore that both Stimson and Frank Knox, the secretary of the navy, were Republicans (Knox had, in fact, run in 1936 as GOP vice presidential candidate against the Roosevelt ticket). They demonstrate their total misreading of character by implying that General Marshall would let people die in so cynical a way and then lie about it. They seem not to realize that, even if Roosevelt had wanted war, he would not have wanted to enter it with his fleet badly weakened. The concocters of these theories are unable to accept that humans sometimes do things wrong or do not do them at all, that accidents happen, that in the complex system that is the world improbable events occur. . . .

KATSUMI USUI

The Chinese-Japanese War

Before Pearl Harbor, China and Japan had been at war intermittently for more than ten years. Although Japan's southward advance and its search for petroleum were the immediate circumstances of the final act of the U.S.-Japanese crisis, you will recall from the documents in Part One that the fundamental obstacle proved to be the China question, with the United States insisting on Japan's withdrawal from China, and Japan refusing to comply.

Because China had been fighting alone against Japanese aggression, thus in a sense enabling the United States and Britain to wait until the last moment to decide on their strategy toward Japan, it is important to understand how the Chinese-Japanese conflict and the U.S.-Japanese crisis became inexorably interconnected. In the following essay, Japan's leading authority on the history of modern Chinese-Japanese relations discusses the different views of the Chinese Nationalists and Communists about possible U.S. and Soviet involvement in the Asian war. Do you agree with the author's view that the Japanese were making substantial concessions in presenting Plans A and B? How does he depict the policies of the U.S. and Chinese governments toward Japan?

. . . China paid very close attention to the development of the U.S.-Japanese negotiations in Washington. China was very aware of the possibility that the United States and Japan might reach a compromise — a Far East Munich — that would neglect Chinese interests.

On May 23, the Chinese ambassador in Washington, Hu Shih, met with Secretary of State Cordell Hull. Hull assured the ambassador that "America would not enter final comprehensive negotiations with Japan about the problem of peace without having prior consultation with China, regardless of the matter that arose."[1]

Katsumi Usui, "China and the Coming of the Pacific War." This essay was originally presented at a conference near Lake Yamanaka, Japan, in November 1991. The conference brought together more than forty scholars from the United States, Japan, Britain, Germany, Russia, Korea, China, and the Philippines for four days of intensive reexamination of the origins of the Pacific war. The papers were translated into Japanese and published as *Taiheiyō sensō* (The Pacific war) (Tokyo: University of Tokyo Press, 1993). The original English texts, however, have not been published elsewhere.

[1] *Shōkaiseki hiroku* (Secret memoirs of Chiang Kai-shek), Japanese translation (Tokyo, 1976), vol. 3, p. 173.

Three days later, on May 26, Hu Shih sent a letter to Hull in which he said that it would be difficult to detach Japan from the Tripartite Pact as long as the British and the Americans did not abandon the principles for which they stood. To prevent Japan from aiding its Axis partners in Europe, he wrote, China had to keep a million Japanese troops and several hundred supply ships bogged down, while the continued presence of the U.S. fleet in the Pacific discouraged Japan from advancing any farther south, from interrupting trade between the English colonies and China, and from cutting off their supply lines. He insisted that any Japanese promises to withdraw troops were mere words and that there was absolutely no possibility of a Japanese withdrawal from Manchuria, Inner Mongolia, the coastal centers of Chinese trade and industry, the base areas for Japanese advances to the south, and Hai-nan Island.[2]

On June 22, the German army began a concerted attack on the Soviet Union, thus opening up a new stage in the war on the European front. The outbreak of the German-Soviet war was a great shock to the rest of the world, and it was inevitable that China would suffer directly from this conflict.

On June 24, Chiang Kai-shek thus summoned the American ambassador, Clarence E. Gauss, and advised America to make a statement promising material assistance to the Soviet Union and expressing hope that the Soviet Union would cooperate with England in Europe and with China in the Far East. Such a statement, Chiang stressed, would give great aid to the Soviet Union in its resistance to Germany and would head off any possibility of the Soviet Union making a compromise with Japan. Without a guarantee of U.S. aid, Chiang thought, the Soviet Union would reach a compromise with Japan to avoid a Japanese attack. Under these circumstances, Japan would advance farther south, and the United States would be drawn into a war with Japan.[3] Chiang asked Gauss to pass his views on to Washington.

Chiang also said that the war between Germany and the Soviet Union would result in a turn for the better in the relations between the Nationalists and the Communists. The Chinese Communists were reducing the tensions that had arisen between themselves and the Nationalists after their clash in January and were calling for the firm maintenance of resistance to Japan on the basis of their united front with the Nationalists.[4]

[2] *Papers Relating to the Foreign Relations of the United States, 1941,* vol. 4 (Washington, D.C.: Government Printing Office, 1956), pp. 225–27, hereafter cited as *FRUS.*

[3] Ibid., pp. 277–78.

[4] Chinese Communist Party Headquarters, "Han-fassho kokusai tōitsu sensen ni tsuite no kettei" (Decision concerning the international anti-fascist front), June 23, 1941, in Japan

At the end of July, in light of the successful Japanese military invasion and occupation of the southern part of French Indochina, the Americans, English, and Dutch froze Japanese assets in their countries and prohibited the export of oil to Japan. Japan's negotiations with the United States thus reached a deadlock.

At this time, the Japanese air force was bombing Chungking day and night on almost a daily basis, shutting off water and electricity to the city, making it difficult for residents to cook and sleep. At the beginning of August, Chiang had a meeting with the American adviser, Owen Lattimore (who had first met with Chiang only on July 20), and through him asked President Franklin D. Roosevelt to undertake either one of two measures. For four years, China had unflinchingly continued its war of resistance against Japan, and because it had done so all alone with no allies, the suggestion should be made that the English and the Soviets should conclude a military alliance, or an invitation should be given to China to attend the Pacific Defense Conference being organized by Britain, the Netherlands, and the United States. Chiang's argument, in sum, was that China had been excluded from the Allies' joint operation conference for the war against Japan and Germany, even though China had already been attacked and had defended democracy from Japan, a partner of Germany.[5]

What lay at the basis of Chiang's proposal was his long-held unhappiness with what he considered the American and British failure to pay proper respect to the position of China in world politics; China had borne the brunt of the fight in an important part of the battlefront. It is not known when Chiang's views were transmitted, since Roosevelt was engaged then in making a secret trip to meet Prime Minister Winston S. Churchill in Newfoundland. During this American-British summit meeting, however, it was decided that the two countries would pay attention to the security of China but that China would not be given concrete information because the leaders feared leaks of their secret deliberations. This decision was made at Churchill's suggestion. On the other hand, Stalin was notified on August 12 that the Americans and the British had agreed to supply the Soviets with as much urgently needed material as possible.[6] The difference in the treatment of China and the Soviet Union was painfully obvious.

Institute for International Affairs, ed., *Chūgoku kyōsantō-shi shiryō-shū* (History of the Chinese Communist Party: a documentary collection) (Tokyo, 1974), vol. 10, pp. 453–54.

[5] *FRUS 1941,* vol. 4, p. 362.

[6] Winston S. Churchill, *The Grand Alliance* (London, 1962), pp. 389–96.

Churchill asked Roosevelt to warn Japan that the United States would be forced to take countermeasures, including even a declaration of war, if Japan made any further incursions in the southwest Pacific. Roosevelt agreed to this request. Immediately after his return to Washington, Roosevelt called Ambassador Kichisaburō Nomura for a meeting on August 17, a Sunday. He warned Nomura against any further military advance by Japan, although he moderated the tone of his warning and did not mention the possibility of war between Japan and the United States.[7]

Meanwhile, in a radio broadcast on August 24, Churchill declared that England would support the United States in any war with Japan.[8] Chiang wrote in his diary on August 25, "The English Prime Minister Churchill made a radio broadcast yesterday, in which he vowed to stop this crazy orgy of invasion and gave a warning to Japan. This is a sign that the English have given serious regard to their Far East policy during this Atlantic meeting."[9] This comment shows Chiang's optimistic nature.

On August 18, the Chinese foreign minister, Kuo T'ai-ch'i, expressed his agreement and support for the Atlantic Charter issued jointly by Churchill and Roosevelt, and he declared that the contents of the charter were the same as the principles of the Nationalist Party. He added, however, that the quickest way to attain the ultimate defeat of the invading powers was to defeat Japan first by an encircling net of Allied powers.[10]

Although Foreign Minister Kuo publicly expressed support for the Atlantic Charter, some Chinese political leaders had their misgivings. Because the charter mentioned nothing about China, they realized that China had not been given the respect and status that they felt it merited as an equal partner. For the same reason, Kuo told Ambassador Gauss on August 26 that China should no longer remain the object of other countries' discussions and that it would decide its destiny for itself.[11]

Another cause of irritation to China was the information that, with the support of Britain, the United States had reached an understanding with Japan. It was said that the United States had proposed that Japan, France, Thailand, China, and other concerned countries agree to the

[7] *Nihon gaikō monjo: Nichi-Bei kōshō, 1941* (Japanese diplomatic documents: Japanese-U.S. negotiations, 1941) (Tokyo: Foreign Ministry, 1990), vol. 1, pp. 224–25.

[8] *Further Correspondence Respecting Far Eastern Affairs,* microfilm (London: Foreign Office), supplement to part 16, no. 132, hereafter cited as *FCFEA.*

[9] *Shōkaiseki,* vol. 13, p. 186.

[10] *FRUS 1941,* vol. 4, p. 377.

[11] Ibid., p. 395.

neutralization of Thailand and French Indochina and that Japan would legitimately be entitled to the supply of necessary raw materials. According to this rumor, Japanese Prime Minister Fumimaro Konoe had made a counterproposal demanding the retention of more than ten thousand Japanese soldiers in French Indochina, while the United States had demanded the maintenance of the status quo of the Japanese military base in French Indochina and the suspension of any further Japanese military action there. Thus, the two countries were rumored to have reached an understanding.

On September 10 in Chungking, Kuo informed Gauss of Chinese anxiety about this news. His points were that China could not welcome such measures by the United States because the agreement's toleration for the continued supply of raw materials to Japan would lower the economic pressure on Japan that had recently begun to be effective and thus reinforce Japan's invasion of China. Kuo stressed that Japanese diplomacy could not be trusted and said that although Britain and the United States wished to avoid a crisis, it was Japan, rather than those two countries, that wanted to buy time.[12] The rumor turned out to be incorrect, but in taking note of China's deep anxiety about its negotiations with Japan, the United States was forced to take some measures to protect China. On September 12, Secretary of State Hull ordered Ambassador Gauss to give informal notice to the Chinese government that the U.S. government would definitely discuss with China in advance all matters that might have an impact on the Chinese situation.[13] On September 15, Gauss relayed this information to Kuo.[14]

The United States informed China of the general principles it was following in its negotiations with Japan, but it had no intention of revealing concrete contents and developments. On the other hand, however, it carried out its promise of material aid to China, including, as promised in August, the dispatch of a military representative group headed by General John A. Magruder.

Chiang remained deeply concerned about the U.S.-Japanese negotiations, however. On September 12, he wrote in his diary, "I can conclude that the United States-Japan negotiations will never come to a fruitful conclusion. The best they can hope for is to put on a good face to one another and buy some time. If in the unlikely situation the United States

12 Ibid., pp. 436–41.
13 Ibid., pp. 445–46.
14 Ibid., p. 450.

reaches a compromise with Japan whereby it makes a concession about the third point of the China problem [i.e., the withdrawal of Japanese troops from China] as a bargaining point to persuade Japan to withdraw from the Axis Pact, China would fall into a disadvantageous situation in world politics. There is no doubt that the psychological impact at home would be serious. Even then, however, our country would do nothing but continue its resistance to Japan and would look forward to the day when the world situation would change and England and America would be attacked by Japan."[15]

Here I would like to discuss the state of affairs in the U.S.-Japanese negotiations from early September. From a comparison of Japan's proposals of September 25 and November 7 it becomes abundantly clear that Japan was willing to make unilateral concessions on the "China Problem."

The "China Problem" had consisted of three important issues: the retention (or withdrawal) of the Japanese army, nondiscriminatory trade, and the fate of the Japanese-established state of Manchukuo (Manchuria, Manshūkoku in Japanese). In addition, there was the problem of how to deal with the Wang Ching-wei government in Nanking. From the start of the negotiations, Japan had assumed a flexible attitude about Wang's government and had virtually agreed to allow Chiang to absorb it.

Japan made extensive concessions about the future location, stay, and withdrawal schedule for its army in China. In the September proposal, Japan originally offered to locate its army in the limited area of north China, Inner Mongolia, Hai-nan Island, the Lower Yangtze delta, and the southeast coastal area of China. In the November proposal, the last two areas were dropped from the list. The Japanese army was to stay in the other three regions for just twenty-five years, while withdrawing from the rest of China over the next two years.

On the issue of fair trade, Japan proposed in September "Japanese-Chinese cooperation for the development and use of important national defense resources in China." In other words, Japan would receive preferential treatment from China in the development of those natural resources in China that it considered vital to its national defense. In its November proposal, Japan made a significant concession in agreeing to fair, equal, and nondiscriminatory trade with China. Back in June, in the

---

[15] *Shōkaiseki,* vol. 13, p. 152.

early stage of the negotiations, Secretary of State Hull had warned Japan about the monopolization and discriminatory trade policies in the occupied areas of China. Hull demanded that Japan terminate its clearly discriminatory treatment against other countries' economic activities in China, as evident in the exclusive policies, trade practices, and currency management undertaken by companies acting under Japanese government supervision (*kokusaku kaisha*) and their branch companies in the development of north and central China. On July 10, Ryōei Saitō, an adviser to the Japanese Ministry of Foreign Affairs, had explained at the Japanese Government High Command Liaison Council that the construction of "a new order in the Far East," that is, the fundamental principles of Japanese policy, would be extremely difficult or virtually impossible, if a policy of nondiscriminatory treatment in trade, which the United States demanded, was forced on Japan.[16] However, by November, Japan had conceded on this point, and in its new proposal it assented to the original U.S. demand for the approval of the principle of nondiscriminatory treatment.

Finally, in earlier discussions, Japan had consistently called for the recognition of the state of Manchukuo. However, the United States had demanded in its June 21 proposal an "amicable negotiation about Manchuria." At the same Liaison Council meeting mentioned above, Saitō gave quite a sharp analysis of this matter. He said, "The American proposal foresees the return of Manchukuo to China, but in our proposal we intend to safeguard the independence of Manchukuo, taking the Japan-Manchukuo-China joint declaration as the fundamental basis for any peace treaty. The American proposal, however, does not approve this joint declaration. It simply demands that the matter be decided through negotiations with Chiang, but it is obvious that Chiang would not give his approval [to our proposal]. Since it is impossible for our country to give up Manchukuo at this stage, United States negotiations with Japan will reach a deadlock about this matter."[17] It is possible, however, that the United States had considered some compromise on the Manchuria issue.

In its final proposal (Plan A) of November 7, Japan refused to budge on two points: the retention of its army in specified areas of China for a limited period of time and the *de facto* existence of the state of Manchukuo.

---

[16] *Nichi-Bei kōshō,* vol. 1, p. 152.
[17] Ibid.

By November, a change was evident in Churchill's policy for coping with the Japanese-Chinese issue. This change was inspired by the emergency appeal sent by Chiang at the very beginning of November about the safeguarding of Yunnan province. On November 5, Churchill proposed to Roosevelt that the United States and Britain warn Japan not to attack Kunming, the capital of Yunnan province, from French Indochina. On November 9, Roosevelt assumed a moderate response in his reply to Churchill, reminding him once again of the importance of buying time in the Pacific and that new warnings to Japan would result in the opposite of what they wanted.[18]

Churchill recognized that Japan had made the decision to wage war. On November 10 at a banquet at the Guildhall in London, he stated that if war broke out between Japan and the United States, Britain would declare war against Japan within one hour. He pointed out the remarkable difference in the productive power of the United States and Japan in steel and iron and urged Japan's political leaders to make a wise decision.[19]

In Washington on November 7, Japan presented its final compromise proposal (Plan A). Seeing that it had not won approval, on November 20 it presented a provisional proposal (Plan B) in its place.

On the morning of November 22, Secretary of State Hull summoned the representatives of Australia, China, Britain, and the Netherlands. In seeking their understanding of the measures the United States would undertake, he explained the present status of the U.S. negotiations with Japan, which had reached their final stage. The Chinese ambassador, Hu Shih, arrived a bit late. The meeting lasted two and a half hours, and there are two documents that inform us of its contents: a memorandum by Secretary of State Hull[20] and a report by Ambassador Halifax to Foreign Minister Anthony Eden.[21] The former is brief and concise; the latter, detailed.

Secretary Hull presented the provisional agreement proposal (Plan B)[22] made by Ambassador Nomura on November 20, and he explained the U.S. counterproposal. This was all done orally.

The gist of the American counterproposal, which was set to last for just two to three months, was Japan's withdrawal of its troops (all but two

---

[18] Churchill, *Grand Alliance*, pp. 526–27.
[19] Ibid., pp. 528–29.
[20] *FRUS 1941*, vol. 4, p. 640.
[21] *FCFEA*, supplement to part 16, no. 189, pp. 100–102.
[22] *Papers Relating to the Foreign Relations of the United States: Japan, 1931–1941*, vol. 2 (Washington, D.C.: Government Printing Office, 1942), pp. 755–56.

to three thousand men) from French Indochina and, in compensation, the partial lifting of the embargo imposed against Japan by the United States, Britain, and Holland. The representatives of three countries — England, Australia, and Holland — took a basically positive stance, giving their approval to the agreement for the withdrawal of Japanese troops from French Indochina as long as they did not have to pay a large compensation. The problem was the Chinese ambassador. According to Hull, the provisional agreement would stop Japanese attacks against the Burma Road, but Ambassador Hu paid no attention to this statement and asked Hull if Japan had agreed not to attack China during these two to three months. Hull replied negatively, saying that this problem belonged in the next stage of negotiations.

According to Lord Halifax, Hu's reasons for opposing the U.S. counterproposal were that Japan could still carry on its war against China during these two or three months and that as China gave great weight to the economic pressure against Japan, it could not approve a large-scale removal of such economic sanctions at this stage.

Foreign Minister Eden was also sharply critical of the American counterproposal.[23] In the instructions he sent on November 24 to Halifax, he imposed certain further restrictions to agreeing with the U.S. proposal: The withdrawal of Japanese troops from French Indochina was to include all air, land, and naval forces; Japan was not to make any military advance against China, Southeast Asia, the south Pacific, and Russia; and there was to be no one-sided relaxing of the embargo against Japan.

On the afternoon of November 24, Hull called together the representatives of Australia, China, Britain, and the Netherlands for the second time. This meeting also lasted two hours. Hull showed each of the representatives the written form of the agreement proposal to be presented to Japan. According to Hull's memorandum,[24] it was Ambassador Hu who stubbornly opposed the U.S. proposal. Hu argued that the twenty-five thousand Japanese troops to remain in French Indochina should be reduced to five thousand men. Hull replied by stressing that gaining time through the provisional agreement should be given priority, as both the U.S. Army and the U.S. Navy regarded time as most important. In this regard, Hull noted that General Marshall had only a few minutes earlier said that twenty-five thousand troops posed no menace. Only the Dutch ambassador, however, supported Hull's view, and thanks to this unexpectedly harsh attack, Hull gave up hope.

[23] *FCFEA,* no. 191, pp. 103–4.
[24] *FRUS 1941,* vol. 4, pp. 646–47.

Lord Halifax was, according to his report to Eden, also right at the frontline of this barrage of criticism against Hull.[25] He raised questions about whether Russia and the Burma Road were included among the areas Japan gave its guarantee not to attack. Along with Hu, he stressed that the Japanese military force of twenty-five thousand troops should be cut. At this meeting, Hu demanded a guarantee that the Japanese army not advance any further against China, and Halifax reports that Hull opposed this request.

Upon the advice of Hull, who felt a sense of crisis from the words and actions of Halifax at this meeting, President Roosevelt late in the evening of November 24 sent a personal telegram to Prime Minister Churchill in an effort to explain the U.S. provisional proposal.[26]

That same night, Ambassador Hu visited Stanley K. Hornbeck, special adviser to Secretary Hull, and again explained his concern about the U.S. provisional proposal presented at the afternoon's meeting.[27] He said that if the Allies were to recognize the stationing of twenty-five thousand Japanese troops in French Indochina, it would be possible for the Japanese army to advance to Kunming (in Yunnan province) and thereby endanger the Burma Road, Free China's lifeline for supplies from the world outside.

In Chungking, Chiang Kai-shek learned of the contents of the U.S. provisional proposal from Ambassador Hu. He flew into a rage, accusing the United States of trying to compromise with Japan by using China as the sacrificial victim.[28] Lattimore reported to President Roosevelt from Chungking that he had never seen Chiang in such a deranged state of mind. According to Lattimore, thanks to this news the power and credibility of the United States in China had fallen just as England's had when it closed the Burma Road.[29]

Chiang took the unusual step of sending a personal telegram to Secretary of War Henry L. Stimson and Secretary of the Navy Frank Knox through his brother-in-law, Sung Tzu-wen, in Washington. Chiang directly told Stimson, who had considerable influence in the Roosevelt cabinet, that if America reached a compromise with Japan, the Chinese resistance to Japan — which had resulted in unspeakable devastation and unprecedented loss of life over five years — would be made meaningless. He stated that the collapse of Chinese resistance would lead to

[25] *FCFEA,* no. 192, pp. 104–6.
[26] *FRUS 1941,* vol. 4, pp. 648–49.
[27] Ibid., pp. 650–51.
[28] Ibid., p. 654.
[29] Ibid., p. 653.

the destruction of the world and asked Stimson to consider how future history would record this episode.[30]

Churchill reported to Roosevelt his concern about the position of Chiang Kai-shek, expressing his own judgment that if China should collapse, it would greatly increase the common danger to both Britain and the United States.[31]

If Hull's provisional proposal (omitting the number of Japanese troops in line with British and Chinese desires) had been presented, it is hard to predict how the situation would have developed. However, it was probably impossible to stop the outbreak of war. The focus of the problem lies in the fact that no one was allowed any longer to deny the energy that China had accumulated in its more than four years of resistance against Japan. Ever since 1937, the Asian mainland had been one of the battlefields of the world, as Chiang had persistently stressed.

The United States had not shown to China, Britain, and the other countries the final proposal of concessions (Plan A) that Japan had presented on November 7. If it had asked China's opinion about Plan A, how would China have responded? Perhaps China would have been amazed by the extent of Japan's concessions, and it might have judged that on the basis of further concessions it would be beneficial to attain peace with Japan under the leadership and supervision of the United States, for the continued war in China had led to a remarkable increase in the power of the Chinese Communist party. Moreover, after the Hull note was presented to Japan, on November 27 and 28 Chiang observed that because Japan was being exhausted due to the economic pressure of the democratic nations and its long-term conflict in China, it would not be able to fight a strong naval power.[32]

The Hull note completely neglected the concessions made by Japan. It demanded the complete and unconditional withdrawal of the Japanese army from all of China, including Manchuria. In other words, it demanded that Japan return to its position in East Asia in 1930 before its conquest of Manchuria. In January 1932, Stimson, then the U.S. Secretary of State, had notified Japan that the United States would not recognize the outcome of the Manchurian incident. Consequently, one can say that U.S. demands had remained consistent from start to finish.

Japanese approval of the Hull note would have meant the collapse of the Greater Japanese Empire established during the Meiji period (1868–

[30] Ibid., pp. 660–61.
[31] Ibid., p. 665.
[32] Ibid., p. 709.

1912). It was impossible for Japan's leaders to submit to the American demands without contemplating the destruction of the Japanese Empire. This is something Hull was very much aware of. It is well known that after he handed over his note to the Japanese on November 26, Hull said that the matter was now up to the army and the navy.

On December 8, the news that the U.S.-Japanese war had broken out due to the Japanese air force's unexpected attack on Pearl Harbor was welcomed in China as salvation from heaven. Han Suyin wrote, "The officials of the Nationalist party exchanged congratulations, walking back and forth repeatedly as if they had won a great victory. In their view, this news was the equivalent of a great victory." [33]

In Chungking, it was commonly thought that China had obtained the Allies' support, that U.S. participation in the war against Japan meant the defeat of Japan, and that by doing nothing China could await victory. One American who observed the mood of celebration then common in Chungking said, "What was Pearl Harbor Day in America was Armistice Day here." [34]

China had grown impatient, feeling that it alone had been fighting against Japan for four and a half years. Now it could rest assured that it would obtain the considerable Allied support it had long awaited. On December 8, Churchill sent a telegram to Chiang, saying, "Always we have been friends; now we face a common enemy." [35]

From the time Chiang knew of the Japanese military attack on the United States, he began taking a diplomatic initiative. On the afternoon of December 8, Chiang summoned Soviet Ambassador Aleksandr S. Panyusikin and American Ambassador Gauss to meet with him and Foreign Minister Kuo.

In addition to saying that China had decided to declare war on Japan and its Axis Pact allies, Germany and Italy, Chiang put forth the following proposals:

1. All of the anti-Axis countries must declare all of the Axis countries as their common enemy, and therefore the United States should declare war on Germany and Italy while the Soviet Union declared war on Japan.

2. To wage war, the Soviet Union, the United States, Britain, Australia, New Zealand, Canada, the Netherlands, and China should form a military pact and set up a unified military command under the leadership of the United States.

[33] Han Suyin, *Birdless Summer,* Japanese translation (Tokyo, 1972), p. 230.
[34] Barbara Tuchman, *Stilwell and the American Experience in China, 1911–1945* (New York, 1972), pp. 233–34.
[35] *FCFEA,* supplement to part 16, no. 1.

3. These countries should make a treaty not to come to a separate peace.

Chiang's principal purpose in making these proposals was to see to it that the Soviet Union was clearly participating in the war against Japan. He relied on the Soviet and American ambassadors to convey these proposals to their leaders.[36] The same request was made to British Ambassador Sir A. Clark Kerr, who was not at this meeting, as he was then in Chengtu.

On the same day, a Soviet military adviser in Chungking told the Chinese that the Soviet Union would not immediately wage war against Japan and that if the Soviet Union did wage war against Japan, the United States would not put all of its power into the Pacific theater of the war.

On December 9, Chiang told Roosevelt that China was awaiting the reply of the Soviet Union and asked whether China should wait until the attitude of the Soviet Union became clear or whether it should immediately declare war.[37] President Roosevelt replied that China should immediately declare war.[38]

On December 16, Stalin rejected Chiang's request that it declare war immediately against Japan. He said that the Soviet Union was presently waging war with Germany, the strongest of the Axis powers. When the time came when Soviet victory over Germany became widely anticipated among the anti-Axis powers, Stalin told Chiang, the Soviet Union would not spare the use of its power in the Far East; but for the time being, war against Japan was unthinkable. The Soviet Union was making preparations for a war with Japan, even though it was in violation of its neutrality pact with Japan, but it needed time before it could wage war. Stalin told Chiang not to ask the Soviet Union again to participate in the war against Japan.[39] Chiang thought that the anti-Axis powers should concentrate their full power in an attack on Japan, the weakest link among the Axis powers. If they concentrated all their power in such a war, they could gain victory over Japan in 1942. By using the south Pacific, Alaska, the American West Coast, and the China coast as their military bases, they could bomb Japan and isolate its army on the China mainland by cutting off its supply lines. The Chinese army would then exterminate the Japanese army. Chiang's strategy of fighting war, with its stress on

[36] *FRUS 1941,* vol. 4, p. 736.
[37] Ibid., p. 737.
[38] Ibid., p. 740.
[39] Ibid., p. 747.

the need to fight against Japan rather than Germany, was frustrated right at the start by the failure of a precondition — namely, the participation of the Soviet Union in the war against Japan.[40]

While Chiang held fast to his efforts to have the Soviet Union participate in the war against Japan, the Chinese Communist party, in contrast, expressed a different stance. On December 9, in its "Declaration at the Time of the Pacific War" and "Instructions on the Unified Front against Japan in the Pacific," the Central Committee of the Chinese Communist party argued for the formation of a military pact among China, England, and the United States.[41] It did not indicate that the Soviet Union was to be one of the allies in this war, and this was based on the view that the Soviet Union should not participate in the war against Japan.

On December 18, an editorial in the Chinese Communist party's newspaper, *Liberation Daily,* analyzed this point clearly. In comparing the three great battlegrounds of the world (Europe, Asia, and Africa), it was clear that Europe and the Atlantic were the center of the world war, and that the Allied powers should first concentrate their might on the task of demolishing Germany. After the defeat of Germany, they should then separately crush Japan and Italy. If they overthrew Hitler's government, the Japanese problem in the Far East would be easily solved. "If there is a change in this basic policy by giving priority to the overthrow of Japan, the Soviet Union would thereby have to shift troops to the Far East while making no change in its war with Germany and the Americans and English would have to concentrate their main force in the Pacific while not changing their present level of opposition to Germany in Europe, Africa, and the Mediterranean. This would mean nothing but the renewed surge of Germany to fight back with increased force. Therefore, this war must proceed with the fight against Germany as first and Japan as second in the list of priorities."[42] Thus, in contrast to Chiang, the Chinese Communist party advocated the priority of the European theater of the war. These statements can be said to reflect the different positions of the Nationalist government (and party) and the Chinese Communist party. . . .

---

[40]Tuchman, *Stilwell,* p. 234.

[41]*Chūgoku kyōsantō-shi,* vol. 10, pp. 555–58.

[42]A January 22 telegram from Yenan found in Foreign Ministry Archives, A7009-67, p. 57.

WANG XI

China and U.S.-Japanese Relations

In the following essay, a distinguished historian from China, a specialist in U.S.-Asian relations, offers his views on the relationship between the Chinese-Japanese war and the Pacific war. Why did the Japanese, who had not been successful in fighting against one country, China, decide to expand the war to include the United States, Britain, and others among its enemies? There was a failure, the author argues, to make decisions in a systematic and consistent fashion, and this failure, in turn, produced other failures. How does this author's interpretation of U.S.-Chinese-Japanese relations differ from those which you have just read?

In the Chinese-Japanese war and the Pacific war, a prominent and surprising fact is that the assessment of the situation by those in power in Japan frequently ran counter to reality. The course of development was completely at variance with Japan's expectations. China, instead of "stumbling at one blow," drew Japan into a never-ending protracted war. Thus we had Fumimaro Konoe's first, second, and third declarations.* Because of mistakes in judgment, each declaration was a contradiction of, and retreat from, the previous declaration. Konoe regarded the misjudgment of the effectiveness of Wang Ching-wei's puppet government as the "greatest defeat." Japan's decision to advance southward was due in many respects to mistaken estimates based on the war in Europe. At the time, Japan's military and political leaders thought that Britain would be unable to fight back against the German blitzkrieg and that Britain's collapse would undermine America's will to fight, forcing it to seek compromise with Japan. Hideki Tōjō even thought Roosevelt was so afraid of

---

*Prime Minister Konoe issued statements on January 16, January 18, and November 12, 1938, containing contradictory positions as to Japan's policy toward Chiang Kai-shek's government in China. At first Konoe indicated that Japan would no longer recognize the Chiang regime, but he steadily retreated from that position and, by the time of the November 12 statement, declared that Tokyo was ready to deal with any government in China that shared Japan's objectives in Asia.

Wang Xi, "The Chinese-Japanese War and the Pacific War," presented at the 1991 Lake Yamanaka conference. (See the source note on page 170 for more information on the conference.)

war that he would not dare to engage Japan in battle.[1] Similarly, the Japanese authorities' appraisal of the effectiveness of the Tripartite Pact was excessively high; they regarded it almost as if it were the key to the Chinese, Soviet, and U.S. problems. The result was that not even one of the problems could be solved. This kind of miscalculation had a major influence on the subsequent development of the situation. At a time when U.S.-Japanese relations were becoming increasingly tense, the Japanese military, on July 19, 1941, occupied the southern part of French Indochina. Six days later, Roosevelt ordered the freezing of all Japanese assets in the United States. This serious step was completely contrary to expectations in Japanese military and political circles. The leadership did not anticipate that its actions could elicit such a strong response from the United States. They lacked the capacity to judge the consequences of their own behavior; this was the fatal flaw of the Japanese decision makers during the Chinese-Japanese and Pacific wars.

Unfortunately, during these crucial years, Japan did not produce a politician with foresight. Some of those in office were myopic and wallowed excessively in colonial history, forgetting that times were changing. In 1931, because Chiang Kai-shek had adopted a policy of nonresistance, the Kwantung Army took over almost the entire northeast region (Manchuria). With very little effort, it used the puppet Manchukuo regime to dominate the northeast for more than six years. The notion that China would "stumble with one blow" was probably a product of this period in history. In 1937, Japan believed it could reenact the same scene and, by establishing puppet organizations, use the "Manchurian model" to achieve the goal of subjugating and controlling China. However, the China of 1937 was not the China of 1931. Certain Japanese leaders were determined to emulate the British East India Company of the seventeenth century, which used gunboats and arms to control India for several hundred years — with force deciding everything. However, the world of the fourth decade of the twentieth century was not the world of the seventeenth century. Japan was adept at using alliances to manipulate relationships among other countries to protect and strengthen itself. The British-Japanese alliance and the Soviet-Japanese secret treaty in the late nineteenth and early twentieth centuries were all for Japan's benefit. This was perhaps the reason for Yōsuke Matsuoka's enthusiasm for the Tripartite Pact, but this time Japan was engaged in a losing

[1] Samuel E. Morison, *The Rising Sun in the Pacific, 1931–April, 1942* (Boston, 1961), p. 72; James W. Morley, ed., *The Fateful Choice: Japan's Advance into Southern Asia, 1939–1941* (New York, 1980), p. 251; Dorothy Borg and Shumpei Okamoto, eds., *Pearl Harbor as History* (New York, 1973), p. 227.

venture. Mistaken strategies and misjudgments made it increasingly difficult to remedy the situation.

The New Order in East Asia and the Greater East Asia CoProsperity Sphere were important Japanese policies during the Chinese-Japanese and Pacific wars. The former took the unification of the economies of Japan, China, and Manchuria as its foundation; the scope of the latter was even broader, encompassing the entire East Asian region, including even Oceania. The Japanese appeal was, taking Japan as the nucleus, to help Asians expel whites from Asia, bringing "coprosperity" to all of Asia. This national policy was so important that almost every cabinet used this slogan to win over Asians, and it became a goal for Japan to fight for. Fighting for the New Order in East Asia became a "holy war" for the Japanese. Right up to the present day, there are still people who think that the Pacific war should be called the Greater East Asian War.

The New Order in East Asia had several inherent characteristics:

1. Japan would be the absolute ruler of the New Order.
2. The members of the New Order would provide resources to support Japan's Great East Asian War.
3. The New Order would be comprehensive; encompassing politics, economics, and culture.[2]

Thus, in actuality, the New Order was a huge colonial system under the absolute control of Japan. The history of the New Order in East Asia is a record of failure. It had already failed before the conclusion of the Pacific war. As soon as this New Order was conceived, it met with the intense opposition of both China and the United States, but the fundamental reason it failed was because neither the design nor the implementation was attractive to Asians. The Chinese people learned from their own blood and tears to believe that a country that massacred civilians, that used naked predation to occupy territory, and that used human beings as guinea pigs absolutely could not "fraternally" bring "coprosperity" to China.[3] Asians certainly abhorred the previous hundred years of white

[2] For the nature and orientation of the New Order in East Asia, see Japanese Foreign Ministry, ed., *Nihon gaikō bunsho narabi shuyō bunsho* (Chronology of Japanese diplomacy, with important documents, hereafter cited as NGN), vol. 2 (Tokyo, 1966), pp. 381–87, 389–91, 401, 405–7, 421–24, 464–66, 544–45, 575–76, 580–81, 583, 588–89, 593, 601, 605.

[3] *Okamura Yasuji senjō kaisō-hen* (Wartime memoirs of Yasuji Okamura) (Tokyo, 1970), pp. 387–88; Han Xiao, "Qin-yu Ri-jun di-731 xi-jun bu-dui zhui-xin-kao" (Textual research on Japan's 731 bacteriological warfare units), paper presented at the international conference on Sino-Japanese relations during the last hundred years (Hong Kong, 1990); Akira Fujiwara, *Nankin dai-gyakusatsu* (The great massacre at Nanjing) (Tokyo, 1988), chaps. 2,

control, but this was not the same as saying that they welcomed an even more cruel form of control under the Japanese. During the Chinese-Japanese and Pacific wars, the Japanese authorities were most concerned with using the framework of a New Order in East Asia as a tool to dominate and plunder Asia. According to a 1943 investigative report, if one takes Japan's domestic productive capacity in 1943 as the base figure, 56 percent of the iron ore, 29.8 percent of the cast iron, 10.8 percent of the coal, and 34 percent of the salt all came from China.[4] Japan used the New Order in East Asia as a mechanism to achieve the goal of "using war to conduct war." Just as Former Foreign Minister Mamoru Shigemitsu says, "So-called 'Sino-Japanese economic cooperation,' and 'co-existence and co-prosperity' followed the plunder of even more of China's resources. In actuality it had already turned into economic extortion."[5] The Japanese occupiers actually sought to "thoroughly explore and acquire resources for national defense" as stipulated in the "Outline for Handling the China Incident (November 13, 1940)."[6]

The Japanese leaders planned to use the New Order to oppose or to replace the Washington Conference system of treaties established in 1921–22. However, the New Order, besides furthering Japanese interests under bayonets, could not promote generally recognized principles of fairness, nor could it promote the welfare of the people under its jurisdiction. Strictly speaking, the New Order in East Asia was not an international system; rather, it was a single colonial system. Following an era of progress, the Washington Conference system would definitely have broken down, but its replacement could not be the New Order in East Asia.

The theoretical basis of the New Order in East Asia was "Great Asianism" and "Datsuaron," or the idea that Japan should "leave Asia" and "join the West." The creator of these doctrines, Yukichi Fukuzawa, was a scholar of the Japanese enlightenment period who was very worthy of respect. He idolized Europe and hoped that Japanese and Asians would leave behind the backwardness of Asia and aspire to the advanced ranks of Europe. He was moved to tears by Japan's victory in the 1894 Chinese-

3, 4; Akira Fujiwara and Seiichi Imai, *Jūgonen sensō-shi* (History of the fifteen years' war) (Tokyo, 1988), vol. 2, pp. 54–59.

[4]Tan Guanchu, "Ri-ben qin-Hua de 'yi-zhan yang-zhan' zhen-ce" (Paying for war by fighting war as Japan's policy in invading China), *Li-shi yan-jiu* (Historical studies), 1991, no. 4, p. 85.

[5]Mamoru Shigemitsu, *Shōwa no dōran* (The turbulent Showa era) (Tokyo, 1952), vol. 2, pp. 158–68.

[6]NGN, vol. 2, p. 465.

Japanese War.[7] But did he shed tears for the expansion and victory of Japanese militarism or for the lesson Japan learned about Chinese backwardness? There is no way to know. But China's poverty, backwardness, and inability to catch up with Europe were not reasonable justification for invasion; this point is not debatable. Unfortunately, "Datsuaron" was rapidly accepted by Japanese militarists and became their bold excuse for the invasion of China. The theoretical basis for the New Order in East Asia was weak. They forgot the most basic point, namely that those who enslave others can never attain freedom themselves.

In modern international diplomatic history, Japan has always been outstanding at using diplomatic procedures to support its national interests. In the Chinese-Japanese and Pacific wars, however, Japan's diplomatic activities unexpectedly did not succeed. Japan was continuously and unexpectedly shaken in diplomatic matters by alliance partners and enemies alike. The 1939 Soviet-German Nonaggression Treaty shook both the government and the public in Japan. After Kiichirō Hiranuma issued his irrelevant and strange declaration saying that international events were truly inexplicable, the entire cabinet resigned. After Yōsuke Matsuoka took charge of diplomacy, he adopted a "lean to one side" policy in foreign affairs, leaning toward Germany. He maintained his determination to sign the Tripartite Pact with Germany and Italy because "one cannot catch a tiger's cub without going into the den."[8] During the process of deliberation over the treaty, the Germans threw out some bait; they would mediate in Soviet-Japanese relations, compel China to engage in peace talks, threaten the United States into an attitude of compromise, quickly destroy the British Empire, and so on. Now there is evidence to prove that at the time of the signing of the Tripartite Pact, Germany had already decided to attack the Soviet Union under Operation Barbarossa, and within three months Hitler approved this secret plan.[9] The Japanese readily believed Germany's cheap promises, but ultimately not a single promise was realized. The Soviet-Japanese treaty of neutrality was signed under conditions of mutual distrust and did not obviate guardedness on either side. Of the two countries, the Soviet Union gained the greater benefit from the treaty. Two months after the signing of the treaty, Germany launched its surprise attack on the Soviet Union,

---

[7] Yukichi Fukuzawa, *Fukuō jiden* (Autobiography) (Tokyo, 1950), p. 402.

[8] This allusion came from Fan Ye (399–446), an outstanding historian of the Southern Song dynasty. He was the author of *Hou-Han shu* (History of the late Han dynasty).

[9] S. P. Platonov, ed., *Victoraia morovaia voina, 1939–1945 gg* (The Second World War) (Moscow, 1958), Chinese translation (Beijing, 1980), vol. 1, p. 143.

once again surprising both the government and the people of Japan. The easily excited Matsuoka had forgotten his warm embrace with Stalin at the Moscow train station and forcefully advocated that Japan advance northward to attack the Soviet Union.

At this time, the attitude of Britain and the United States toward Japan was becoming more hard-line. China and the United States had also moved closer together. China rejected the proposal of peace talks, and the threat from the Soviet Union still had not been removed. On September 6, 1941, the Imperial Conference decided on the strategic direction of "not allowing the Soviet Union and the United States to establish a combined front against Japan," [10] but this also fell through. The results of Japan's diplomatic activities were all contrary to expectations. Ultimately, the situation turned into a total debacle. Kijūrō Shidehara criticized Matsuoka's engaging in "aimless diplomacy regarding childish matters." [11] Cordell Hull also commented that Japan's diplomacy at that time seemed as if it were "galloping off on a wild horse." [12] Although Matsuoka had entered the "tiger's den," he never managed to capture the "tiger's cub." When the Pacific war finally broke out, he shed tears, saying, "Concluding the Tripartite Pact was the biggest mistake of my life." [13] While, of course, this "mistake" was Matsuoka's, it is not fair to place the blame for this kind of failure completely on him. More fundamentally, it was the result of an accumulation of strategic errors and misjudgments made under the guidance of militarist thinking.

Japan's impulsiveness and lack of strategic thinking in foreign affairs were manifested in the U.S.-Japanese negotiations. During the prolonged, nine-month negotiations, the United States was much more mature and prudent. Concerning economic sanctions, for example, Roosevelt as early as the 1920s considered implementing economic sanctions against Japan as a strategic measure.[14] The economic blockade against Japan was an important part of the content of the U.S. Navy's Orange Plan.[15] However, before the Pacific war, the United States, in implementing sanctions against Japan, employed the relatively cautious tactics of "gaining mastery by striking only after the enemy has struck" and

[10] NGN, vol. 2, p. 544.

[11] Shidehara Heiwa Zaidan, ed., *Shidehara Kijūrō* (Tokyo, 1955), p. 517.

[12] Cordell Hull, *Memoirs* (New York, 1948), vol. 1, p. 895.

[13] James W. Morley, ed., *Deterrent Diplomacy: Japan, Germany, and the USSR, 1935–1940* (New York, 1976), p. 275.

[14] Franklin D. Roosevelt, "Shall We Trust Japan?" *Asia,* vol. 23, p. 476 (July 1923), quoted in Borg and Okamoto, *Pearl Harbor,* pp. 213, 218.

[15] Edward S. Miller, *War Plan Orange: The U.S. Strategy to Defeat Japan, 1897–1945* (College Park, MD, 1991), pp. 4, 28, 35.

of leaving itself some room to maneuver. During the two and a half years from the announcement on January 4, 1939, of the prohibition on the export of aircraft and spare parts to Japan, to the total ban on the export of oil on August 1, 1941, the United States implemented economic sanctions on approximately twelve occasions. Each instance was a reaction to a Japanese invasion. As Japan's southern advance became increasingly intense, the scope of U.S. sanctions expanded as well. Warren Cohen correctly summarizes this relationship; he says that Roosevelt's actions were based on Japanese intentions. Thus it was the Japanese themselves, and not other people or groups, who determined Roosevelt's course of action with respect to economic sanctions against Japan.[16] It is worth noting that even though the United States at that time had implemented economic sanctions, it still had room to maneuver. The United States did not want to trap the Japanese in a corner. Although the U.S. president had issued declarations on July 2 and July 16, 1940, limiting the exports of petroleum and scrap iron, in December Japan imported 2.8 times more aviation fuel and 3.6 times more fuel of other types from the United States than it had in July. Although the export of certain high-grade fuels was prohibited, Japan could still blend ethyl and regular gasoline (the export of which was not banned) and, through a chemical process, attain the high-octane fuel it needed. This took place right under the nose of the U.S. government. The State Department directed the relevant departments to employ lenient policies toward the export embargo on Japan.[17] The U.S. tactic of flexibility, even under the export embargo, was intended, first, to avoid pushing Japan toward war and, second, to allow room for compromise. The tactics of "gaining mastery by striking only after the enemy has struck" and of allowing maneuvering room were cautious and prudent tactics on the part of the United States.

There were also diverse opinions regarding economic sanctions within the United States at that time. The U.S. Navy, because it was becoming increasingly involved in the European theater, did not support economic sanctions against Japan. On July 22, 1941, responding to Roosevelt's request, Admiral Stark ordered the naval war planners to provide a report that concluded with the following proposal: "We should not implement an embargo against Japanese trade at this time."[18] Within the State Department there were two schools of thought regarding whether to implement economic sanctions. This illustrates that economic sanc-

---

[16] Borg and Okamoto, *Pearl Harbor*, p. 458.

[17] James H. Herzog, "The Influence of the United States Navy in the Embargo of Oil to Japan, 1940–1941," *Pacific Historical Review,* vol. 25, no. 3 (August 1966), p. 322.

[18] Ibid., p. 323.

tions were used as a kind of deterrent. It was not that Japan lacked room to maneuver, but rather that Japan did not take advantage of the flexibility in U.S. policy. Similarly, the Japanese navy at that time was a powerful force that could have been used as a bargaining chip with the United States to find a means other than warfare of resolving problems. The use of latent deterrent power is perhaps even more effective when there is no guarantee of sure victory. Unfortunately, Japan did not deport itself in this way; rather, its aggressive and bellicose attitude casually risked war, and its readily usable deterrent power vanished. Roosevelt certainly did intend to appease the Japanese; even after Japan invaded northeast China, he still paid attention to cultivating friendly U.S.-Japanese relations. In Washington during February 1939, the Japanese ambassador to the United States, Hiroshi Saitō, died in office as a result of an illness. Roosevelt specially ordered a U.S. carrier to return Saitō's remains to Japan in a highly honorable way.[19] This was a very unusual expression of goodwill, and the events of 1939 were even more unusual. However, the Japanese did not fully consider using this goodwill. This kind of slow diplomatic reaction cannot be attributed to any single individual. Its roots are located in the aggressive nature of militarist thinking. The force of militarist thinking compelled the Japanese to advocate war and may have prevented them from wanting or daring to advocate peace.

Impediments in the Japanese decision-making mechanism influenced both domestic and international decision making and thus also influenced the development of the situation. This is an issue worth discussing further.

In foreign relations, Japan simultaneously implemented contradictory policies (such as wanting both to become a member of the Axis and to improve relations with the United States, wanting both to hold peace talks with China and to not abandon its position as aggressor, etc.). This often put Japanese decision makers in a difficult position. One of the fundamental reasons for this is that there were irreconcilable contradictions within the decision-making circle itself. The contradictions between the army and the navy are well known. They quarreled endlessly over major issues (such as the issue of northern or southern advances; the issue of the Tripartite Pact; the issue of withdrawal from China; the issue of whether the Pacific war would be characterized by "swift attack, swift victory" or by protracted warfare; etc.). Factions formed within the army

---

[19] Layton Horner, "Hiroshi Saito: A Most Remarkable Diplomat," in *Pull Together,* published by the Naval Historical Center, vol. 27, no. 2, p. 8 (Fall-Winter 1990).

and navy themselves. Within the navy there were disputes between the two Katō factions; within the army there were disputes between the China division and the Soviet division, between the Chongqing faction and the Wang Ching-wei faction, between the young, middle-rank officers and the senior officers, and so on.* All the factions handicapped one another, sometimes even withholding information. (Following the Battle of Midway, the navy informed then-Prime Minister Hideki Tōjō of the Japanese defeat only after one month had passed, and even then, it omitted many details.)[20] Controversy surrounds policy in any country; this is not strange. During the Chinese-Japanese and Pacific wars, for example, U.S. policy also had internal contradictions: Henry Morgenthau and Cordell Hull always held different opinions; within the State Department, Stanley Hornbeck and Maxwell Hamilton held different views as well. However, the crucial point is that once the differences had been discussed, Roosevelt gave the final word and made the final decision. However, Japan was not like this. There was no way to resolve controversies over major questions or divergences of opinion over strategy. Even the emperor was powerless in this regard. Therefore, those with great power (generally the Ministry of War, and especially the army because of its control over arms and its ability to carry out a coup) could persist in holding onto their own views; and even when they were fully aware that they were wrong, they acted rashly, as, for example, in getting bogged down in the Chinese "quagmire," in striving for the Tripartite Pact, in abruptly advancing southward, and so on. There were different opinions to start with, but there was no mechanism by which to establish the correct opinion. (Shigenori Tōgō, the Japanese ambassador to Germany, firmly opposed the Tripartite Pact and, as a result, was dismissed.) Because it was not possible to form a comprehensive and stable policy on a fully democratic basis, major decisions tended to be erratic and subject to influences from the outside. The knowledge of Germany's transient victory during the European blitzkrieg and other factors that were impossible to foresee ultimately became the major impetus for Japan's southern advance. Just as Joseph Grew, the U.S. ambassador to Japan, said, "The German military machine and system and their brilliant suc-

---

*The "two Katō factions" refers to Admirals Tomosaburō Katō and Kanji Katō. The former was a "moderate" and supported various agreements on naval arms limitation with the United States and Britain, while the latter opposed them, adamantly insisting on Japan's "parity" with these other powers. The Chongqing (also spelled Chungking) faction refers to the Nationalists under Chiang Kai-shek. They were opposed by a faction led by Wang Ching-wei (also spelled Wang Jingwei). Wang was willing to cooperate with the Japanese and, in 1940, set up his own pro-Japanese regime in Nanking (Nanjing).

[20]Shigemitsu, *Shōwa,* vol. 2, pp. 130–40.

cesses have gone to the Japanese head like strong wine."[21] Matsuoka also excitedly said to Hitler that Japan could not abandon such a golden opportunity.[22] Making and implementing strategic decisions in such a "drunk and silly" state definitely led to opportunism and adventurism.

At times, major decisions were not carefully considered from an over-all strategic perspective, but rather from the awkward predicament of the decision makers themselves. On July 26 and 27, 1940, the "Outline of the Basic Principles of National Policy" and the "Outline for Handling the Current Situation"[23] were adopted; even though the "China Incident" had not been brought to a conclusion, it seemed as if the conditions existed for southern advance. That is to say, Japan would advance south-ward while bearing the burden of the war in China. This was a crucial decision. The emperor commented about this decision that "it was as if Prime Minister Konoe had decided to transfer the low national morale created by the failure of the China Incident to the south."[24] If the emperor's commentary accords with reality, then this decision was made entirely too rashly. The decision maker did not thoroughly understand either his enemies or his allies; he just relied on impulse to decide. This is one important reason why Japan was placed in a passive position. As a military history series notes, "Perhaps there was not much real under-standing on the part of government leaders" in Japan of the high level of national consciousness of the Chinese people and of China's relations with other countries.[25] Under these circumstances, politicians harbor-ing personal ambitions made the situation even more complicated.

Shigemitsu's analysis of Matsuoka was that "in building a new Japan, his intention to build up his own achievements was quite strong. He meddled in the domestic political situation, intending to realize his own political ambition. . . . He was eager to succeed; therefore, he was, at times, even more aggressive than the Ministry of War."[26] He would see which way the wind was blowing and behave accordingly. To realize his personal ambition, he closely followed the Ministry of War, but he did not hesitate to be even more aggressive than those in the ministry. This kind of politician inevitably led Japan to disaster.

Before the Second World War, Japan was a poorly developed capital-ist country. The bourgeois capitalist system had not yet been estab-lished; therefore, the existence of impediments in the decision-making

[21] Joseph C. Grew, *Ten Years in Japan* (New York, 1944), p. 325.

[22] Winston S. Churchill, *The Grand Alliance* (Boston, 1950), p. 166.

[23] NGN, vol. 2, pp. 436–38.

[24] Kōichi Kido, *Kido Kōichi nikki* (Diary of Kōichi Kido) (Tokyo, 1966), p. 812.

[25] Defense Agency, War History Division, *Shina jihen rikugun sakusen* (The army's strategy during the China Incident), vol. 2 (Tokyo, 1976), foreword.

[26] Shigemitsu, *Shōwa*, vol. 2, chapt. 7.

mechanism had especially deep social roots. Moreover, there was the traditional militarist education and imperiousness of soldiers. Thus, militarist thinking could control everything for a period of time and, moreover, could be accepted by the people. For this, Japan paid a heavy price.

ANTHONY BEST

The British Perspective

Britain was traditionally a major Asian power, with its colonies and spheres of influence all over the region. In 1941, however, its hands were tied because of the war closer to home against Germany. The following essay by a British historian details the predicament. In your opinion, how much sway did Britain have over the United States?

The question of Japan's attitude towards the European war presented Britain with a myriad of problems. Whitehall's fear was that Japan would seize upon the conflict to strengthen its position in the Far East, either by pressuring Britain into concessions in China or by taking the extreme measure of striking at British possessions in Southeast Asia. Britain's concern was compounded by the close relations between Japan and Germany that had developed since the mid-1930s. Although these relations had turned sour due to the signing of the Nazi-Soviet Pact, there remained the possibility that Japan would become a neutral benevolent towards Germany or even be persuaded to join the war as Berlin's ally. Furthermore, there was the danger that renewed cooperation between Japan and Germany could also lead to an improvement in Soviet-Japanese relations. This had the potential to affect adversely Britain's position, as Anglo-Soviet relations were poor and a relaxing of tensions in Northeast Asia would remove an important restraint from Moscow. A Chiefs of Staff *aide-mémoire* of February 1941 summed up the dangers of a conflict in the East by noting that "such a war will lay open to attack our communications with Australia and New Zealand, our trade in the

Anthony Best, "Britain and the Coming of the Pacific War," presented at the 1991 Lake Yamanaka conference. (See the source note on page 170 for more information on the conference.)

Far East and the Indian Ocean, and will even jeopardise our communications with the Middle East. The efforts which we shall be bound to make to prevent excessive damage to our vital interests will weaken our whole war effort against Germany."[1] The natural conclusion from this was, as the Chiefs of Staff earlier reported to the War Cabinet on 28 September 1939, that "a possible extension of the war to the Far East must be prevented by any means in our power."[2]

There was then a serious need to keep Japan neutral and pacified. Theoretically this could be achieved through one of two means, deterrence or appeasement, but in fact both of these paths were closed off. Deterrence was not a serious option because the British forces in the Far East were simply inadequate for such a task. Resistance to Japanese pressure could only be sanctioned if there was clear evidence that Britain could get support from the United States, and there seemed little likelihood of that. Appeasement, which could have freed Britain from the need to defend East Asia, faced two obstacles. First, it was clear, particularly after the Tientsin crisis of the summer of 1939, that the price of achieving a reconciliation with Japan would be very high, probably amounting to official recognition of Japan's political and economic dominance of the region with all the attendant effects such an action would have on Britain's prestige in South and Southeast Asia and with no guarantee that even then Japan would be satiated. Second, there was the problem that a policy of appeasement would antagonize opinion in the United States, which had little sympathy for Japanese expansionism: Not only would this risk losing American support in the Pacific, which was vital should appeasement of Japan fail, but it would also jeopardize their financial and economic support for Britain in Europe.

Washington's unwillingness either to underpin a policy of resistance or to approve one of outright appeasement meant that Britain was forced to work within very limited parameters in its effort to keep Japan neutral. To an extent, Britain could rely on the American interest in the region and the continuing stalemate in the Sino-Japanese conflict as means of ensuring this, but there was also a need to defuse Anglo-Japanese tensions. Britain's motives were twofold: first to prevent any crisis from occurring, and second to try, within the limits laid down by the war effort and the watchful eye of the Americans, to support the delicate position of the "moderates" in the Abe and Yonai cabinets, which governed Japan

[1] Public Record Office (PRO) PREM 3 157/1, Chiefs of Staff Aide-Mémoire, 8 February 1941.

[2] PRO CAB 66/2 WP(41)56, Chiefs of Staff Memorandum, "Sino-Japanese Hostilities," 28 September 1939.

between September 1939 and July 1940, who were trying to keep Japan strictly neutral in the European war.

This policy led to a number of efforts to conciliate Japanese opinion. In East Asia Britain agreed in November 1939 to the renewal of negotiations with Japan to solve the economic problems left over from the Tientsin crisis, a decision that Lord Halifax, Foreign Secretary, justified to the War Cabinet by explaining that "A struggle was going on in Japan between those who favoured a rapprochement with Germany through the Soviets, and those who desired Japan to draw nearer to the democracies. Everything pointed to the near approach of a turning point in Japanese policy, and it would be wrong to miss any chance of drawing Japan closer to our side."[3] The Tientsin negotiations stood until an agreement was signed in mid-June 1940 as the chief hope for improved relations, but there was also the vague chance that the issue of the Soviet Union could act as a catalyst for conciliation. To both countries Stalin's Russia stood as a dangerous and unpredictable threat, and in particular the start of the Russo-Finnish war, which seriously alienated opinion in Japan, led to speculation in both London and Tokyo about the possibilities of forming an anti-Soviet front.[4] Such a radical diplomatic revolution could, however, not be seriously contemplated, no matter how useful this would have been to the war effort, because Britain was faced with two perennial problems, differences with Japan over China and the attitude of the United States.

In parallel to these largely political considerations the Foreign Office also pushed for Japan to be treated leniently over economic matters that arose from the necessities of the British war effort, such as the introduction of a blockade of Germany and the reserving of strategic raw materials from the British Empire for war production. This approach was largely the initiative of R. A. Butler, the Parliamentary Under-Secretary at the Foreign Office, who in late September 1939 provoked a major interministry debate in Whitehall by asking how Britain could conciliate Japan in the economic sphere.[5] This finally in November led to the draft-

[3] PRO CAB 65/2 96(39), War Cabinet Meeting, 27 November 1939.

[4] Discussions of the Soviet issue in relation to Anglo-Japanese relations in the winter of 1939–40 can be seen in PRO FO371/24708 F1462/193/61, Sir R. Craigie to Lord Halifax, 29 February 1940, FO371/24724 F2169/23/23, Sir R. Craigie to Lord Halifax, 31 March 1940, W0106/2436 MO2 Memorandum, "Japan as an Ally," 31 March 1940.

[5] PRO FO371/23567 F10429/1054/23 Shackle (Board of Trade) to Hutchinson (Import Duties Advisory Committee), 23 September 1939. For discussion of the debate see P. Lowe, *Great Britain and the Origins of the Pacific War: A Study of British Policy in East Asia 1937–1941* (Oxford Univ. Press, Oxford, 1977), pp. 109–12, and W. N. Medlicott, *The Economic Blockade,* vol. 1 (HMSO, London, 1952), pp. 388–92.

ing of a Foreign Office memorandum for the War Cabinet that recommended that Britain should conclude an informal trade agreement with Japan where Britain would guarantee to purchase a certain amount of Japanese exports and to sell to Japan commodities from the Empire. The memorandum noted, "It is not suggested that the political advantages which would accrue from the successful conclusion of a trade agreement would be immediately apparent or that they could at once be brought into account in respect of Anglo-Japanese differences in respect of China. What is hoped for rather is a demonstration that although we cannot come to terms with her on the question of principle which divides us in respect of China, we are otherwise well disposed towards Japan and anxious to be friendly." [6] However, this attempt to ease relations failed to bear fruit as it ran into strong opposition from the Treasury, which pointed to the dangers to the stability of sterling should the latter be used to buy goods in large quantities from the Japanese, who might very well decide to sell the currency on the open market. Support was also prejudiced because at the very time that an agreement was being considered the Americans were preparing to denounce their 1911 Commercial Agreement with Japan and pressing Britain to restrict sales of nickel and wolfram to Japan. [7] This defeat for a concerted effort to conciliate Japan meant that the Foreign Office had instead to rely on a piecemeal policy of meeting Japanese desires over a variety of small-scale issues. For example, Britain tried to avoid antagonizing Japan by strictly limiting the interception of Japanese merchant ships that entered or left European ports, one case being the decision in December 1939 not to search the *Sanyo Maru,* even though there was intelligence to suggest that it was carrying contraband.

The need to pursue a policy of conciliation also influenced the first wartime crisis with Japan, which occurred in January 1940 when HMS *Liverpool* intercepted the *Asama Maru,* a Japanese merchant ship carrying a large number of Germans eligible for conscription who were seeking to return to the Reich, just thirty miles off Yokohama. [8] At first it appeared that this had the makings of a serious clash, but the wish on both

---

[6] PRO FO371/23568 F11899/1054/23, Undated Foreign Office Memorandum for the War Cabinet.

[7] PRO FO371/23568 F12160/1054/23, Sir G. Sansom Minute, 27 November 1939, T160/1054 F16224/1, S. Waley (Treasury) to R. Howe (Foreign Office), 20 December 1939.

[8] The interception of the *Asama Maru* was supposed to have taken place sixty miles off Japan, which was thought not to be too provocative; circumstances, however, eventually dictated that the action took place "within sight of Mount Fuji." See PRO ADM 116/4157. For greater detail on the various crises mentioned in this paper see Lowe, *Great Britain and the Origins of the Pacific War.*

sides to avoid confrontation at this stage of the war meant that a mutually acceptable compromise was found that ended any possible recurrence of the problem. The incident showed clearly the potential damage that could be done to relations by a severe application by Britain of belligerent rights and also shed a spotlight on one of the gravest disputes arising from the blockade: the use of the Trans-Siberian Railway as a trading link between Japan and Germany and as a route for Germans to reach the Reich from East Asia.

The threat posed by the railway to the blockade of Germany first became apparent to Britain in October 1939 when Sir Robert Craigie, the British ambassador in Tokyo, reported that arrangements were being made for supplies to be sent by that route.[9] The main issue was that the railway allowed Japan to send exports to Germany and evade the blockade and even to reexport goods and raw materials vital to Germany's war effort, such as rubber and copper. Britain saw this as a serious threat and restricted the sale to Japan of commodities that could be useful to Germany in an effort to force Japan to close this loophole. In April 1940, talks were started to settle the problem with Britain tying a War Trade Agreement to a Japanese promise not to reexport goods to Germany, but the Japanese refused to compromise, and in June the talks broke up without any success.[10]

Japan's neutrality could not, however, be guaranteed simply by Britain's attempts to lower tensions; it also relied on the success of the British war effort. In May and June 1940, with Germany's dramatic series of victories in Western Europe, the mood in Japan began to change. The German triumphs presented Japan with a power vacuum in Southeast Asia, where the empires of France, the Netherlands, and Britain lay virtually unprotected. Here was an opportunity not only to cut off China's lifelines to the outside world, but also to achieve autarky by acquiring, through diplomatic pressure or force, the rich resources of the region. Britain's policy of limited conciliation had little to offer to stem the tide, and when on 19 June, two days after the end of French resistance in Europe, the initial demand for Britain to close the Burma Road was made, British policy in East Asia was thrown into confusion.

The crisis presented Britain with a simple choice between resistance and appeasement, with no middle way available anymore. Resistance could, due to the dire situation in Europe, only be sanctioned if there was

---

[9] PRO FO371/23568 F11195/1054/23, Sir R. Craigie to Lord Halifax, 20 October 1939.
[10] PRO FO837 C9/16 1940, Sir F. Leith Ross (Ministry of Economic Warfare) to R. A. Butler, 27 June 1940. See also Medlicott, *The Economic Blockade,* vol. 1, pp. 403–11.

a definite and public measure of support from the United States. In desperation Britain turned to Washington in the hope that some tangible aid would be forthcoming, and Lord Lothian, the British ambassador, was ordered to tell the State Department that "we cannot maintain our position in both spheres alone and unaided, and to the extent that the struggle in which we are engaged is in defence of our common interests and way of living, it is surely to the advantage of the United States to take what action they can to prevent an attack upon us in the Far East."[11] The lacklustre American response to this plea was to offer no support but to state that Britain should not give way to force. This made Britain's decision inevitable, and on 5 July, with the threat that Vichy France might imminently enter the war against Britain in retaliation for the bombardment of Mers-el-Kebir, Craigie was given permission by the War Cabinet to seek a settlement with the Japanese. On 17 July an agreement to close the Burma Road for three months was signed in Tokyo. In the Admiralty the Deputy Chief of Naval Staff Vice Admiral Sir Tom Phillips summed up the position: "It seems to me quite clear that our policy in the Far East at the moment must be directed to the avoidance of war with Japan, even if that means some temporary loss of prestige and giving in to Japanese views. We know quite well that we cannot take on Japan in addition to the rest of the world at the present time, and every sign goes to show that the United States will not back a strong policy in the Far East by force."[12]

Japan's new aggressiveness forced Britain to reconsider its long-term policy in East Asia. Some officials, such as Craigie, Lothian, and R. A. Butler, believed that Britain, in the light of the desperate European position, should build on the forced agreement with Japan to try to mediate a general settlement for the Far East. This policy, however, depended on Japan's willingness to compromise, a hope that was belied by the tide of events. Japan, under the direction of the new foreign minister, Yōsuke Matsuoka, markedly increased its influence in Southeast Asia from July to September 1940 and by signing the Tripartite Pact with Italy and Germany openly aligned itself with Britain's enemies. Japan's alliance with the Axis powers, more than any other factor, forced a change in British policy. Low-key appeasement had been appropriate when Japan had been undecided about its course, but once Japan had taken sides, the emphasis changed to persuading her that to go one step further and enter the conflict on the side of the Axis powers would be a fatal mistake, and this objective could only be brought about by a policy of deterrence.

[11] PRO FO371/24725 F3465/23/23, Lord Halifax to Lord Lothian, 25 June 1940.
[12] PRO ADM/116 5757, Vice Admiral T. Phillips Minute, 4 July 1940.

Britain's resolve was strengthened by the coincidence of these events with a relative improvement in her international position: Victory in the Battle of Britain, and evidence that the United States was showing a greater willingness to collaborate with Britain in both Europe and the Pacific and was taking a more assertive stand against Japan, meant that from late September the restraints that had forced Britain into appeasement over the Burma Road no longer applied. In fact the tougher American stance towards Japan, as demonstrated by its embargo on 26 September of scrap iron and aviation fuel, required Britain to follow suit. To Craigie this acceptance of American hostility towards Japan appeared to be against British interests, and he wrote to the Foreign Office on 19 September, "However gratifying may be the increasing American disposition to collaborate with us in the Far East, it remains as true as ever that actual American involvement in hostilities with Japan would in present circumstances mean a serious weakening of America's power to assist us in Europe."[13] Although there was merit on the surface with this observation, it revealed that Craigie had failed to realize how Britain's perceptions of what was necessary for victory had changed. Churchill minuted to Halifax on 4 October 1940 that it should be explained to Craigie that "the entry of the United States into the war either with Germany and Italy or with Japan, is fully compatible with British interests. That nothing in the munitions sphere can compare with the importance of the British Empire and the United States being co-belligerent. That if Japan attacked the United States without declaring war on us we should at once range ourselves at the side of the United States and declare war on Japan."[14] In Churchill's mind, Japan had become a possible backdoor route for American entry into the war against Germany, and the latter had become such a necessity that it even outweighed the need to keep Japan neutral.

This new strategy did not, however, mean that Britain now viewed the prospect of war in the Pacific with equanimity. Except for the scenario sketched out by Churchill, Britain's aim was still to avoid a conflict with Japan through a policy of deterrence and containment, ideally in close cooperation with the United States. The need for such a policy was underlined by evidence from intelligence sources of increasing cooperation between Japan and Germany, as demonstrated by German raiders entering Japanese waters and Japan apparently acting as a transit route for the passage of raw materials from Latin America to Germany, which the Ministry of Economic Warfare believed included the transport of

---

[13] PRO FO371/24670 F4328/43/10, Sir R. Craigie to Lord Halifax, 19 September 1940.
[14] PRO FO371/24729 F4634/60/23, Churchill Minute for Halifax, 4 October 1940.

Brazilian rubber worth $1 million for the Reich.[15] The problem, however, with developing a tough line was that Britain and the United States did not share the same interests in the region, and though Britain was careful to act in parallel with American actions, this was not reciprocated. In particular, Britain was concerned with the defense of its imperial possessions and the maintenance of a strict blockade of Germany, both unsympathetic issues for the United States, and this raised the danger that Britain might, through the protection of these interests, provoke a war with Japan that would not bring in Washington. Britain was thus forced to continue to show restraint in its attitude towards Japan, even though there was a desire to take a tough stance and even if the failure to act decisively led to an undermining of Britain's position in the Far East or affected the course of the European war.

The policy that Britain was forced to adopt was described by Lord Halifax to the War Cabinet as aiming "to cause inconvenience to Japan without ceasing to be polite,"[16] with the ultimate aim of bringing about a situation where, through the use of embargoes, commodity shortages would seriously hamper Japan's entry into the war and restrict her ability to reexport vital raw materials such as rubber and zinc to Germany. This policy was based on the extension of restrictions over a broad range of exports to Japan, the keeping of sales to prewar levels, and the stricter application of blockade rules to Japanese ships attempting to reach Europe. This had to be done within the parameters of not provoking Japan or compromising American support, and this was made all the more difficult as America seriously lagged behind Britain in its economic measures, which consisted only of singling out a few individual items to be embargoed. The limitations placed on Britain were noted by R. A. Butler, who was the chairman of the Far Eastern Committee that coordinated these economic measures, when he wrote to Lord Halifax, "The screw will have to be applied, more or less firmly, in proportion as the Japanese control their wayward tendencies, or as our hand grows stronger in Europe and the Middle East or as the United States Administration interests itself more in the Far East."[17]

---

[15] The best source for the naval material is J. Chapman (ed.), *The Price of Admiralty: The War Diary of the German Naval Attaché in Japan 1939–1943*. Vol. 2 & 3 23 Aug. 1940–9 Sept. 1941. (Univ. of Sussex Press, Lewes, 1984). On the transport of goods for Germany from Latin America via Japan see PRO PREM 3 156/6, Cranborne to Canada, 27 February 1941, and FO837/440 L. 1/3/6/Z Summaries of Enemy Economic Developments, No. 71, 27 January 1941, see also Medlicott, *The Economic Blockade,* vol. 1, pp. 649–51.

[16] PRO CAB66/12 WP (40)398, Lord Halifax Memorandum, "The German-Italian-Japanese Treaty," 2 October 1940.

[17] PRO CAB66/14 WP(40)484, R. A. Butler Memorandum for Halifax, 18 December 1940. Also quoted in C. Thorne, *Allies of a Kind: The United States, Britain and the*

Britain's inability to effectively counter the growing German-Japanese cooperation had its gravest consequences in Southeast Asia, where in the winter of 1940–41 the two powers attempted to establish a preponderant position through the encouragement of Thai territorial claims against French Indochina and pressure on the Vichy regime of Admiral Decoux in Saigon to make economic concessions. The crisis peaked in the first two weeks of February, when it became apparent that Japan's price for its help in mediating between the French and the Thais would be military bases and closer political and economic ties with the two countries and that it was willing to back up its demands with force. These developments were extremely serious for Britain, as they threatened to jeopardize the security of Singapore and undermine the effectiveness of economic restrictions by allowing Japan and Germany to draw on the rich resources of the region. In addition, there was concern that Japanese gains in Indochina and Thailand may not be an end in themselves but rather a precondition for an imminent direct attack on either British territory or the Dutch East Indies, which could be synchronized with a new German offensive in Europe.[18]

Despite the fact that the issues raised by the crisis were so important for both Europe and the Pacific, Britain was not in any position to counter or preempt a Japanese strike. This was not simply due to British military weakness in the region, but also because any attempt to forestall Japan's entry into the region through military force or economic pressure would not necessarily have the support of the United States, which remained largely inactive in Southeast Asia. The need for Britain to avoid igniting any sparks not only counted against any increase in economic restrictions in the Pacific, but also forced Britain into a compromise over its blockade policy in Europe. In the same week as the crisis reached its height, reports reached Britain that a Japanese armed merchantman,

---

War against Japan 1941–45 (Hamish Hamilton, London, 1978), p. 69. For the work of the Far Eastern Committee see Lowe, *Great Britain and the Origins of the Pacific War,* Appendix C, pp. 292–94, and Medlicott, *The Economic Blockade,* vol. 2 (HMSO, London, 1959), pp. 63–76.

[18] The exact nature of the information that led Britain to conclude that a Japanese attack was imminent is not available in the Public Record Office, but it must be assumed that much of it came from Britain's reading of the Japanese diplomatic code, information referred to as BJs; more details can be found on this source in J. Rusbridger and E. Nave, *Betrayal at Pearl Harbor: How Churchill Lured Roosevelt into War* (Michael O'Mara, London, 1991). Material in PREM 3 252/6A and W0208/896 suggests that British fears were more justified than is often assumed. The details revealed in the chapters by Nagaoka and Tsunoda in J. W. Morley (ed.), *The Fateful Choice. Japan's Advance into South East Asia 1939–1941* (Columbia Univ. Press, New York, 1980) would seem to add some credence to this view (p. 231 & pp. 283–84).

the *Asaka Maru,* had set sail for Portugal with a Japanese naval mission to Germany on board and that it was likely that the ship would be carrying strategic material on its return voyage. The issues raised were of grave importance; to let the ship pass through the blockade threatened to set a dangerous precedent, but to intercept it risked provoking a serious incident or even war over a matter in which the United States was clearly uninterested. Foreign Secretary Anthony Eden explained the dangers to the War Cabinet on 8 February 1941 when he stated, "It is essential that, if we become involved in war with Japan, it should be as a result of clear aggression by Japan, and it would be disastrous from the point of view of American sympathy and assistance if it could be represented that we had provoked war on such an issue as the searching of the *Asaka Maru.*"[19] This cautious line was judged to be realistic, particularly in the light of advice from Roosevelt not to make an issue out of this case, and the ship was allowed to arrive and depart unhindered.

The need not to provoke war meant that the only weapon Britain could safely use was propaganda, intended to show Japan that Britain was prepared to fight and to counteract Japanese claims to the native peoples of Southeast Asia that Britain was in decline.[20] Apart from broadcasting an image of apparent readiness, Britain could only hope that the United States would act as a deterrent. Churchill on 15 February wrote to Roosevelt, "Everything that you can do to inspire the Japanese with fear of a double war may avert the danger. If however they come in against us and we are alone, the grave consequences cannot easily be overstated."[21] Britain could not, however, afford to press the Americans too hard, and when Admiral Roger M. Bellairs, the head of the British delegation to the Anglo-American staff talks in Washington, angered his hosts by using the crisis to press the importance of Singapore in Pacific strategy, Churchill reprimanded the Navy Chief of Staff, Admiral Sir Dudley Pound, and wrote, in a sentence that summed up Britain's position, "The first thing is to get the United States into the war; we can then settle how to fight it afterwards."[22]

[19] PRO CAB66/15 WP(41)28, A. Eden Memorandum, "The 'Asaka Maru'," 8 February 1941.

[20] PRO CAB96/3 FE(41)38, Report of Ad-Hoc Sub-Committee on Propaganda, 11 Feb. 1941.

[21] PRO FO371/27887 F1086/17/23, Former Naval Person (Churchill) to Roosevelt, 15 Feb. 1941. Quoted in S. O. Agbi, "The Pacific War Controversy in Britain: Sir Robert Craigie versus The Foreign Office," *Modern Asian Studies,* No. 17/3 (1983), p. 512.

[22] PRO ADM116/4877, W. Churchill to Admiral D. Pound, 17 February 1941. Quoted in J. R. Leutze, *Bargaining for Supremacy. Anglo-American Naval Co-operation 1937–1941* (Univ. of North Carolina Press, Chapel Hill, N.C., 1977), p. 241.

The crisis mysteriously died away as rapidly as it had appeared,[23] but it had an important effect on the United States, which was now more co-operative about introducing stricter restraints on Japan, although this was also linked to the successful conclusion of the staff talks and the passing of Lend-Lease. By the spring of 1941, a rough framework for co-operation over economic sanctions had been constructed, and this laid the grounds for a concerted effort to reduce Japan's ability to come in on Germany's side and even, as Eden noted in a War Cabinet memorandum, to "bring home to an increasing number of Japanese the solid advantages to be gained by renewing Japan's former relations with us and re-nouncing her connexion with the Axis."[24] It was soon clear that this policy began to cause Japan great discomfort and led not only to the Hull-Nomura talks in Washington, but also to Japanese pressure in London in May to revitalize the issue of an economic deal with Britain. Japan's hope was that, by agreeing to sign a Payments Agreement and promising to use their reserves of sterling solely to finance the purchase of imports from the British Empire rather than selling them on the open market, they would be able to persuade Britain to enter into trade talks that would lead to a lessening of economic restrictions. To the Japanese Ambassador in London, Mamoru Shigemitsu, this was the last chance for an improvement in Anglo-Japanese relations, but he was soon dis-abused of any false hopes when Britain rejected the agreement on the grounds of Japan's continued belligerency. In reality, the British decision was due to the Far Eastern Committee concluding that "any agreement with the Japanese at the present juncture would be likely to be misun-derstood both in China and the United States of America and would arouse suspicions (however groundless) that H.M. Government were embarking on a policy of appeasement vis-à-vis Japan."[25]

The growing desperation in Japan due to the damage caused by West-ern sanctions led Sir Robert Craigie to become apprehensive, and he warned the Foreign Office that they could lead to a "serious dispute at a crucial juncture."[26] He advised that the motives for British policy ought

[23]The British assumed that the Japanese had suddenly got cold feet, and interpreted the news that reached them through the BJ source on 15 February that Matsuoka intended to visit Rome and Berlin as a means of mollifying Axis feeling. See PRO PREM 3 252/6A, W. Churchill to Sir A. Cadogan, 16 February 1941.

[24]PRO CAB66/17 WP(41)155 A. Eden Memorandum "Nature and Extent of Our Eco-nomic Restrictions," 7 July 1941.

[25]PRO CAB96/2 FE(41) 16th Meeting, 8 May 1941. For Shigemitsu's perspective see A. Best, "Shigemitsu Mamoru as Ambassador to Great Britain 1938–1941," *International Studies,* 1990/2 (LSE, London, 1990).

[26]PRO FO371/27833 F4376/1732/61, Sir R. Craigie to A. Eden, 23 May 1941.

to be explained to Japan, that it had to be made clear what Japan could expect should further adventures occur, and that Japan could encourage British flexibility by agreeing to stop reexports to Germany. He concluded, "The Japanese realisation that such machinery (for reprisals) had been perfected, combined with the knowledge that we were at present using our powers with discretion and moderation would in itself constitute one of the best deterrents against unwise or hasty action by Japan in South East Asia."[27] Craigie's fears did not impress the Far Eastern Committee, which was convinced that Japanese concern only showed that the economic restrictions were working and that therefore there was no need for the noose to be loosened. This conviction also influenced the decision not to take a more lenient line with Japan even after the Trans-Siberian Railway had been closed due to Germany's attack on the Soviet Union.[28] The Committee did, however, still recognize the dangers of going too far, and Eden reported to the War Cabinet that "constant care and attention is being exercised . . . not to push restrictions to the point of provoking Japan to war either by reducing too drastically and suddenly supplies, e.g. of oil, considered vital by the Japanese Government or by striking too brusquely at Japanese enterprises within British territory."[29]

This caution was evident in Britain's initial response to intelligence reports in early July that Japan was planning to extend its control of Indochina, which was to recommend only a slight turning of the screw.[30] This policy was, however, swept aside when it was learned that America intended to freeze Japanese assets and put virtually all trade under license, despite the recognition that such a severe stance could lead to a showdown in the Pacific. Eden warned his War Cabinet colleagues of "the dangers inherent in our lagging behind the United States Government in dealing with Japan, *a fortiori* in our attempting to dissuade them from firm action. The risk of creating another Simon-Stimson incident* and

[27] PRO CAB96/3 FE(41)104, Joint Secretaries Note, 11 June 1941 (Based on Sir R. Craigie to A. Eden 30 April 1941).

[28] PRO CAB66/17 WP(41)155, A. Eden Memorandum, "Nature and Extent of Our Economic Restrictions," 7 July 1941.

[29] PRO CAB96/4 FE(41)126, Ministry of Economic Warfare Memorandum, 25 June 1941.

[30] This cautious attitude also applied to the contingency plans for action in case of a Japanese attack on the Soviet Union. For more detail, see P. Lowe, "The Soviet Union in Britain's Far Eastern Policy," *International Studies,* 1981/1 (LSE, London, 1981).

* Refers to the lack of close coordination between Foreign Secretary John Simon in London and Secretary of State Henry L. Stimson in Washington during the Japanese invasion of Manchuria in 1931–32. The United States and Britain failed to act together to restrain Japan.

of seriously weakening the ties between us and America is real."[31] Once the American line was accepted Britain was sidelined as the final act was played out; warnings from Craigie that Britain must take its place in the Hull-Nomura talks to avoid their breakdown were ignored on the usual grounds that Britain could not afford to tell the Americans their business. Any British concerns were eased by the likelihood that, should war occur, America would be involved and that Japan would anyway not be foolish enough to resist the overpowering combination ranged against her. This complacency rested on a gross underestimation of Japan's martial abilities, a sentiment that permeated Churchill's memoranda on the naval reinforcements to Singapore and a reference by Eden to Japan as "probably over-valued,"[32] and a failure to see that in reality the West's harsh stance rested on foundations of sand, as sanctions were not backed up by a military deterrent. The power that America and Britain had in the Pacific could only be measured in potential.

It is surely only too understandable that Britain should have viewed events in the Pacific from 1939 to 1941 largely through the perspective of how they affected the life or death struggle with Germany. What may seem surprising or, as some critics would have it, misguided, is that Britain, while fighting for its very existence, failed to prevent the emergence of a conflict in the East. This view only holds water if the Pacific is treated as a discrete compartment, which it never was. Events in the Pacific were frequently the result of European influences or were interpreted by how they affected the European situation. From the first, Britain's range of alternatives was cut down due to the existence of the United States both as a Pacific and an Atlantic power; Britain could not appease Japan without its affecting American attitudes to the European situation. The result was that Britain could only attempt a very limited policy of conciliation towards Japan that did little to stem the tide that drove Japan towards the Axis powers. This policy ended in the autumn of 1940 due to the perception that Japan had become part and parcel of the Axis camp, cooperating in the economic and naval spheres with Germany and with the ever-present threat that it could launch a devastating assault in Southeast Asia in concert with renewed German offensives in Europe. It was recognized in both London and Washington that the Japanese threat had to be countered and its link with Germany broken

---

[31] PRO CAB66/17 WP(41)172, A. Eden Memorandum, "Japanese Plans in Indo-China," 20 July 1941. Also quoted in C. Thorne, *Allies of a Kind,* p. 72.

[32] For Churchill's views see PRO PREM 3 163/3; for Eden see CAB120/517, A. Eden to W. Churchill, 12 Sept. 1941.

and that this could be achieved through a policy of Anglo-American eco-nomic restrictions that always carried with it the danger that if applied too vigorously it could go beyond its remit and challenge Japan's very ex-istence as a state.[33] The British had, however, little means to influence the Americans once the latter had entered the driving seat and pushed for an increasingly tough line with Japan, due to the desperate need to drag the United States into the European war; this forced London to co-operate with Washington in the Pacific even if this might lead to war. In the end, the advantages to be gained from having America as a full ally outweighed the risks entailed from having both Germany and Japan as enemies. The reaction in the upper echelons of the British government to news of the attack on Pearl Harbor showed that even at this late stage East Asia was primarily seen as important in relation to its effect on the war against Germany. Eden recorded in his memoirs that when he heard the news of Pearl Harbor his thoughts were of American entry into the war: "I could not conceal my relief and did not have to try to. I felt that whatever happened now, it was merely a matter of time."[34]

[33] For the American view of how Japan was linked to the conflict in Europe and for the rationale behind its sanctions policy, see C. Hosoya, "Miscalculations in Deterrent Policy: Japanese–US Relations 1938–1941," *Journal of Peace Research* 1968, and A. Ben-Zvi, *The Illusion of Deterrence. The Roosevelt Presidency and the Origins of the Pacific War* (Westview Press, Boulder, Colorado, 1987).

[34] Lord Avon, *The Reckoning* (Cassell & Co., London, 1965), pp. 285–86.

KEN'ICHI GOTŌ

The Indonesian Perspective

How did other Asians feel about Japanese imperialism and about its pan-Asianist rhetoric in the late 1930s and the early 1940s? Here is a study of one prominent Indonesian leader, written by a Japanese authority on mod-ern Indonesian history. Mohammad Hatta, the subject of the study, was a nationalist, like so many of his contemporaries, but he was far more at-tracted to Western ideas of democracy and freedom than to Japanese slo-gans. Not every Asian leader would have agreed, but even pro-Japanese na-tionalists were alienated by Japanese rule in the wake of Pearl Harbor. In

Ken'ichi Gotō, *"Return to Asia": Japanese-Indonesian Relations, 1930s–1942* (Tokyo: Ryūkei Shosha, 1997), 300–12.

the light of Hatta's views, how justified was Japan's claim for leadership in Asia? To the extent that his ideas were widely shared in Indonesia and elsewhere in Southeast Asia, what problems or opportunities would they have presented to the United States?

In the wake of the breakup of the Indonesian Nationalist Party in April 1931, Mohammad Hatta (1902–80) parted company with Sukarno and, along with Sutan Sjahrir, became co-leader of the new Indonesian National Education Association. Hatta published numerous essays on politics and economics in the journal of this association, *Daulat Rakjat* (The People's Sovereignty), earning a reputation as a sharp-witted polemicist. In contrast to his comrade Sjahrir's relative lack of discussion of Asia in general and of "the Japan question" in particular (apart from a number of brief, negative comments), Hatta approached the process of Japan's development from the Meiji era onward with the characteristic zeal of a student of economics, also devoting careful attention to Japan's contemporary foreign policy. Self-assured in his understanding of Western modernity, he was, like a number of his peers, also comfortable with Sun Yat-sen's * Asianist assertion that "if the people of Asia truly unite, Asia's own progress is possible."

In his article, "Japanese Imperialism in China," published immediately after the Manchurian Incident, Hatta criticized the actions of the Japanese military as a violation of the League of Nations Charter. He objectively argued that Japan's actions in Manchuria were rooted in that region's great attractiveness to Japan as a late industrializer — as a source of natural resources, as a commercial market for Japanese goods, and as a solution to Japan's population problem — and that Japan had undertaken these actions in light of both the wavering of the Western Powers in the wake of the Great Depression and the Soviet Union's absorption with its own internal economic development. Having thus condemned the Manchurian Incident as rooted in the particular disposition of "Modern Japan," Hatta then turned his fire toward the League of Nations (which was also criticizing Japan), attacking the League itself as a collection of imperialists and arguing that "the Western Powers fear that if they supply China with weapons, those weapons will at some point be

---

*Sun Yat-sen (1866–1925) is known as "the father of modern China" because of his role in the overthrow of the Qing (Ch'ing) dynasty in 1911 and in the founding of the Nationalist Party. He often spoke of the need to unite Asians against Western imperialism, although he never accepted the Japanese idea of pan-Asianism which placed Japan as the leader of an Asian coalition.

pointed at them. Therefore, China will have to oppose Japan through her own moral power."[1]

Hatta's Visit to Japan and His Views on Asianism

Hatta was aware that self-interested power politics was the logic that permeated international politics. One year after publishing the above essay, in April 1933, Hatta chose to visit Japan, the object of his interest, arriving there just after Japan's withdrawal from the League of Nations and the founding convention of the Greater Asia Association. . . . Held in the Tokyo Convention Hall, the convention had been attended by over one hundred influential members of political, military, and opinion circles, and had caused a great stir both within the country and abroad. It was in this context that Hatta received an enthusiastic welcome from the Greater Asia Association's leader, Yasaburō Shimonaka, and others as "The Gandhi of the Netherlands East Indies." Their conversation with Hatta was subsequently published in the second issue of the Association's journal, *Dai Ajia Shugi* (Greater Asianism), under the title "Indonesia's Nationalist Movement."

Hatta had traveled to Japan in the company of his uncle Ayub Rais, general manager of the well-known *pribumi* (native Indonesian) firm Djohan Djohor, and according to his own statements, which had been reported at the time, Hatta had not come to Japan for political reasons. Rather, he maintained that he had come purely "to observe the culture and industry of the great Japanese nation," as well as to promote discussions about "direct trade between Japan and Indonesia" [i.e., rather than via the Dutch or *peranakan* (Indonesian-born) Chinese —*Author*] within the business community.[2] Indeed, in his later memoirs, Hatta writes that his motivation for visiting Japan was as a "consultant" for his uncle Rais, who had come to Japan to have business talks with Japanese trading companies. He adds, however, that he was also motivated by discussions with his colleagues in the Indonesian National Education Association who argued that "considering the recent rise of fascism and militarism there, it would be worthwhile to see Japan's activities firsthand."[3] . . .

As has already been noted, March 1933 was a time in which Japan witnessed slogans such as "Anti–Anglo-Americanism" and "Asia for the

---

[1] Mohammad Hatta, *Kumpulan Karangan* (Jakarta: Penerbitan Balai Buku Indonesia, 1953), pp. 18–23.
[2] *Dai Ajia Shugi* (May 1933), p. 64.
[3] Mohammad Hatta, *Memoirs* (Jakarta: Tintamas, 1979), p. 293.

Asians!" and which saw, both at the government level and in private circles, the rise of an argument for "the abandonment of the Versailles-Washington system" and calls for "a return to Asia." Whatever Hatta's own intentions and aims may have been, in the context of this atmosphere of "Asianism" into which he was thrust, Hatta's visit itself was interpreted politically, and the Japanese made frequent attempts to make political capital out of it.[4]

On his way to Japan, Hatta had in fact already witnessed Western colonial apprehensions about Japan first-hand, when he was questioned about his trip by English police authorities in Singapore. Upon his arrival in Kōbe harbor, Hatta was mobbed by Japanese reporters who bombarded him with questions about his reasons for coming to Japan, the situation with the Indonesian people, and the recent cabinet reforms in the Netherlands. . . .

Despite his cautious approach, however, Hatta was widely reported as saying at a news conference that "The League of Nations is a European affair—we must find life in Greater Asianism."[5] While encouraging those on the Japanese side, this also moved Hatta to be all the more careful. After arriving in Kōbe, Hatta followed the same itinerary as Rais, touring factories and schools specializing in cotton textiles in the Osaka and Tokyo regions, with enough time remaining to enjoy springtime Japan with trips to tourist destinations such as Nikkō and Hakone. In his memoirs, Hatta goes into detail about his experiences at this time. His writings reveal the perspective one might expect of a student of economics and are of great interest in understanding his views on Japan.

For example, when he toured a certain industrial college, Hatta watched as students took apart an American-made Ford automobile, then carefully put it back together again. Hatta comments here that the key to Japan's success in catching up with the West was its skill at "first

---

[4]For example, the *Osaka Asahi Shinbun* of April 15, 1933, carried an article welcoming the trend that said: "Since the Manchurian Incident, Indonesian admiration of Japan has become very warm. There were some from among the native troops that shook the world by their anti-Dutch uprising of the Dutch warship *Seven Provincien,* who visited the Japanese Consulate-General asking that they be allowed to work as members of the Japanese military. In this atmosphere, Asian leader Hatta is now to visit Japan, in the name of commercial inspection. Their slogan is to learn from Japan and develop the native economy through their own efforts." Arifin, representative of the Indonesian Communist Party to the 13th Comintern executive committee plenary meeting in Moscow, December 1933, argued that the purpose of Hatta's visit to Japan was not academic inspection but to "get in touch with Japan's imperialists and fascists." Tō-A Kenkyūjo, eds., *Ran-in ni okeru Kominterun no Katsudō* [Activities of the Comintern in the Netherlands East Indies] (August 1941), p. 125.

[5]*Dai Ajia Shugi* (May 1933), p. 64.

copying something, and then improving on it."[6] When touring modern enterprises and factories in different areas, Hatta was inevitably first served refreshments and subjected to lengthy sessions of polite conversation, a practice which provoked a frustration at the Japanese commercial custom of taking ages to get to the point. In another statement, Hatta attributes the success of Japan's fiber industry in surpassing the West not only to the importation of technology (imitation), but also to such cultural factors as Japanese diligence and Japanese workers' fondness for cleanliness (as evidenced in their habit of daily bathing), which led them to maintain a spotless workplace.[7]

As episodes such as this reveal, Hatta identified Japan's success at copying the West as the fundamental reason for its modernization. It seems he gave only secondary attention to the subjective, internal factors that made Japanese importation of Western technology possible. Hatta showed little inclination to praise Japan as Asia's only country to succeed by combining "Western technological civilization and Asian spiritual culture." Rather, Hatta's view of Japan is strongly tied to his assessment of Japan as "a late-developing nation" in his 1932 essay, along with his later statement in an essay written upon his return from Japan that "[the Japanese] people do not understand their government's policies." Hatta was familiar with European society, and felt a deep affinity with its democracy; these comments seem to reflect a sense that while Japan may have succeeded in its program of "rich country, strong military" (*fukoku kyōhei*), it had yet to attain a mature, Western-type civilian society. Indeed, Indonesian intellectuals who had received an elitist European education in the 1930s were more likely to see Japan as "a bad version of Europe" than to see Japan as "a first-class Asian country" that might represent a model for Indonesia's own modernization.

The year of Hatta's visit to Japan, 1933, was also a time in which the first Indonesian students were coming to Japan to study abroad. One of them was Mahjuddin Gaus, a student at Jikei Medical College. He, along with Madjid Usman, a student at Meiji University, were of the same Minangkabau (West Sumatra) ethnic group as Hatta. They frequently visited their well-known elder kinsman when he was in Tokyo, and also accompanied him on his trip to Nikkō.

During one of their times together, Gaus asked Hatta his opinion of Japan's policies in Asia. Hatta replied: "In the area of politics, we need to be wary. Japan is a strong country economically. Politics is always

---

[6] Hatta, *Memoirs,* p. 301.
[7] Ibid., pp. 296, 297–98.

connected to economics, and it is difficult to separate the two. We should develop contacts with more liberal and progressive, idealistic groups. No country offers aid without some motive of its own. We have to rely on our belief in self-help and self-reliance."[8] To Gaus, who felt a strong affinity with Japan's "Pan-Asianism," and who was at the time himself participating as an associate in the Greater Asia Association, it may have been a disappointment to hear these measured, objective words from Hatta.[9]

In response to another of Gaus's questions, on "the issue of development in New Guinea and Japan's serious population problem," Hatta had this to say: "New Guinea is a huge, undeveloped area. It is rich in mineral resources and lumber resources, both waiting to be developed. The Netherlands lacks the developmental capital, and our own power is still insufficient. As far as lumber development is concerned, Japanese involvement is a blessing. Japan has both capital and technology. If New Guinea is not developed, it will never amount to anything."[10] The "New Guinea question," which included the issue of purchasing, was often raised within the context of discussions on Japan's possible move southward in the mid-1930s. Leaving aside the issue of whether Hatta approved of Japan's intentions or not, his statement seems to demonstrate a desire that the government of the Netherlands East Indies should open to Japan's economy.

After a brief but stimulating month in Japan, Hatta returned home. Immediately afterward, he discussed his Japan experience and appealed to Indonesian society in an essay entitled, "Does Japan Want a 'Return to Asia'?"

In the eyes of Ahmad Subardjo — a nationalist of the same generation as Hatta who came to Japan in the autumn of 1935 — Japan's 1933 withdrawal from the League of Nations and its open advocacy of a "return to Asia" were a great turning point in Japan's foreign policy. Subardjo further characterized Japan's victory in the Russo-Japanese War as "the turning point in the history of Asia." . . . It is interesting to note that Hatta did not share Subardjo's positive assessment of Japan as a catalyst for political and psychological change in Asia, nor was he inclined to emphasize any shared heritage between Japan and other Asian nations. Never-

---

[8]Ken'ichi Gotō, "Senzenki Indoneshia ryūgakusei no Nihonkan" (Prewar Indonesian Students' Views of Japan — Concerning Mahjuddin Gaus's *Memoirs*), *Shakai Kagaku Tokyu*, vol. 28, no. 2 (February 1982), p. 200.

[9]As an episode illustrating Gaus's inclination toward Asianism, in his *Memoirs*, Gaus describes in detail the circumstances when Hatta asked him if he could have a meeting with Behari Bose. See Chapter 14: *Mohammad Hatta and Indonesian Students in Japan.*

[10]Ken'ichi Gotō, "Senzenki Indoneshia ryūgakusei," p. 200.

theless, the fact that Hatta chose to write an essay on the "return to Asia" fever upon his return to Java indicates, at the very least, a strong interest in the subject.

How did Hatta himself interpret the Japanese "return to Asia" movement, and how did he feel Indonesians should best respond to it? Hatta first argued that Japan's growing interest in Asia was a direct consequence of Japan's reaction against the League of Nations in the wake of the Manchurian problem. From a more historical standpoint, however, Hatta maintained that Japan's growing concern with Asia could be attributed to a sequence of "unfortunate encounters" with the Western powers dating back to the tumultuous end of the Edo period (ca. 1853–68). Namely, the various unequal treaties that the Powers had forced Japan to sign "enveloped the Japanese in a feeling of inferiority. This feeling was strengthened further when Japanese people compared themselves to whites. It was precisely this feeling of inferiority that became the psychological basis for Japanese policy from then on. And this feeling also gave rise to a desire to attain the same status as Europeans."[11]

Citing "the desire to overcome this feeling of inferiority" as the motivating force behind Japan's modernization, Hatta went on to state that "Japan has continued to imitate the Western races. It has gone so far as to imitate Western imperialism in its dealings with the Asian races. . . . This desire to be seen as racially equal to the West, and the resultant willingness to behave just as they do — this is the psychological basis for Japan's mistaken policies. Japan's recent belated realization of this error has come too late."[12]

Outlining the course of Japan's abandonment of Asia for Europe and citing Japan's experience over the previous half century as the reason for its return to Asia, Hatta worked toward his conclusion. Having pursued Western-followerism to the point of becoming "a Far Eastern watchman for the Western Powers" and yet still failing to attain recognition of equal status with the West, Japan was finally "beginning to have doubts about being treated as a mere tool of the West. Now the feeling of inferiority toward the West, so long the driving force behind Japanese policy, has disappeared. In its place Japan has discovered its 'own personal values.' At the same time, the unrequited yearning for the West has been replaced by the flames of hatred; a malice toward the West has taken shape in the hearts of the Japanese. This is precisely the reason that Japan now seeks to return to Asia once again."[13]

[11] Hatta, *Kumpulan,* p. 25.
[12] Ibid., p. 27.
[13] Ibid.

In this way, Hatta perceptively analyzed the "return to Asia" phenomenon of early 1930s Japan in light of Japan's setbacks in her attempts to leave Asia and join the West. . . . At the same time, Hatta — himself a member of one of Asia's oppressed peoples — rejected Japan's desire to "return to Asia" as a result of rejection by the West as "coming too late." In particular, in its installation of a puppet government in Manchuria, Japan exhibited the "go in before others, feast more heartily than others" *modus operandi* of imperialism. For this reason, "once Japan had entered the imperialist fray in order to satisfy its desire to be equal with the West, its desire to feast upon China all by itself could no longer be suppressed."[14]

Hatta thus took an extremely critical view of the "Asianism" that Japan extolled, after contrasting it to the reality of Japan's policies in Asia. Given that his ultimate goal was independence and that much of Asia remained colonized or semi-colonized, however, Hatta was not necessarily against the idea of "the promotion of the Asian spirit, the encouragement of the Pan-Asian movement, and the desire to restore Asia to Asian hands" itself. In fact, whereas Sun Yat-sen had termed Japan's "Greater Asianism" a "friendly warning" in light of Japan's naked outward expansionism, Hatta attempted to take a more positive view. To Hatta, the problem that needed to be considered was the connection between the reality of the "Asianism" that Japan was extolling and attempting to realize, and the ideal of "Asianism" as a positive concept for Asian solidarity. The gap between what Japan was saying and what it was doing in its policies toward China represented the litmus test for Japan's Asianism in general. In order to prove that Japan's proclamation of "Asia for the Asians" was really anything more than a hollow slogan, Hatta claimed that two essential conditions had to be met. The first was the realization of a permanent peace between Japan and China, and the second was the confirmation of complete equality among all the peoples of Asia.[15]

But Hatta was skeptical about the possibility that Japan's Asianism could ever succeed in developing into a full-fledged movement. He astutely ascertained that "[Japan's Asianism] is being tainted by the influence of Japanese fascism, which dreams of Japan becoming Asia's leader. This fascist movement is not prominent as yet, but it could eventually push Japan toward the acquisition of new colonies in Asia. What is more, Japanese people do not understand the policies of their own government."[16]

[14] Ibid.
[15] Ibid., p. 28.
[16] Ibid.

Thus, at an extremely early juncture, Hatta pointed out the contradictions inherent in Japan's conception of Asianism, in particular, its potential as a premise for expansionism. How then should Indonesians confront Japan and its desire for a "return to Asia"? In the course of his essay, Hatta drew on the examples of contemporary China (which was at that time moving closer toward Britain) and of Turkey during World War I — where nationalists had made overtures to Germany — to illustrate his point that relying on foreign countries for assistance is no way to achieve total independence. These examples helped to illustrate his main point, that Indonesians must take a steadfast attitude in the face of Japan's alluring overtures. Hatta's argument may be summarized in his statement that, "if we make plain our intentions for independence, this might well be enough to cool the greedy ambitions of Japan's fascists who would hope to sink their teeth into Indonesia."[17] With this, Hatta both confirmed Japan's Asianism as nothing more than a fascist ploy and flatly rejected Japan's call for a "return to Asia."

Views of the Pacific War

Hatta's desire to maintain a distance from political issues while in Japan, in spite of, or perhaps because of, the great expectations of his Japanese hosts, has already been noted. Hatta's cautious attitude is also referred to in a number of contemporary Japanese documents. For example, Tenkai Takei, who visited Hatta when he was staying at the Imperial Hotel, writes that Hatta "said absolutely nothing about anything concerning the nationalist movement or political issues. He said only that he had come with his uncle and was just a simple tourist in Japan."[18]

Hatta was thus politically cautious while in Japan, but nine months after his return home in February 1934 he was arrested by the Netherlands East Indies government along with fellow Indonesian National Education Association colleagues Sutan Sjahrir, Bondan, and others and sent first, along with Sjahrir, to the Digul region of West New Guinea (now Irian Jaya). He was later forced to live in exile on the remote island of Bandaneira. A number of Japanese were among those who felt at the time that one of the reasons for Hatta's exile was his "political contact" with Japan,[19] but it should probably be understood as part of a general

---

[17] Ibid.

[18] Jūrō Takei, *Indoneshian* [Indonesian] (Tokyo: Okakura Shobō, 1941), p. 261. On Takei, see Chapter 4.

[19] Takei's observation on Hatta's arrest upon his return home was that "it was suspected that his visit to Japan had political purposes. The Netherlands East Indies government

government crackdown on the nationalist movement. Sukarno, who had been conducting a rigorous debate with Hatta over the best way to carry on the nationalist movement, was himself arrested and sent into exile at Ende on the island of Flores at almost the same time.

It was in 1936 that Hatta was moved, along with Sjahrir, to exile on Bandaneira island. There they joined other nationalists already imprisoned, including Tjipto Mangunkusumo and Iwa Kusuma Sumantri. Iwa wrote in his memoirs that "living in exile, it is possible to hone one's intellect and spirit. One can think more calmly and deeply about things." [20] Hatta was to share a life of exile on Bandaneira with his colleague Sjahrir, seven years his junior, until after the outbreak of the Pacific War.

For Hatta and Sjahrir, both of whom possessed a strong faith in Western democracy, news of the tectonic shifts occurring in both Europe and Asia during the late 1930s — which did not fail to reach even their remote island in the Banda Sea — was a source of great concern. Based on personal observation, Hatta had judged Japan's Asianism to be a variety of fascism and was strongly critical of its expansion. Now, as he witnessed Japan's alliance with the "enemies of democracy" Germany and Italy (though it must be remembered that under the special conditions of exile, information was manipulated by the Dutch authorities), Hatta believed that fascism was challenging democracy on a worldwide scale.

Within this context, Hatta anxiously viewed the beginning of Japan's sustained military action in China as a step toward a future grab at Indonesia itself. At the same time, he began to carefully reconsider the attitude the nationalist movement ought to take vis-à-vis the Netherlands East Indies government. Sjahrir thus describes Hatta's mixed emotions at the time:

> [Despite Hatta's intense criticism of the Netherlands East Indies government,] he was still a Netherlander in the sense that he did not really regard that government as a foreign and enemy element, but considered it in the same way that, for example, a left-wing socialist opponent considers the Netherlands government in Holland. [21]

suspected him of being communist and maintained that his visit to Japan was to meet Japanese communists. But his past career makes it clear that he is not a communist." Jūrō Takei, *Indoneshian*, p. 262. Tatsuji Kubo also argues that Hatta was arrested because he visited Japan to ask Japan and Japanese comrades to aid Indonesian independence. Tatsuji Kubo, "Indonesia Minzoku Undō" [Nationalist movement in Indonesia], *Ranryō Indo Sōsho (jo)* [Series on the Netherlands East Indies (1)] (Tokyo: Aikoku Shinbunsha, 1940), p. 172.

[20] Iwa Kusuma Sumantri (translated by Ken'ichi Gotō), *Indoneshia Minzokushugi no Genryū: Iwa Kusuma Sumantri-den* [Origin of the Indonesian nationalism: An autobiography of Iwa Kusuma Sumantri] (Tokyo: Waseda University Press, 1975), p. 89.

[21] Sutan Sjahrir (translated by Charles Wolf, Jr.), *Out of Exile* (New York: John Day, 1949), p. 201.

Of course, this statement might be equally revealing of Sjahrir's own feelings towards the Netherlands (and Europe). And this type of thinking — that cooperation might be possible between the ruler, the Netherlands, and the ruled, Indonesia, through the medium of democracy as a common value — was in that sense in line with the notion of association put forward by the Dutch "Ethical Policy" supporters of the early 20th century. Moreover, it also represents a step closer to the assertion that in order to protect democracy from the spectre of Japanese fascism, it is necessary to keep a lid on resistance against the Dutch government until the period of crisis has passed and fascism has been toppled. . . .

. . . Both Sjahrir and Hatta were convinced that both the war in Europe that began in September 1939 and the Pacific War that began in December 1941 represented a worldwide struggle between democracy and fascist ideology.[22] Particularly after the Dutch home government went into exile in London in May 1940, the colonial government began to view Japan's southward advance as a real threat. It was at this juncture that it began to take precautions against the possibility that Japan might take advantage of the influence that the exiled nationalist leaders still wielded from their cells. In order to avoid this, the colonial authorities hoped to bring Hatta and the others — who were proclaiming their support of, and loyalty to, "democracy" — into their camp.[23] According to Sjahrir, the situation was such that "by the end of the year, our influence had [be]come so strong on the little island that the civil officials even came to seek our advice on various problems. . . . We were no longer treated as exiles by the authorities."[24] In the beginning of February 1942, it was thus allowed that Hatta and Sjahrir be brought back to Sukabumi, West Java. . . .

Hatta had understood the dangerous symptoms of the "return to Asia" fever that was sweeping Japan during his visit there in 1933. Now, eight and a half years later, Hatta asserted that "all who know the dynamism of Japanese imperialism have believed from long before that war in the Pacific would be the result. . . . And ever since Japan joined the Tripartite Alliance, we have been convinced that Japan desired this."[25] He

[22] *See* "The War of Ideology," in Hatta, *Kumpulan.*

[23] Nationalists in exile also were aware of it. Iwa Kusuma Sumantri stated, "the Netherlands was afraid that we would oppose them by becoming Japan's tool. That is why we were dragged out of Bandaneira and moved around from place to place." (Iwa Kusuma Sumantri, *Indoneshia Minzokushugi,* p. 89.) On the other hand, Sjahrir wrote that "We were told we had been taken from Banda because the government felt responsible for our lives and safety, and we would surely have been killed by the Japanese if we had remained. . . . removal from Banda remained a riddle." Sjahrir, *Out of Exile,* p. 231.

[24] Sjahrir, *Out of Exile,* pp. 221–23.

[25] Hatta, *Kumpulan,* p. 141.

thus held that war in the Pacific had been the ultimate aim of Japan's foreign policy in the late 1930s, and perceived it as one link in the expansion of imperialism. Hatta paid no heed to Japan's slogan at the time of "liberation of the peoples of Asia," which was drawing the attention of many Indonesians and must have reached his own ears as well. Rather, he asserted that Japan's aim was "to invade Indonesia and place eastern and southern Asia under it."[26] For Hatta, who believed in the democratic ideals of the colonial ruler Holland, this war was not one of "Asia versus Europe," nor one of "Asian imperialism versus European imperialism." It was rather to be understood in the framework of a showdown between "fascism and democracy." . . .

Thus, Hatta wrote, "as long as the menace of Japanese imperialism exists, there is no hope of national self-determination."[27] What type of response to Japan, then, would best serve the interests of Indonesian nationalism? Unlike the situation of eight years before, the crush of events made it clear that soon enough "like it or not, Indonesia will be embroiled in a Pacific War."[28] Hatta was aware of the urgency with which a decision had to be reached.

As war approached, beginning with the disappointment over the contents of the Pacific Charter, a group within the Indonesian nationalist movement had come to believe that cooperation with Japan was one way of achieving independence. Known as the "pro-Japanese faction," this group within the Parindra [Greater Indonesian Party] momentarily faded from view after the suspiciously sudden death of its leader Mohammad Husri Thamrin. . . . But its pro-Japanese policy line was maintained under the subsequent leadership of Sukardjo Wirjopranoto and others. And as Sjahrir repeatedly pointed out with some irritation, the Indonesian people continued to exhibit a deep-rooted pro-Japanese sentiment.[29]

Fervently aware of these developments, Hatta called for the people to free themselves from the grip of such illogical fantasies as the "Joyoboyo legend," in which it was prophesied that a race of yellow-skinned liberators would come from the north. These sorts of fantasies, he argued, would forever entrap Indonesians in misfortune. And he harshly denounced those nationalists who favored cooperating with Japan and thus relying on the strength of others. . . . He argued that hope for assistance from "their enemy's enemy," even if it was motivated by patriotism,

[26] Ibid., p. 142.
[27] Ibid., p. 144.
[28] Ibid., p. 142.
[29] Sjahrir, *Out of Exile*, pp. 155, 186–87.

would in the end only invite "misfortunes many times worse than those of today."[30] With these two examples as contrast, Hatta then praised [India's Jawaharlal] Nehru, writing that "he clearly opposes English imperialism. Yet he does not despise English people; in fact he admires them. And he does not request assistance from the Nazis or fascists, nor would he accept it from them."[31] If we exchange the Netherlands for England, and Hatta for Nehru, we have precisely the basic pattern of thinking of the democratic-minded Hatta.

In any case, with "fascism at our doorstep,"[32] Hatta argued, "Indonesians cannot simply remain passive onlookers in the Pacific War. . . . For those Indonesians who love their fatherland and believe in democracy, there is no alternative but to oppose Japanese imperialism."[33] He declared that "we must fight alongside the Western democracies." Hatta's argument in this 1941 essay thus logically led to the conclusion that "it is better to die with our principles than to live in shame."[34]

[30] Hatta, *Kumpulan,* p. 142.
[31] Ibid., p. 143.
[32] Ibid., p. 145.
[33] Ibid., p. 144.
[34] Ibid., p. 145.

BERND MARTIN

The German Perspective

Japan and Germany were allies, yet they never coordinated their strategies the way the United States and Britain did. Still, Germany was never absent from the prelude to Pearl Harbor, as this study of German-Japanese relations by a leading German historian demonstrates. The author notes a lack of cooperation between Germany and Japan despite their 1940 alliance. Do you think American fears of close German-Japanese ties were exaggerated?

Bernd Martin, *Japan and Germany in the Modern World* (Providence, R.I.: Berghahn Books, 1995), 249–59, 262–64.

Hitler's basic plan for Operation Barbarossa, dated 18 December 1940, did not include a single word about Germany's strongest ally, Japan.[1] By contrast, Germany's European partners were assigned roles in the coming offensive against the Soviet Union. Hitler believed the annexation of territory in the East should be carried out exclusively by the German "master race." Trapped in traditional concepts of a contained land war, the German General Staff also omitted Japan from their plans. Due to his ideological prejudices Hitler could not comprehend the global aspects of prosecuting a war in a coalition, and the highest ranking officers of the army were not open to this possibility due to their own one-sided expertise. Only the relatively small German navy, always on the lookout for strong comrades-in-arms at sea, regarded the alliance with Japan positively.

Japan was referred to in Hitler's directives to the *Wehrmachtsführungsstab* (German High Command) solely about promoting a strike against Singapore, and finally in his "Führer Directive," "Collaboration with Japan" (5 March 1941): The Japanese were to rout the British with a combined land-sea operation on the Malayan Peninsula.[2] In this way, the United States would be restrained from further helping her ally Britain in Europe well as in East Asia. Hints to this effect, however, fell on deaf ears in Japan at this time. The Imperial Navy thought the idea of separating American and British military interests illusory, and had long planned accordingly. Nor was this request welcomed by Foreign Minister [Yōsuke] Matsuoka. He wanted to force the Americans to withdraw from East Asia from a position of overwhelming strength. At the beginning of April 1941, during his talks in Berlin,[3] Matsuoka was told repeatedly by Hitler and his Foreign Minister [Joachim von] Ribbentrop that this was a once-in-a-lifetime chance to take Singapore. Though diplomatically open to the Germans' arguments, he still had to admit that he did not rule alone in Japan. In early 1941 a consensus among the leaders of Japan approving such an operation was not to be expected.

Hitler's strategy was summarized succinctly by Foreign Minister Ribbentrop in a discussion with his Japanese counterpart; should war break out between Germany and the Soviet Union, Japanese participa-

---

[1] A basic study on the origins of the German attack on the Soviet Union is Andreas Hillgruber, *Hitlers Strategie, Politik und Kriegführung 1940–41,* Frankfurt a. M., 1965. For Hitler's war directives, see Walter Hubatsch, ed., *Hitlers Weisungen für die Kriegführung 1939–1945: Dokumente des Oberkommandos der Wehrmacht* (Frankfurt a. M., 1962).

[2] For the deliberations about a Japanese attack on Singapore, see Jun Tsunoda, "Matsuoka und Singapore," in *Wehrwissenschaftliche Rundschau,* vol. 19, 1969, pp. 68–74.

[3] Records of all diplomatic talks Matsuoka had in Berlin, in *Akten zur deutschen auswärtigen Politik,* series D, vol. 12. *Documents on German Foreign Policy,* series D, vol. 12 (London, 1949–64).

tion would be unnecessary. Instead, the best assistance would be a Japanese attack on Singapore. The double guarantee given by Hitler and confirmed by Ribbentrop that Germany would support Japan, should either the Russians or Americans attack her, obviated the risks involved. With the beginning of the German offensive, which was originally planned for May 1941, the Japanese were to attack Singapore. Britain would then be involved in a war in the Far East making retaliation against Germany impossible in Europe or North Africa during the campaign in Eastern Europe.

The relationship between Germany's surprise attack on the Soviets and the proposed Japanese attack on Singapore was not entirely clear to the latter, due to a lack of information from Germany about the coming operations. Matsuoka's report to the Liaison Conference, as well as to the Privy Council, about what German leaders had told him regarding a possible war between Germany and the Soviet Union was correct. In the Privy Council he even put the eventual probability of such a war at fifty percent and for the first time proposed deliberating if, in this event, Japan ought to participate in subduing the Soviet Union. The United States' inflexible posture in the negotiations with Japan — Secretary of State [Cordell] Hull insisted in his "four principles" on Japan's withdrawal from China — meant that there was no doubt that the United States would react militarily to a Japanese assault on Singapore. Matsuoka for the first time pleaded, therefore, for a German-Japanese military union and extolled Germany as a worthy model for the final transformation of Japan into an authoritarian state.[4] The Foreign Minister's display of independence violated the Japanese "holy principle" of governing by consensus. Matsuoka expounded his ideas ceaselessly with the result that he isolated himself in the cabinet and came to represent himself personally, and not Japanese foreign policy. The traditionalists around Minister of the Interior [Kiichirō] Hiranuma regarded Matsuoka simply as a fascist whose public statements were quite correctly redlined by the censors.[5]

Japanese foreign policy lacked clear direction due to the diverging ideas of the country's individual leaders. This confusion and cacophony came to a head during the negotiations with the United States when, against the Foreign Minister's will, Japan appeared ready to distance herself from the Tripartite Pact while at the same time this Pact was being praised as fundamental to Tokyo's entire foreign policy. Matsuoka then

---

[4] Records of the Liaison Conferences in Nobutake Ike, ed., *Japan's Decision for War. Records of the 1941 Policy Conferences* (Stanford, Calif., 1967).

[5] Gerhard Krebs, *Japans Deutschlandpolitik, 1935–1941* (Japanese policy toward Germany, 1935–1941) (Hamburg, 1984).

attempted to acquire a clear picture of German intentions, and at the end of May he sent his ambassador to Hitler and Ribbentrop to advise against a *coup de main* in Eastern Europe. The German leaders, who were not at all happy about the Japanese-American negotiations, because they were contrary to the German policy of isolating the United States, sought anew to bind Japan closer to Germany. Therefore, at the beginning of June they informed the Japanese leaders of the upcoming offensive in the East.[6] Hitler left it up to Tokyo to decide on Japanese participation in this conflict, but Ribbentrop came out clearly in favor of Imperial Army collaboration. He proposed a coordinated pincer operation against the Soviet Union. This fundamental dissension among German leaders concerning Japanese participation in the Russian campaign lasted until January 1943 when the *Wehrmacht* came to their Waterloo at Stalingrad. Finally, Hitler adopted the line of his Foreign Minister and called unequivocally for Japan to intervene militarily in Russia.[7] However, by this time Japan was likewise on the defensive on all fronts and was in no position to respond. This open difference of opinion between the leader of the government and his foreign minister is difficult to imagine in a democracy, and it completely discredited the reports to Tokyo from Ambassador [Hiroshi] Ōshima in Berlin. Not even the Japanese, long accustomed to factional feuds, could imagine a head of state tolerating such contrariety in a key minister.

In fact, before the German offensive began, the Japanese decided in a Liaison Conference, during which Matsuoka presented the newest information from Germany, not to attempt to pursue a two-front war. Instead, from that time onwards, in the shadow of Germany's successes, Japan would venture into Southeast Asia as originally desired by her European "ally." This began with the nonviolent occupation of southern Indochina. Even the army explicitly acknowledged in a memorandum the priority of the southern operation and communicated this to their German partners. In the Liaison Conference of 16 June 1941 Matsuoka read the reports from his ambassador in Berlin. They revealed that the war with Russia would begin within a week. Matsuoka stood alone with

---

[6] For Japanese reports from Berlin, translated into German, see Andreas Hillgruber, "Japan und der Fall 'Barbarossa,'" in *Wehrwissenschaftliche Rundschau*, vol. 18, 1968, pp. 312–36. Furthermore, see Gerhard Krebs, "Japan und der deutsch-sowjetische Krieg 1941," in Bernd Wegner, ed., *Zwei Wege nach Moskau: Vom Hitler-Stalin-Pakt zum "Unternehmen Barbarossa"* (München, 1991), pp. 564–83, and Bernd Martin, "Japan and Barbarossa," paper, University of Waterloo, Ontario, Center for Soviet Studies, 18 May 1991.

[7] Bernd Martin, *Deutschland und Japan im Zweiten Weltkrieg* (Germany and Japan during the Second World War), p. 173 (Conversation Hitler-Oshima, 21 January 1943). (Göttingen, 1969).

his request for a change of policy. The representatives of the army and navy would not consider abandoning their hard-won compromise. The ponderous character of collective leadership in Japan, faced with the necessity of reacting quickly and adequately to a new situation, is clearly evident. "However, it is not good to alter what was decided the other day," stated the Navy Minister. To which Matsuoka could only retort sarcastically, "I'm not very intelligent. . . ."[8] The shock over the Hitler-Stalin Pact had not been forgotten, and on 21 June 1941 Prince [Fumimaro] Konoe, head of the government, attempted to resign due to the most recent change in Germany's Eastern Europe policy. Lord Privy Seal [Kōichi] Kido, the Emperor's political advisor and the most powerful bureaucrat at court, informed the Prime Minister, however, that the German government had correctly informed Japan of their plans and they had in no way objected to them.[9]

With the onset of the German assault, Ribbentrop assailed the Japanese ambassador in Berlin, and in Tokyo Matsuoka implored the Emperor and court officials to immediately join in the German operation. Both argued from the basic standpoint of the Eurasian block concept which they had previously advocated. Since the peaceful integration of the Soviet Union into this block was not possible, the continental landbridge necessary for a military coalition against the Western powers was now to be constructed by force. However, neither of the Foreign Ministers was able to gain acceptance of this policy among the leaders of their respective governments. Ribbentrop's exhortations were unconvincing as long as Hitler, for ideological reasons, did not support him. Matsuoka, on the other hand, was unable to break through the united opposition of the army, navy, and imperial court to a Japanese expedition in the north. Only Hiranuma's traditionalist anticommunist camp, with their Bolshevik phobia, changed their evaluation of Matsuoka and seconded the Foreign Minister.

In a total of six Liaison Conferences the question of a Japanese operation against the Soviet Union was the central topic of discussion. Foreign Minister Matsuoka argued, convincingly from our point of view fifty years later, that a quick attack in the north would forestall American intervention, but a strike south would surely bring the United States into the conflict. He also stated that there was the danger that the war in China might have to be put on hold, should Japan venture northward. This latter comment aroused the premodern, prestige-oriented

---

[8] Ike, *Decision for War* (Liaison Conference, 16 June 1941).
[9] Krebs, *Japans Deutschlandpolitik,* p. 541.

leaders of the army. Army Minister [Hideki] Tōjō immediately voiced opposition to any cutbacks in the China war effort.[10] The Japanese Imperial Army was so preoccupied with the stalemated war in China that it rejected any strategic alternatives and, later, possible political solutions. The continuing conflict in China and the inability of the army leaders to accept some sort of compromise with respect to this thorny issue eventually brought Japan onto an inescapable collision course with the United States.

Matsuoka's position was further weakened by the lack of an official request from Germany for Japanese participation in the war with Russia. Clearly, Ribbentrop did not wish to openly disagree with Hitler. Hitler appears to have purposely waited for the initial victories of his army before he approved a corresponding démarche by his Foreign Minister. Thereafter, Japan's retarded entry into the conflict could not diminish the great achievements of the "Aryan Race" in the battle against the "subhuman Slavs." Finally, one week after the surprise invasion an official request from Ribbentrop was sent to the Japanese side requesting that Japan enter the war against the Soviet Union without delay. In a personal message[11] to Matsuoka, Ribbentrop indicated that a Japanese push to the north, contrary to his earlier recommendation, was now a prerequisite to a subsequent, successful strike south. German recognition of the puppet government under Wang Ching-wei in Nanking was regarded as a demonstration of German-Japanese unity. However, the Imperial Army would not consider even a six-month delay of the southern operation, and it frustrated the Japanese Foreign Minister's last attempt at achieving a compromise.

On 2 July 1941 an Imperial Conference, the highest government council in the land, approved a plan for the occupation of southern Indochina.[12] Japan reserved for itself the possibility of participation in the German war against the Soviet Union, should the German operations go well, and increased the strength of Japanese forces in Manchuria from four hundred thousand to seven hundred thousand men. The following day, Matsuoka communicated this historic decision to the Germans. Japan and the Axis Powers had squandered, fortunately, their best chance of winning the war. From this point onwards the independently chosen paths of the German and Japanese war machines diverged, even before

[10] Ike, *Decision for War* (Liaison Conference, 27 June 1941).

[11] *Documents on German Foreign Policy*, D XIII, Doc. No. 53, telegram from Ribbentrop to Ambassador Ott (Tokyo), 1 July 1941.

[12] Ike, *Decision for War*, pp. 77–90.

the Japanese challenged the United States militarily in the Pacific. All that remained for Foreign Minister Matsuoka to do was to seal his complete defeat with his own resignation.

In mid-July 1941 the collapse of the Soviet Union appeared imminent. Even the United States government had written off Stalin. With this turn of events, the possibility of a combined German-Japanese offensive briefly reemerged. On 14 July 1941, when German forces were at the height of their seemingly unstoppable march on Moscow, Hitler received Japanese Ambassador Ōshima, who had been sent to make a tour of the front, at his headquarters in East Prussia. Exalting in the string of German victories, Hitler exhorted the Japanese to participate in the destruction of Russia so that afterwards they could embark together upon the battle between the continents — the struggle with the United States.[13] This vision of German-Japanese world hegemony, never again proposed by Hitler in this form, was enticing for the Japanese up until the first week of August. They seriously considered taking advantage of this suggestion, now coming directly from Hitler. Even the Japanese General Staff, in talks with the highest-ranking representative of the German military in Tokyo, spoke of the imminent unleashing of the Kwantung Army in Manchuria. Similar reports piled up in Berlin — Japan would invade the Soviet Union in October at the latest. The Japanese Foreign Ministry, in its diplomatic negotiations with the Soviet Union, also assumed that the latter would be ultimately defeated. Matsuoka had remained purposefully unclear about the Japanese position *vis-à-vis* the neutrality treaty, but the Ministry under his successor [Teijirō] Toyoda wanted to use it to force the Russians to cede Amur Province and northern Sakhalin to Japan through diplomatic measures.

However, the course of the war along the middle of the Eastern Front, which the ambassador in general's uniform Ōshima reported in detail to Tokyo, prompted a revision of the Japanese estimate of the situation. Bitter defensive fighting by the Russians in the area of Smolensk had stalled the middle of the *Wehrmacht* line, and the Japanese General Staff began to have doubts about a quick victory over the Soviet Union.[14] An order sent to the units stationed in Manchuria on 6 August strictly

[13] For the meeting between Hitler and Ōshima on 14 July 1941, see Andreas Hillgruber, *Der Zenit des Zweiten Weltkrieges Juli 1941* (Wiesbaden, 1977).

[14] For the political repercussions of the battle of Smolensk, see Andreas Hillgruber, "Die Bedeutung der Schlacht von Smolensk in der zweiten Juli-Hälfte 1941 für den Ausgang des Ostkrieges," in Inge Auerbach et al., eds., *Felder und Vorfelder russischer Geschichte: Studien zu Ehren von Peter Scheibert* (Freiburg i. Br., 1985), pp. 266–79.

prohibited them from engaging in border skirmishes of any sort.[15] Three days later the leaders of the Japanese army decided not to intervene in the German-Soviet conflict of 1941. Instead, they intensified their preparations for the strike south.[16]

On 24 July 1941 Japan began the occupation of southern Indochina. The northern half had already been occupied one year earlier. The move further south was answered by the United States two days later with a total trade embargo. The government in Washington froze all Japanese assets in the United States and banned oil deliveries to Japan. Britain and the Netherlands joined this embargo, and the Japanese were able to calculate, based on their oil reserves, when the fleet would be forced to give their sailors permanent leave ashore. Matsuoka's warning that a strike south would result in an intractable conflict with the United States was confirmed within a few weeks. On 6 September 1941 the decision was taken in an Imperial Conference that Japan would go to war with the United States if the situation did not improve dramatically within a month.[17] This was to take place regardless of what happened on the Russian front. The Japanese still hoped for a German victory, but no longer expected the rapid destruction of Stalin's régime. Shortly thereafter, an internal discussion began in the Foreign Ministry and among leaders of the military about the possibility of Japan providing mediation in the conflict between Germany and the Soviet Union. Displaying rare unanimity, the Japanese leaders returned to their position of 1940 — the building of a continental block against the Western powers. With the ever increasing probability of war with the Allies, Japanese leaders wanted to secure access to German technology, vastly superior to their own at the time, and eventually to military help.

Just as the final German assault on Moscow had started (2 October 1941), the Japanese military brought up the possibility of a political solution to the war in Russia with German diplomats in Tokyo.[18] In order to emphasize the proposal, they also communicated to the Germans their decision made two months earlier not to join in the war against the

---

[15] For the attitude of the Japanese army, see Takushirō Hattori, *The Complete History of the Greater East Asia War,* Tokyo, 1953 (American translation, unpublished, copy on microfilm), vol. 1, part 1, p. 153.

[16] On the origin of Pearl Harbor, see the recent anthology by Hilary Conroy and Harry Wray, eds., *Pearl Harbor Reexamined: Prologue to the Pacific War* (Honolulu, 1990), and the papers from the International Conference, "Fifty Years After — The Pacific War Re-examined." Lake Yamanaka 14–17 Nov. 1991, edited, in Japanese, by Chihiro Hosaya (Tokyo, 1993).

[17] Ike, *Decision for War,* p. 158.

[18] Martin, *Deutschland und Japan,* p. 110.

Soviet Union that year. Hitler, who had never insisted on Japan entering the war, and with his confidence in a quick victory restored, returned to his former position: the Japanese should be restrained from entering the war so as to increase the chances of making peace with Britain. German and Japanese interests diverged before the alliance between them was of any practical consequence. The Germans were transfixed by the war with Russia in the east, the Japanese by the conflict in the Pacific with the United States.

Japanese foreign policy, even under Matsuoka's successor, the moderate Admiral Toyoda, gradually leaned towards formally withdrawing from the negotiations in Washington. Viewing the dark war clouds gathering over the Pacific after the United States had imposed a total embargo on Japan, the leaders in Tokyo once again looked to their two potential allies in Europe. During the three months prior to the opening of hostilities, Japanese leaders made their decisions about the coming war independently of promises of aid from their German and Italian partners. However, the Japanese sought and received assurances from Berlin and Rome that they would not have to stand alone against the United States. Thus, the Tripartite Pact had no direct influence on the Japanese decision to go to war, but may have reassured the Japanese leaders indirectly in their conclusion that war was inevitable.[19]

During the decisive Imperial Conference of 6 September 1941, in which, for all practical purposes, war against the Western powers was decided upon, Chief of Staff Gen Sugiyama specifically referred to the two allies: Germany and Italy should be informed in due course of the decision to go to war, and it should be ensured contractually that they would not conclude a separate peace.[20] The final resolution stated that Japan, to be sure, would have to rely on her own resources, but close ties with Germany and Italy were to be established. Japanese diplomacy remained true to this policy up until Japan entered the war.

After Prime Minister Konoe had worked himself into a hopeless situation politically — the great war appearing ever more probable — he resigned. The Emperor then approved the formation of a government by

---

[19] See Krebs, *Japans Deutschlandpolitik,* and Peter Herde, *Pearl Harbor, 7. Dezember 1941. Der Ausbruch des Krieges zwischen Japan und den Vereinigten Staaten und die Ausweitung des europäischen Krieges zum Zweiten Weltkrieg* (Darmstadt, 1980); on Italy's Far Eastern policy, see Valdo Ferretti, *Il Giappone e la Politica Estera Italiana 1935–1941* (Roma, 1983). Most recent anthology, stressing cultural relations: Gerhard Krebs and Bernd Martin, eds., *Formierung und Fall der Achse Berlin–Tokyo* (München, 1994).

[20] See note 17 above.

General Hideki Tōjō, telling him not only to review the 6 September decision to go to war, but also reminding him of Japan's German ally.

Although the Japanese plans for the war,[21] first completed on 20 October, did not provide for a coalition with Germany to direct the war or corresponding consultations on strategy, representatives of the navy brought up this possibility in the next Liaison Conference. According to the admirals, the British placed a high priority on the defense of Singapore and the Suez Canal. A German advance in the Middle East would turn it into a battleground, opening up the possibility of a maritime connection between the two war zones across the Indian Ocean. A few days later, the conference decided on this strategic proposal of united action in the Middle East together with the demand that Germany immediately declare war on the United States and not agree to any separate peace accord. Because this plan came from the army, the navy relinquished the hoped-for collaboration with their German counterparts and proposed to agree to a division of operational areas along a line extending north-south through Colombo.

Japanese deliberations about bringing Germany into the war against the United States coincided with the German navy's desire to move the German Reich in the same direction. A conflict with the United States, an acknowledged power at sea, was deemed inevitable, and it would be better to enter the war together. A navy memorandum to this effect, which may have accelerated reconsideration of this possibility, circulated through the high command of the armed forces and the Foreign Ministry. Hitler's original principle of avoiding any provocation of the United States during the campaign in Russia in order to keep Washington out of the war at least temporarily became untenable with the collapse of the *Blitzkrieg* on the Eastern front. The German dictator revealed for the first time, in a secret conference on 19 November 1941, his doubts about a German victory.[22] At the same time, he began to reconcile himself to the United States' entry into the war, and within ten days in mid-November opinion in Berlin reoriented itself completely.[23] At the beginning of November, Ribbentrop had reacted as before to the first re-

[21]Takushirō Hattori, "Japans Operationsplan für den Beginn des Pazifischen Krieges," in *Wehrwissenschaftliche Rundschau*, vol. 7 (1957), pp. 247–74.

[22]Hillgruber, *Hitlers Strategie*, pp. 551–52 (Hitler in a conversation with General Halder and other military leaders).

[23]For the German decision to declare war upon the United States, see Jürgen Rohwer and Ernst Jäckel, eds., *Kriegswende Dezember 1941* (Frankfurt a. M., 1981) and Martin, *Deutschland und Japan*, pp. 34ff. With special regard to the topic of this article, Gerhard Krebs, "Deutschland und Pearl Harbour," in *Historische Zeitschrift*, 253 (October 1991), pp. 313–70.

ports from Tokyo about the approaching war in the Pacific: the American threat against Japan was simply a bluff. The Axis allies should persevere and preferably begin an attack on the Soviet Union which involved no risks. But on 21 November Ribbentrop suddenly changed course and moved in the direction of Japanese wishes.

In Japan, after giving the German ambassador in Tokyo advance warning and reendorsing the agreement in the event of war which had been reached at the Liaison Conference, the Japanese officially approached, for the first time, the German military attaché on 18 November and requested that Germany enter the upcoming war. The ambassador immediately reported this unanimous wish of the Japanese armed forces to Berlin. He asked for new instructions covering these "situations not included in the scope of the Tripartite Pact." Ribbentrop at once sent the desired directives which, however, were to be transmitted discreetly and only verbally to the Japanese. The German Reich would stand by Japan and sign the agreement not to settle for a separate peace treaty, "if Japan or Germany, regardless of the grounds, becomes involved in a war with the United States."[24] This new tune from Berlin sounded so unusual to the Japanese that the German ambassador was requested to reconfirm the promise. This he did, and when the United States' rejection of Japan's latest compromise proposal arrived in Tokyo, Japanese leaders already had an oral promise from Germany to enter the war. Two days later Ribbentrop underscored Japanese-German shoulder-to-shoulder cooperation in a talk with Ōshima, and encouraged the Japanese directly to take up the fight with the Americans.

Japanese soundings in Berlin corresponded with the timing of enquiries in Moscow about the neutrality treaty.[25] Would the Soviet Union grant foreign powers the use of air bases — in Vladivostok, for example? The answer from Moscow was also positive: No. As a result the Japanese were strategically well prepared. They need not fear an attack from the rear in a war with the United States, and they had obliged the Germans to accompany them in their risky venture.

With these assurances in hand, Japanese leaders decided irrevocably on war in the Imperial Conference of 1 December 1941.[26] Now, for the first time, the Japanese ambassador in Berlin received formal

[24] Martin, *Deutschland und Japan,* p. 34 (Telegram Ribbentrop–Ambassador Ott in Tokyo from 21 November 1941).

[25] On Japanese-Soviet relations, see Hubertus Lupke, *Japans Russlandpolitik von 1939– 1941* (Frankfurt a. M., 1962), and George A. Lensen, *The Strange Neutrality: Soviet-Japanese Relations during the Second World War* (Tallahassee, Florida, 1972).

[26] Ike, *Decision for War,* pp. 262–83.

instructions that he should have the oral promises reconfirmed in written form. The no-separate-peace agreement proposed long ago by the Japanese, and accepted by the Germans, should be quickly concluded and ratified by the Tripartite Pact signatories. When Ribbentrop delayed the proceedings because he wanted first to consult with Hitler, who was touring the Eastern front, the Japanese turned to the Germans' junior partner, the Italians. Leaders in Rome were flattered and, without equivocating, immediately agreed. In Berlin, where [Benito] Mussolini was obliged to report the entire course of action, Ribbentrop followed suit after consulting with Hitler. On 5 December at four o'clock in the morning, the German Foreign Minister handed the Japanese ambassador the German-Italian counterproposal for a no-separate-peace agreement.[27] Thereby, some sixty hours before the surprise attack on Pearl Harbor, the European Axis Powers had committed themselves in writing to entering an eventual war with the United States. Of course, at the time they had no idea when and where this war might break out.

The role of the German-Italian no-separate-peace promise in Japanese decision making is very difficult to ascertain. It is doubtful that this reassurance from their pact partners was meaningless to the Japanese, but it seems finally to have had little influence on their decision for war. Dwelling on possible Japanese reactions to a clear refusal from Germany and Italy to join in such an agreement is, therefore, mere speculation. Basically, German leaders had already reconciled themselves to the inevitability of a war with the United States, and this agreement can be viewed as acknowledging a self-evident situation. It hardly implies, as Cordell Hull thought, the spawning of a worldwide conspiracy. . . .

[27] Key documents in Martin, *Deutschland und Japan,* pp. 224–28.

ALEXEI M. FILITOV

The Soviet Perspective

The recent partial opening of Soviet archives has enabled historians to reexamine the Soviet Union's foreign policy during the era of Stalin's dictatorship. However, as this essay by a Russian historian notes, not all records

Alexei M. Filitov, "Japan's Entry into the Pacific War and Soviet-Japanese Relations," in Sophia University Institute of American and Canadian Studies, ed., *Beginnings of the Soviet-German and the U.S.-Japanese Wars and 50 Years After* (Tokyo: Sophia University Institute for the Culture of German-Speaking Areas, 1993), 49–60.

were kept, and some that were are not yet available to researchers. Still, the
essay provides a glimpse into the thinking of Stalin and his officials as they
struggled to prevent Germany and Japan from attacking Soviet territory.
The gathering and evaluating of information was of critical importance,
and the study suggests that Soviet officials were by no means unanimous in
interpreting world events. How does this analysis of the Soviet leaders' per-
ceptions of Japan in 1941 add to our understanding of events at that time?
How did the Soviet leaders view U.S.-Japanese relations, and what did they
tell the Americans? What did the American leaders, in their turn, tell the
Soviets? Is there a gap between what is revealed in this study and the pic-
ture of U.S. policy toward the Soviet Union that emerges from the docu-
ments in this volume?

We still know little about the decision-making process in Stalin's Soviet
Union, in particular as regards his Far Eastern policies on the eve of and
during World War II. Taking into consideration the highly secretive manner in which these decisions were reached and Stalin's care to "keep
records clean" (that is, to have all the evidence, not necessarily incrimi-
nating, destroyed), we should not be overoptimistic even with the welcome prospect of more openness in Soviet archival practices.

Perhaps a good beginning would be the study of the "background information" files: the collections of the analytical papers, press reviews
and other similar materials prepared by low-level officials in the Foreign
Ministry. These files convey a true glimpse of the mentality, conceptual
framework and basic approaches characteristic of the Soviet diplomatic
establishment that affected (to some degree, at least) the attitudes of the
decision-makers, and were, in turn, affected by them.

Japan's political life and its trends were the subject of close scrutiny
by Soviet diplomats in the field and their counterparts in Moscow. An
elaborate system of selecting basic data, and of assessing and cross-
checking it, was in operation in the period covered by this presentation
(1940–41). Samples of those analyses will be quoted to show the interesting mixture of ideological clichés, attempts to follow the facts objectively and the resulting contradictions.

Two phenomena of Japan's situation attracted the most attention:
"new political structure" and "new economic structure" (these loose
terms were applied to the efforts by the authorities to concentrate all
the political activities in the "Association of Support for the Throne"

[commonly known as the Imperial Rule Assistance Association] and to intensify the state's interference in private business). The first report, dated November 27, 1940 and sent from Tokyo by the Second Secretary of the Soviet Embassy, Generalov, emphasized the lack of support for these measures from not only the "broad masses," but also a "sizable part of the Japanese bourgeoisie." "Most skeptical," the report continued, "are the Privy Council and the majority in the Upper House of the Diet, as well as a considerable part of the former parties and of the Court." The only supporters were reported to be the "military clique." Due to the widespread opposition, an evolutionary path to a military takeover was thought to be improbable. It was only by a coup d'état that militaristic policies might prevail. The phraseology of the report was extremely awkward and sometimes hardly decipherable, e.g.: "Exacerbation of the internal contradictions is increased by the conversion of the petty and middle bourgeoisie, traditionally a social base for the financial capital into their own opposite, which resulted in the considerable weakening and narrowing of the positions of Japanese fascism." Still, the basic message was clear enough: Japan has not yet become a fascist state and is hardly about to become it; the militaristic trend was likely to be checked; it did not reflect the attitudes of not only the "masses," but also of "ruling circles"; it was only after a coup d'état (if any) that a change might occur.[1]

On May 25, 1941, the same diplomat, now in Moscow, reviewed a report just sent from Tokyo by his successor, Khalin (all the incoming "research papers" were subject to such reviewing procedures). Khalin's analysis was more skeptical concerning the estimated strength of the anti-militarist forces, while presuming that the conflict between "hawks" and "doves" had not yet been resolved. Generalov (who had himself shared this idea earlier) strongly disagreed: the new legislation reflected not only the views of the extremists (Khalin's point), but also the wishes and program of "all the ruling class as a whole." The differentiated image of the Japanese political scene was thus repudiated and replaced by a monochromatic, dogmatic picture, in which no alternatives to the expansion by force and growing militarization were seen.[2]

It might seem paradoxical that a gloomier picture of Japan's policies emerged after the marked improvement in Soviet-Japanese relations, the conclusion of the Neutrality Treaty being a sign of it. Again, the piece

---

[1] AVP SSSR, fond 725, opis' 24, papka 78, delo 34, list 32.
[2] AVP SSSR, f. 725, op. 24, p. 147, d. 32, l. 23.

of semi-information semi-research from the files of the Soviet Foreign Ministry may help to unravel the intricacies of Stalin's political thinking. The source is several mimeographed pages from the TASS bulletin for the restricted list of users, entitled "Internal Political Situation in Japan."[3] Too petty an evidence to draw a direct line to high-level decisions? Not quite so.

The TASS correspondents served often as a better link between foreign and Soviet politicians than the career diplomats (much the same may be said of the other information agencies' and media representatives). As for this specific piece of TASS reporting, it was circulated very actively in the various branches of the Soviet foreign policy apparatus: several copies of it, retyped, abridged, sometimes even without dates and other insignia, were found by this author in the different ministerial files, which testify to the significance attached to it.

The text of this report began with the very definite statement: "The serious situation in Japan is being exacerbated by two factors: 1. the war in China is delayed indefinitely with no sign of its termination; 2. Japan is getting ready for a new, more large-scale war against the USA and Great Britain for the re-distribution of the colonies in South-East Asia."

The conclusions (most frequently retyped and circulated) read as follows: "The international constellation made Japan raise the question of a fundamental settlement with the USSR. A sharp turn took place after Japan made a decision to proceed with its southward expansion. . . . It is characteristic to note that the ruling circles of Japan are unanimous in their intention to settle relations with the USSR. Foreign Minister Yōsuke Matsuoka in several statements expressed the necessity to settle relations with the USSR. . . . The ruling circles of Japan want the USSR to reduce its armed forces in the Far East, to obtain oil, metals and other materials from the USSR, to conclude a fishery convention, etc. In a conversation with the TASS correspondent, the representative of the Information Council Ishii indicated that Japan would wish to conclude an agreement on neutrality with the Soviet Union. 'In case we are compelled to fight a third power, we would like the USSR to keep neutral toward Japan,' Ishii said."

The ideas contained in this piece of TASS reporting and attention given to it in Moscow may suggest that the Soviet decision to sign the Neutrality Treaty with Japan was made in clear anticipation of the coming Pacific war and because of it. The parallel with the Soviet-German

<hr>

[3] AVP SSSR, f. 725, op. 24, p. 78, d. 34, ll. 65–72.

Treaty of 1939 unavoidably arises. Important distinctions are also evident, however.

First, there were no signs of the Western Powers' wishing even to discuss with the Soviet Union any plans for collective security in the Far East. There was no analogy to the tripartite talks of July–August 1939 to stem Hitler's expansion. British plans for joint British-Japanese action against the Soviet Union were of quite recent vintage.[4] No other option for the USSR, except of trying to avert the danger of Japanese assault by "channeling-off" tactics, seemed to be in sight.

Secondly, the Soviet-Japanese Treaty, unlike its Soviet-German predecessors, did not provide for any "spheres of interests" settlement. Interestingly enough, some Western commentators, while perceptively guessing at the eventuality of Soviet-Japanese rapprochement, predicted the "division of China" as its main feature.[5] These predictions did not come true.

Thirdly, there was too long a time-lag between the signing of the Soviet-Japanese Treaty and the outbreak of the Pacific War to try and construe a direct (or causal) connection between the two events, while it is arguable that there was such a connection between the Molotov-Ribbentrop pact [the Nazi-Soviet non-aggression treaty of 1939] and the German attack on Poland, even though it still remains a moot question.

Fourthly, while the European war was absolutely unjust for the Axis Powers and absolutely just for the anti-Axis countries, this clear line was somewhat blurred in the conflict between Japan and the "ABCD" countries. With the exception of China, the remaining members of this bloc (was it really a "bloc"?) were the colonial powers defending (albeit not primarily, it may be argued) their colonial interests. The stance of non-interference and even aloofness by the Soviet Union, preaching its anti-colonialism, may look less repugnant than it seemed in 1939 in the context of Hitlerite aggression in Europe.

The outbreak of the Soviet-German War strained further the uneasy situation in the Far East. Military action by Japan was widely perceived to become more probable. The question was — where and when? For the Soviet decision-makers the situation looked very much like that on the eve of "Barbarossa."

---

[4] Cf. M. Kitchen, *British Foreign Policy Toward the Soviet Union during the Second World War* (London, 1986), pp. 25, 27.

[5] Wilfried Fleischer, ex-editor of "Japan Advertizer" as quoted in *China Weekly Review*, Nov. 30, 1940, in files: AVP SSSR, f. 140, op. 24, d. 49, 1. 8.

Again the torrents of warnings of imminent attack (this time, by Japan) followed from the West. Again various Soviet attempts to "appease" the dangerous partner took place — stretching from the more cordial treatment of the Japanese fishermen to the re-routing of the lend-lease supply line in order to avoid any complications with the Japanese authorities.[6] Still again, the analogy is in many respects misleading.

First, the information supplied by the Western side on Japanese intentions was, in contrast to the pre-Barbarossa case, very contradictory. Undersecretary [of State Sumner] Welles told Soviet Ambassador [Constantine] Oumansky on July 3, 1941, in rather categorical terms: "According to the most reliable sources, the Japanese government intends to break the Neutrality Treaty with the USSR and attack the USSR. The American government is as sure of the accuracy of this information, as it was sure of the reliability of information given to the Soviet ambassador in January on the aggressive intentions of Germany against the USSR."[7] He changed his tone to a more contemplative one during the next meeting with Oumansky on July 7, however. On the other side, he repudiated, again rather categorically, "all talks of the southward expansion" (by Japan) as a "piece of disinformation."[8]

Roosevelt, in his conversation with Oumansky on July 10, was even more reluctant to make any predictions. He confined himself to recital of three intelligence reports of very different contents: the first (allegedly of Chinese origin) confirmed "the firm Japanese decision to attack the USSR" to be preceded by the closure of the Sangar and La Perouse straits; the second (from a non-specified source) indicated the southbound direction of the Japanese thrust, allegedly recommended by Germans; the third (from a "Chinese source in Berlin") combined both versions: first penetration into Indo-China, then immediately a blockade of the Soviet Far East and attack.[9]

Quite different was the information supplied by the Secretary of the Treasury Henry Morgenthau. Welles's predictions of an imminent Japanese attack against the Soviet Union were summarily rejected as "overdrawn and simplified." According to his "own intelligence network,"

[6] *Kokumin*, Aug. 19 (translation of an article in files: f. 146, op. 24, d. 49, 1. 8). The problem of re-routing lend-lease delivery's lines was discussed by the Soviet Ambassador with Hornbeck and Hull on Aug. 24, Sept. 4 (AVP SSSR, f. 048z, op. 24, p. 23, d. 2, u. 298–99, 301).

[7] *Sovetsko-Amerikanskie Otnosheniia vo Vremiia Velikos Otechestvennoi Voiny 1941–1945*, t. 1, m. 1984, s. 52–53.

[8] AVP SSSR, f. 48z, op. 24, p. 23, d. 2, l. 276.

[9] *Sovetsko-Amerikanskie Otnosheniia*, t. 1, s. 62–63.

Japan is getting prepared for some military move, but his guess on the most probable actions is: "the completion of the occupation of South Indo-China, the thrust into Siam and Indonesia."[10]

The forecast of Navy Secretary [Frank] Knox was again in favor of the "Northern" variant (a blockade of Vladivostok was specifically mentioned).[11]

The alarmist line taken by the American officials (with the notable exception of Morgenthau, and later, less emphatically, [Presidential advisor Harry] Hopkins, with the President vacillating between the different points of view) was in marked contrast to the restrained, even leisurely manner in which the problem of the American reaction to the supposed outbreak of the Soviet-Japanese war was discussed by them. The total trade embargo, maybe some kind of blockade and some "new method of the fighters' delivery" were promised — not more. Roosevelt hinted that the USSR could easily check Japanese aggression without American aid: "He hopes that the Soviet air force would choose some fine windy day and cover the cardboard towns of Japan with a good portion of incendiary bombs. The Japanese people are not at fault, but there is no other way to demonstrate to the Japanese rulers the madness of their policies." On the other side, Roosevelt, during the same conversation, advocated the continuation of oil exports to Japan ("too abrupt and hard measures would rather provoke Japanese aggression against the Dutch Indies") and practically evaded discussion on the non-public Soviet proposal for some American declaration (or diplomatic move) with the purpose "to explain to the Japanese that in case of any adventurist actions in relation to the USSR they would face such and such specific (American) measures."[12]

The texts of the diplomatic exchanges, which this author was able to look into, indicate rather conclusively that the line of "keeping the Japanese in the dark" on possible American actions in case of the outbreak of a Soviet-Japanese conflict was articulated most emphatically by Undersecretary Welles, while Navy Secretary Knox expressed (at least, to the Soviet Ambassador) some doubts about its practicability.[13] Still, it remained the stated policy of the Administration.

At the end of July and beginning of August the forecasts on the course of Japanese moves, as they were given by American officials to the Soviet side, became even more bizarre. Harry Hopkins, while in Moscow,

[10] AVP SSSR, f. 048z, op. 24, p. 23, d. 2, l. 282.
[11] Ibid., l. 283.
[12] *Sovetsko-Amerikanskie Otnosheniia*, t. 1, s. 62–63.
[13] AVP SSSR, f. 048z, op. 24, p. 23, d. 2, l. 290.

told [Foreign Secretary Vyacheslav] Molotov, on July 31, that "they (the Japanese) would not attack Siberia" and advocated, just on this ground, American "aloofness" with respect to Japanese policies; another argument was that "the U.S. dislikes sending notes on its disapproval of measures taken by Japan."[14]

The State Department continued to raise the specter of a "clear and present danger" for the Soviet Union in the Far East. On August 4, Welles informed Oumansky of the impending Japanese invasion of Siam, repeating again his warnings on "the concentration of Japanese troops in Manchuria."[15] On August 8, [Secretary of State Cordell] Hull stressed the "reality of the northward movement by Japan." The Soviet Ambassador criticized on this occasion, once again, the lack of a clear formulation of American policy on the Far Eastern crisis; the Secretary of State expressed his personal agreement with this criticism, but evaded a positive answer.[16]

At last, on August 19, Welles informed Oumansky ("strictly confidentially") of Roosevelt's warning allegedly made to the Japanese Ambassador on August 17, that any new aggressive action by Japan in the Pacific, either in the South, or in the North, would trigger corresponding American counter-measures.[17] Still, the information obtained by the Soviet Ambassador from the Australian envoy [Richard C.] Casey (whose comments in the past were quite accurate) and from another, unspecified "well informed source" was different. "Roosevelt's warning concerned mainly the Singapore-Siam complex," reported Oumansky to Moscow.[18] On September 8, he received a directive from the Foreign Ministry to abstain from any further discussion of Far Eastern matters.[19] After that, the subject faded away from the agenda of Soviet-American diplomacy and reemerged only after Pearl Harbor.

The conclusions drawn from these exchanges by the Soviet decision-makers were clear enough. The image of the United States as a source of information and potential ally suffered badly. As an exercise in "confidence-building" this experience was rather counter-productive. Perceptions gained of the leading American political figures varied in terms of their accuracy: while the image of Welles as an insincere and unreliable partner was probably not quite untrue, that of Morgenthau

---

[14] *Sovetsko-Amerikanskie Otnosheniia*, t. 1, s. 87.
[15] AVP SSSR, f. 043z, op. 24, p. 23, d. 2, l. 290.
[16] *Sovetsko-Amerikanskie Otnosheniia*, t. 1, s. 101.
[17] Ibid., s. 104.
[18] AVP SSSR, f. 048z, op. 24, p. 23, d. 2, ll. 293–94.
[19] Ibid., l. 302.

as a sort of "omniscient friend" turned out to be misleading and might play a role in the later Soviet reaction (or rather lack of it) to the ill-fated "Morgenthau Plan" of 1944 concerning the treatment of Germany, which in turn contributed to confusion in Allied planning for a post-war German settlement.

The immediate short-range consequences were far from satisfactory, too. The "black-out" in Soviet-American communications on the very eve of the crisis in the Far East, and the "benign neglect" seemingly demonstrated by both sides to its prospects was not unwelcome to the proponents of the "hard line" in Japan. Perhaps, the only positive thing was the clear perception by the Soviet side — contrary to American "warnings"— of the unwillingness of Japan to attack the Soviet Union.

This conclusion was not drawn primarily from the realm of Soviet-American exchanges, of course. It was rather the "input" from Japan itself that contributed mainly to the Soviet reluctance to give credence to American warnings. What was this "input"? The official diplomatic intercourse was, it seems, of minor significance. The files in the Foreign Ministry archive contain the stories of some small conflicts (concerning the property of the Italian Embassy in Moscow, or the land rights of the Soviet Consulate in Yokohama, or border violations, etc.), but nothing that could elucidate possible trends in Japanese policies or Soviet perceptions of them.

More revealing are the files of the "research branch" in the Foreign Ministry. Especially, the "reviews of the Japanese press" are an interesting source for the history of Soviet perceptions of Japan. The impression created by the contents of these surveys — and obviously not lost on those who should have read them in the decision-making branch of the Ministry — was clear enough: Japan was not likely to start war with the Soviet Union. There was a deep skepticism in Japan concerning German propaganda claims of an early and unavoidable Soviet defeat. There was, all in all, a quite correct (Soviet) perception of the quite correct (Japanese) perceptions!

It is not to say, of course, that this Soviet perception was due to the careful reading of the carefully prepared "Japanese press reviews." The role of the intelligence information (Sorge* group) was great. The main thing was that all the sources, considered as reliable, corroborated

---

* Richard Sorge (1895–1944) was a German press correspondent who worked for the Comintern and organized spy rings in China and Japan. He sent information to Moscow in May 1941 that Germany was preparing for an attack on the Soviet Union. He was arrested by the Japanese police in October 1941 and executed in November 1944.

each other. To identify the "signals" and the "noise" in the information flow turned out to be an easier task than was the case on the eve of "Barbarossa."

As for the reasons for the relatively accurate Japanese perceptions of the dim prospects for Hitler's adventure and thus of the inadvisability of Japan's joining it, some more explanations may be added to those put forward at the conference "December 1941 — the Turning Point of War" held in Stuttgart ten years ago. Apart from the impressions gained by Japanese military experts . . . , the experiences of the "war of attrition" with China seemed to be the strongest inhibiting factor against the "Siberian option."[20]

The outbreak of the Pacific War confirmed the correctness of the "non-alarmist" stance taken by the Soviet side in their East Asian policies. Now, it was quite clear that there would be no acute danger for the Soviet Union in the region. Still, other aspects of the situation looked less positive. First, the probability of concerted German-Japanese action at some later date could not be ruled out. American predictions pointed to the spring of 1942 as the moment of Japan's entering the Soviet-German war,[21] and while these predictions again turned out to be untrue, they weighed heavily on Soviet leaders. On the other side, the practical cessation of the lend-lease deliveries (at least by the American freighters) through the Pacific route was a clear liability. The same could be said of the diminishing prospects of the "Second Front" in Europe. In fact, Stalin practically dropped this issue from the catalogue of his demands during talks with Foreign Secretary Anthony Eden in December 1941,[22] replacing it with an insistence on Western recognition of the Soviet pre-war frontiers. It was only in May 1942 that this trend was reversed and the "Second Front" became again the priority item in Soviet diplomacy.

The consequences of the delay in the opening of the "Second Front" were well-known: the prolongation of the war, more losses and sufferings, even, it may be argued, the creation of preconditions for the outbreak of the Cold War. Even though the latter proposition seems to be too far-fetched, still, the fatal aftermath of the events in the Pacific extended far beyond this region.

[20]Text of the interview with Rear-Admiral Maeda in "Fuji," 1941, N9, in files: AVP SSSR, f. 146, op. 24, d. 47, ll. 178–83.

[21]AVP SSSR, f. 048z, op. 24, p. 23, d. 2, l. 329 (transcript of Litvinov-Roosevelt talk on Dec. 18, 1941).

[22]Public Record Office, Cab. 66/20, W.P. 42 (8), p. 29 (Stalin: "We dropped our insistence on the creation of the second front").

The most immediate concern for Soviet diplomacy in the wake of Pearl Harbor was, however, to resist what may be termed as a rather heavy-handed American pressure to get involved in the Pacific war. It is not to say that the U.S. leaders demanded that the USSR should declare war on Japan. Still, some suggestions by them sounded very much as implying just that (the idea of the bombing missions by the U.S. Air Force, with Manila and Vladivostok(!) as landing and take-off sites, of a joint Soviet-American, or Soviet, declaration on "freedom of action" in regard to Japan, of a conference to be held in China with Soviet participation, etc.).[23]

The Soviet diplomatic files show an interesting dispute between the Soviet Ambassador in the United States, Maxim Litvinov (who arrived in Washington, as a replacement for Oumansky, just in time to hear of the beginning of the American-Japanese war), and the Foreign Ministry. Both sides were unanimous in rejecting any American proposals which could possibly lead to Soviet involvement in the Pacific War. Still, Litvinov was in favor of pure military neutrality, while objecting to what he termed "political and ideological" neutrality.[24] He meant that the Soviet government should not hesitate to voice its condemnation of Japanese actions and its solidarity with the Anglo-American war efforts. He was in favor of accepting, in principle, the American proposal of a "Supreme War Council" to be set up in Washington under chairmanship of the American president. On both counts, the Foreign Ministry strongly disagreed with his recommendations.

The story of this dispute and of its outcome (Litvinov lost it, of course) raises some interesting questions. Was Stalin's totalitarian system so monolithic, as it was usually described? As for the merits of the arguments employed by both sides, one may ask: was not Litvinov's idea of *"military* neutrality" (*only*) preferable? Were not there some opportunities missed? The open statement of Soviet sympathies for the Allied cause would hardly be provocative, while it would mean putting an end to the speculations on the split in the anti-Axis coalition. It, in turn, would strengthen the moderate wing in the Japanese political elite who could possibly prevail with the idea of a compromise peace or even (at the later stage) of surrender on more favorable conditions. Unless this alternative materialized, the Soviet entry into the Pacific war, as it took place in 1945, would look more understandable and justified.

---

[23]Transcript of Litvinov-Roosevelt talk on Dec. 8, 1941. (AVP SSSR, f. 048z, op. 24, p. 23, d. 2, ll. 309–10, 313–14, 317–18).

[24]Litvinov to Molotov, Dec. 9, 1941 (ibid., l. 310).

As for the second point in the Molotov-Litvinov controversy, the latter's arguments seemed to be less strong. He counted on the separation of the prospective "War Council" into two "Sub-Councils": one — for Far Eastern matters (in which the Soviet Union would not participate), the second — for Europe (in which it would). Molotov correctly remarked: there were no signs of America agreeing to such a separation: the idea of a joint "War Council" seemed to be invented largely as an incentive for the Soviet Union to get involved in the Pacific war. Litvinov's reasoning on the opportunities of exerting more influence on the U.S. within the Council's framework (in matters relating to the lend-lease deliveries and the Second Front) was not quite convincing, either.

Some of Molotov's counter-arguments sounded rather odd, indeed; the creation of a "War Council" would, in his opinion, mean "the submission of Soviet military planning to the whims of Washington."[25] The suspicions toward the new ally seemed to be strong — not less than toward the Japanese "neutral." It was only step by step that these suspicions lost their intensity. The positive Soviet reaction to Roosevelt's "Four Policemen" offer made to Molotov during his visit to the U.S. in June 1942 may be indicative of this change. Under the circumstances of the period covered by this study, the mentality of total distrust — of all to all — prevailed and contributed strongly to a tragic turn of events.

---

[25] Litvinov to Molotov, Dec. 23, Molotov to Litvinov, Dec. 24, Litvinov to Molotov, Dec. 24, Molotov to Litvinov, Dec. 25 (ibid., ll. 322–25).

Chronology of Events
Related to Pearl Harbor and
the Coming of the Pacific War
(1931–1941)

1931

September   The Japanese army begins its conquest of Manchuria.

1932

January   The United States says it will not recognize the new situation in Manchuria (Stimson Nonrecognition Doctrine).

March   Manchuria declares independence (Manchukuo).

1933

January   Adolf Hitler becomes chancellor of Germany (Third Reich).

February   The League of Nations accepts the Lytton Commission report calling on Japan to restore the status quo in Manchuria.

March   Franklin D. Roosevelt becomes president of the United States. Japan withdraws from the League of Nations.

June   The London economic conference opens (ends in failure in July).

October   Germany withdraws from the League of Nations.

November   The U.S. and the Soviet Union establish diplomatic relations.

1934

April   Japan declares that it will oppose the powers' assistance to China (Amō Doctrine).

September   The Soviet Union joins the League of Nations.

October   Chinese Communists begin their "Long March" toward the northwest (completed in October 1935).

December   Japan abrogates the Washington naval treaty of 1922.

1935

February   Italy begins its invasion of Ethiopia (completed in 1936).

August   The Communist International (Comintern) issues a call for a worldwide anti-Fascist front. The U.S. Congress passes the Neutrality Act.

1936

March   The German army occupies the Rhineland in violation of the peace treaty of 1919.

July   The civil war begins in Spain (the Fascists win by 1939).

November   Roosevelt is reelected president.

Japan and Germany sign the Anti-Comintern Pact.

December   The Xian (Sian) incident occurs: the beginning of the "united front" in China.

1937

July   Japanese and Chinese forces clash outside Beijing (Peiping): the beginning of the Chinese-Japanese war (through 1945).

October   Roosevelt gives his "quarantine speech" in Chicago. The League of Nations condemns Japanese aggression in China.

December   Japanese troops occupy Nanking (Nanjing): "the rape of Nanking." Japanese naval planes attack the U.S. gunboat *Panay;* Japanese government apologizes.

1938

March   Germany annexes Austria.

July   The U.S. adopts a moral embargo on the export of aircraft to Japan.

September   Britain and France agree to the cession of part of Czechoslovakia to Germany (the Munich Conference).

November   Japan declares its policy to establish a "new order in East Asia."

December   The first U.S. loan to China is granted.

1939

January   U.S. adopts an embargo of aircraft and aircraft parts against Japan.

March   Germany annexes Czechoslovakia.

July   The United States notifies Japan of its intention to abrogate the treaty of commerce in six months. Japanese and Soviet forces clash in Nomonhan, Mongolia (armistice reached in September).

August   The Germans and Soviets sign a nonaggression pact.

September Germany invades Poland. Britain and France declare war against Germany.

November U.S. neutrality laws are amended, enabling the United States to sell arms on a "cash-and-carry" basis.

1940

March A pro-Japanese ("puppet") government is set up in Nanking under Wang Ching-wei (Wang Jingwei).

April German spring offensive occurs in northern and western Europe.

July The Burma Road is closed by Britain for three months under Japanese pressure. Prince Fumimaro Konoe is appointed prime minister of Japan.

September Japanese forces occupy northern French Indochina. The Tripartite (Axis) Pact is signed by Japan, Germany, and Italy.

November Roosevelt is reelected president for the third time.

1941

January Japanese negotiations with Dutch East Indies authorities on petroleum shipments to Japan produce no agreement.

March The U.S. Congress passes the Lend-Lease Act.

April The Japanese-Soviet neutrality treaty is signed.

June Germany declares war on the Soviet Union.

July The United States freezes Japanese assets (followed by Britain and the Dutch East Indies). Japanese forces occupy southern Indochina.

August The United States imposes a de facto embargo of oil shipments to Japan. Japan proposes a summit meeting between Roosevelt and Konoe. Roosevelt and Churchill meet off Newfoundland and issue the Atlantic Charter.

September Japan's imperial conference decides on war against the United States and Britain unless their differences are resolved.

October Hideki Tōjō is appointed prime minister of Japan.

November Japan adopts final terms (Plans A and B) for negotiation with the United States. At negotiations in Washington, the United States presents the Hull note.

December Japan's imperial conference decides on war against the United States (December 1). Japan attacks Pearl Harbor, then declares war (December 7).

Selected Bibliography

An enormous amount has been written about Pearl Harbor. Here are some books that contain additional information that may be useful as you consider the background and immediate circumstances of the Japanese attack.

The international context of the deteriorating U.S.-Japanese relations is sketched in Akira Iriye, *The Origins of the Second World War in Asia and the Pacific* (London: Longman, 1987). The book seeks to examine why Japan's attack on China in 1931 provoked little international reaction, whereas ten years later the war between the two countries brought about massive U.S. support of China, thus making China the major point of contention in U.S.-Japanese relations. For further details on U.S. policy toward China, see Michael Schaller, *The U.S. Crusade in China, 1938–1949* (New York: Columbia University Press, 1979). One of the most recent and best reflections on the United States–Japan–China triangle that provided the setting for Pearl Harbor is offered by Walter LaFeber, *The Clash* (New York: W. W. Norton, 1997).

China, however, was not the only contentious issue between the United States and Japan. They also collided over Japanese designs on Southeast Asia and over Japan's alliance with Germany (the Tripartite Pact). On the first question, the best recent treatment is Jonathan Marshall, *To Have and Have Not* (Stanford: Stanford University Press, 1995). See also Irvine H. Anderson, *The Standard Vacuum Oil Company and United States East Asian Policy* (Princeton: Princeton University Press, 1975), a study of how an American company involved in refining oil in East and Southeast Asia kept in close touch with the U.S. government. On the second question, Saul Friedlander, *Prelude to Downfall* (New York: Knopf, 1967), examines how Hitler viewed U.S.-Japanese relations during 1941, while Paul W. Schroeder, *The Axis Alliance and Japanese-American Relations* (Ithaca: Cornell University Press, 1958), argues that the alliance was no longer a major stumbling block in preventing further deterioration of U.S.-Japanese relations in the fall of 1941.

There are excellent studies of U.S. and Japanese policymakers, the dramatis personae in the final act before Pearl Harbor. The best study of President Roosevelt's handling of the Japanese crisis in 1941 is Waldo Heinrichs,

Threshold of War (New York: Oxford University Press, 1988). For Roosevelt's foreign policy throughout his four terms in office, see Robert Dallek, *Franklin D. Roosevelt and American Foreign Policy* (New York: Knopf; Oxford University Press, 1979). A far more critical account, representing the "conspiracy theory" school of thought on FDR, is Charles A. Beard, *President Roosevelt and the Coming of the War* (New Haven: Yale University Press, 1948). For the Japanese emperor, the most balanced account is Stephen S. Large, *Emperor Hirohito and Showa Japan* (London: Routledge, 1992). On Prime Minister Tōjō, see Robert Butow, *Tojo and the Coming of the War* (Stanford: Stanford University Press, 1961). For the Japanese army's thinking on national mobilization, including a vision of a self-sufficient empire that collided with the U.S. Open Door policy, the most important book is Michael Barnhart, *Japan Prepares for Total War* (Ithaca: Cornell University Press, 1987). For a detailed look at many Japanese officials and officers who played various roles in the events leading up to Pearl Harbor, see James Morley, ed., *The Final Confrontation* (New York: Columbia University Press, 1994). This is an English translation of a Japanese study that was originally published in 1963 and includes an excellent introduction by the translator, David Titus. See also Dorothy Borg and Shumpei Okamoto, eds., *Pearl Harbor as History* (New York: Columbia University Press, 1973), in which U.S. and Japanese historians compare the two countries' political, military, economic, and cultural institutions in the years before 1941.

On Pearl Harbor itself, the most comprehensive study is Gordon W. Prange, *At Dawn We Slept* (New York: McGraw-Hill, 1981). The book details Japanese planning for the attack as well as U.S. strategy for defending its territory. The same author's *Pearl Harbor: The Verdict of History* (New York: McGraw-Hill, 1986) discusses what went wrong and what might have prevented the disaster. In addition to David Kahn's article on U.S. intelligence in this book, you may also wish to consult his book, *The Codebreakers* (New York: Macmillan, 1967). See also Roberta Wohlstetter, *Pearl Harbor: Warning and Decision* (Stanford: Stanford University Press, 1962), which offers a close analysis of why, despite the decoding of secret Japanese messages, crucial information regarding the initial offensive was never brought to the attention of the highest authorities.

In Part Two of this book, you read essays dealing with several countries other than the United States and Japan that were also involved in the Pearl Harbor story, directly or indirectly. If you are interested in learning more about those countries, there are some excellent studies of their foreign policies during the 1930s and the early 1940s. For Great Britain, for instance, a good place to start is David Reynolds, *The Creation of the Anglo-American Alliance, 1931–1941* (London: Europa Publications, 1981). For a study with a sharper focus on Asia and the Pacific, consult Peter Lowe, *Great Britain and the Origins of the Pacific War* (Oxford: Clarendon Press, 1977). On the Soviet Union, Jonathan Haslam, *The Soviet Union and the Threat in the East, 1933–41* (Pittsburgh: University of Pittsburgh Press, 1992), and Robert C. Tucker,

Stalin in Power (New York: W. W. Norton, 1990), contain fascinating details. There is no comprehensive study in English of Germany's Asian policy after the signing of the 1940 alliance with Japan, but for the earlier period, see the excellent monograph by John Fox, *Germany and the Far Eastern Crisis, 1931–1938* (Oxford: Clarendon Press, 1982). An increasing number of historians are reexamining Chinese foreign policy during the 1930s on the basis of recently declassified documents. Such works as Parks Coble, *Facing Japan* (Cambridge: Harvard University Press, 1991), and Youli Sun, *China and the Origins of the Pacific War, 1931–1941* (New York: St. Martin's Press, 1993), examine the close connection between China's foreign policy and domestic affairs.

The above books, as well as this volume itself, approach the Pearl Harbor event as the product of a series of decisions made by Japanese, U.S., and other leaders. In other words, they are all studies in decision making. This is the most common approach to the study of international affairs. It may be pointed out, however, that historians have also proposed additional approaches to the subject. For instance, instead of focusing on decisions and decision makers, some prefer to put the U.S.-Japanese crisis in a larger context, for instance as part of the geopolitical struggle between two great Asian-Pacific powers. In such a framework, the Pearl Harbor attack becomes an episode, grave as it was, in the long history of the rise and fall of the great powers. See Paul Kennedy, *The Rise and Fall of the Great Powers* (New York: Random House, 1987), for the best example of this type of study. Others, in contrast, view the United States and Japan not simply as powers but also as distinctive cultures, defined by their respective histories and ways of life, and they see in the U.S.-Japanese war something more than a conventional international conflict; it was, in their view, a collision of two civilizations, ideologies, and moral systems, even an inevitable clash between a Western and an Asian people. Each was convinced of its own justice, and so, in the end there could be no compromise. The tone of these cultural differences is graphically described by John Dower, *War without Mercy* (New York: Pantheon, 1986). Still others believe that there was nothing inevitable, either geopolitically or culturally, about the U.S.-Japanese conflict and that the whole disaster could have been prevented if international relations during the 1930s had not so cavalierly reversed the hopeful beginnings of the 1920s, when a far more promising world order, based on economic interdependence and cultural communication, had emerged. Put this way, to inquire into the Pearl Harbor tragedy must ultimately lead to questions about the nature of international relations in general. I provide a hint of this broader approach in *The Globalizing of America, 1913–1945* (Cambridge: Cambridge University Press, 1993). Whatever perspective you choose, it is to be hoped that the focus on the Pearl Harbor attack will serve as a window into understanding the shape of the world in the mid-twentieth century, out of which yet another definition of international relations has emerged.

Acknowledgments (*continued*)

Anthony Best. "Britain and the Coming of Pacific War." Reprinted by permission of the International House of Japan. Originally presented at a conference titled "China and the Coming of the Pacific War" (Japan, November 1991).

Henry C. Clausen and Bruce Lee. Excerpt taken from *Pearl Harbor: Final Judgment* by Henry C. Clausen and Bruce Lee, pp. 334–41. Copyright © 1992 by Henry C. Clausen and Bruce Lee. Reprinted by permission of Crown Publishers, Inc.

Alexei M. Filtov. "Japan's Entry into the Pacific War and Soviet-Japanese Relations." Excerpt taken from *Beginnings of the Soviet-German and the U.S.-Japanese Wars and 50 Years After* (1993), pp. 49–60. Reprinted by Sophia University Institute for the Culture of German-Speaking Areas.

Ken'ichi Goto. "Return to Asia: Japanese-Indonesian Relations 1930s–1942." Excerpt taken from *Ryukei Shosha*, 1997, pp. 300–12. Reprinted by permission.

Sumio Hatano and Sadao Asada. "The Japanese Decision to Move South." Excerpt taken from *Paths to War: New Essays on the Origins of the Second World War* edited by Robert Boyce and Esmonde M. Robertson, pp. 391–400. Copyright © 1989 Robert Boyce and Esmonde E. Robertson (eds). Reprinted with permission of St. Martin's Press, Incorporated and Macmillan Press Ltd.

Waldo Heinrichs. "Japan as Enemy." Excerpt taken from *American Ambassador: Joseph C. Drew and the Development of the United States Diplomatic Tradition* by Waldo Heinrichs, pp. 351–61. Copyright © 1986 by Waldo Heinrichs. Used by permission of Oxford University Press.

Nobutaka Ike. Excerpts taken from *Japan's Decision for War: Records of the 1941 Policy Conferences,* edited and translated by Nobutaka Ike, pp. 209–20, 222–39, 262–64, 270–74, 279–83. © 1967 by the Board of Trustees of the Leland Stanford Junior University. Reprinted with the permission of the publishers, Stanford University Press.

David Kahn. "The Intelligence Failure of Pearl Harbor." From *Foreign Affairs,* vol. 70, no. 5 (Winter 1991–92), 138–50. Copyright © 1991 by the Council on Foreign Relations, Inc. Reprinted by permission of *Foreign Affairs.*

Warren F. Kimball. Excerpt taken from *Churchill and Roosevelt: The Complete Correspondence,* vol. 1, 1984, pp. 275–78, edited by Warren F. Kimball. Copyright © Reprinted by permission of Princeton University Press.

Minoru Nomura. "Japan's Plans for World War II." Excerpt taken from *Revue Internationale d'Histoire Militaire,* no. 38 (1978), pp. 201–17. Reprinted by permission.

Katsumi Usui. "The Chinese-Japanese War." Reprinted by permission of the International House of Japan. Originally presented at a conference titled "China and the Coming of the Pacific War" (Japan, November 1991).

Wang Xi. "China and U.S.–Japanese Relations." Reprinted by permission of the International House of Japan. Originally presented at a conference titled "China and the Coming of the Pacific War" (Japan, November 1991).

Excerpt from *This Is Yomiuri,* March 1998, pp. 220–21. Reprinted by permission of Yomiuri Research Institute, The Yomiuri Shimbun, Tokyo, Japan.

Index